AF096712

DWELLING ON EARTH

ALSO BY STEFAN AL

Supertall:
How the World's Tallest Buildings Are
Reshaping Our Cities and Our Lives

Adapting Cities to Sea Level Rise:
Green and Gray Strategies

The Strip:
Las Vegas and the Architecture
of the American Dream

Villages in the City:
A Guide to South China's Informal Settlements (editor)

Mall City:
Hong Kong's Dreamworlds of Consumption (editor)

Factory Towns of South China:
An Illustrated Guidebook (editor)

Macau and the Casino Complex (editor)

The Urbanism Reader:
Design, Technology, Culture and the Future of Cities
(editor, with Tom Verebes)

Beyond Mobility:
Planning Cities for People and Places
(with Robert Cervero and Erick Guerra)

DWELLING ON EARTH

The Past and
Future of the
Places We Call Home

STEFAN AL

W. W. NORTON & COMPANY
Independent Publishers Since 1923

Copyright © 2026 by Stefan Al
Illustrations © 2025 by David M. Dugas

All rights reserved
Printed in the United States of America
First Edition

For information about permission to reproduce selections from this book, write to
Permissions, W. W. Norton & Company, Inc., 500 Fifth Avenue, New York, NY 10110

For information about special discounts for bulk purchases, please contact
W. W. Norton Special Sales at specialsales@wwnorton.com or 800-233-4830

Manufacturing by Lakeside Book Company
Production manager: Lauren Abbate

ISBN: 978-1-324-06572-2

W. W. Norton & Company, Inc.
500 Fifth Avenue, New York, NY 10110
www.wwnorton.com

W. W. Norton & Company Ltd.
15 Carlisle Street, London W1D 3BS

Authorized EU representative:
EAS, Mustamäe tee 50, 10621 Tallinn, Estonia

10 9 8 7 6 5 4 3 2 1

For Natalie

By means of our hands we struggle to create, as it were,
a second world within the world of nature.
—Marcus Tullius Cicero,
On the Nature of the Gods 2.61,
translation adapted from H. Rackham

CONTENTS

LIST OF ILLUSTRATIONS   xiii

INTRODUCTION   Dwelling on Earth   1
         ONE   A Permanent Place   19
         TWO   Cities of Mud   52
       THREE   Order and Ornament   87
        FOUR   The Industrial Home   121
        FIVE   Machines for Living   158
         SIX   The Intelligent Envelope   193
       SEVEN   Nature as Blueprint   225

ACKNOWLEDGMENTS   257
NOTES   259
INDEX   289

LIST OF ILLUSTRATIONS

1. Rock-shelter, Abrigo de Navalmaíllo, Spain, ca. 73,000 BC.   22
2. Temporary Neanderthal camp "La Folie," near present-day Poitiers, France, ca. 60,000 BC.   25
3. Bone hut, Mezhirich, Ukraine, ca. 15,000 BC.   27
4. Traditional Inuit igloo, Nunavut, Canada.   28
5. Brush hut at Ohalo II, Sea of Galilee, Israel, ca. 21,000 BC.   29
6. Natufian pit dwellings, 'Ain Mallaha ('Eynan), Israel, ca. 12,500 BC.   31
7. Five-room mud brick house, Abu Hureyra, Syria, ca. 6500 BC.   38
8. Village of Çatalhöyük, Turkey, ca. 6700 BC.   44
9. Packed-mud house, Tell Hassuna, Northern Iraq, ca. 5500 BC.   53
10. Traditional reed house (*mudhif*), Southern Iraq.   58
11. Tripartite house, Tell Madhur, Iraq, ca. 4500 BC.   59
12. Traditional courtyard houses, Marrakech, Morocco.   75
13. *Pastas* houses, Olynthus, North Hill Section, Greece, 432–348 BC.   89
14. Classic Beijing courtyard house (*siheyuan*), ca. 1300–1900 AD.   95

15. Roman house (domus), Roman Empire, ca. 100 BC–200 AD. 98
16. Insula Diana, Ostia, ca. 150 AD. 107
17. Reconstruction of Angkor's central area, Cambodia, twelfth century AD. 117
18. Canal house, 319 Keizersgracht, Amsterdam, Philips Vingboons, architect, 1639. 126
19. Victorian terraced row houses, Voelas Street (part of the Welsh Streets), Richard Owens, architect, Liverpool, 1880s. 136
20. Dakota Apartments, Upper West Side, New York City, Henry Janeway Hardenbergh, architect, 1884. 145
21. Schermerhorn residence, Riverside, Illinois, William LeBaron Jenney, architect, 1869. 156
22. Siedlung Westhausen, Frankfurt am Main, Ernst May, architect, 1931. 159
23. Edith Farnsworth House, Illinois, Ludwig Mies van der Rohe, architect, 1951. 165
24. Levittown, New York, Levitt & Sons, developers, 1947. 168
25. Kin Ming Estate, Hong Kong, Hong Kong Housing Authority, architects, 2003. 183
26. Quinta Monroy (Half a House), Iquique, Chile, Elemental, architects, 2004. 190
27. Solar Hemicycle, Madison, Wisconsin, Frank Lloyd Wright, architect, 1948. 197
28. Solar Settlement, Freiburg, Rolf Disch SolarArchitektur, 2006. 204
29. Nakagin Capsule Tower, Tokyo, Kisho Kurokawa, architect, 1972. 207
30. 3D-printed home, Project Milestone, Eindhoven, Netherlands, Houben & Van Mierlo Architects, 2021. 211
31. Culdesac, Tempe, Arizona, Opticos Design, 2023. 217

LIST OF ILLUSTRATIONS   xiii

32. Mjøstårnet, Brumunddal, Norway, Voll Arkitekter, 2019.   226
33. Resource Rows, Copenhagen, Lendager Arkitekter, 2019.   234
34. Cardboard shelters, Kobe, Japan, Shigeru Ban
    Architects, 1995.   237
35. Schoonschip floating neighborhood, Amsterdam,
    Space&Matter (master plan), 2019.   242
36. House for Trees, Ho Chi Minh City, Vietnam,
    VTN Architects, 2014.   248
37. Bosco Verticale, Milan, Stefano Boeri Architetti, 2014. 252

DWELLING ON EARTH

INTRODUCTION

Dwelling on Earth

One of the oldest known traces of early human habitation lies deep in Olduvai Gorge in Eastern Africa and dates back nearly two million years—marked by little more than scattered stone tools and fossilized animal bones. Though the first gestures of dwelling likely began even earlier and are lost to time, their significance was profound. When our ancestors began returning to familiar ground and reshaping their surroundings, they did more than rewrite human destiny—they began to rewrite the story of the Earth itself.

From these humble beginnings, our dwellings rose ever higher. Temporary shelters of mammoth bones gave way to Mesopotamian mud brick homes. In time, Roman multistory apartment buildings rose over ancient cities, housing thousands in the early concrete structures called *insulae*, meaning "islands," rising from streets like stone archipelagos. Today, skyscrapers of glass and steel pierce the clouds in Shanghai and Dubai. And now, in our quest for survival and adaptation, we dare to imagine homes on distant planets—carrying the ancient idea of dwelling beyond our world.

As we shaped our dwellings to suit our needs, they in turn shaped us. In an era when survival meant grappling with the elements and nomadic wandering in search of resources, permanent dwellings emerged as sanctuaries. They sheltered us from storms, provided comfort and security, and became the seedbeds of civilization.

Dwellings allowed us to store possessions and accumulate wealth, luxuries that had eluded hunter-gatherers. They offered new degrees of privacy without the risk of venturing far from the community. As populations concentrated, these clusters of dwellings functioned as social catalysts. Larger settlements accelerated the rapid exchange of ideas and spurred cultural development. In a single day, a villager might encounter more people than a forager met in months—sometimes years.

Homes also became places to make sense of the world and express shared values. We filled them with symbols of belief, setting aside spaces for ritual and ceremony. About nine thousand years ago in the Stone Age town of Çatalhöyük on the Southern Anatolian Plateau, residents built walls incorporating vulture beaks and human skulls—precursors, perhaps, to the souvenirs and portraits we display on mantelpieces today.

Behind these walls and under these roofs, an extraordinary transformation took place, altering our habits, relationships, and the course of civilization. With shelter securing our fundamental requirements—anchored at the base of Maslow's hierarchy of human needs—people could turn their energy to higher pursuits: building villages, founding cities, and raising monumental temples and pyramids.

Between our first basic huts and today's towering structures lies an extraordinary and hard-won journey of innovation—from Roman concrete to modern steel frames, from wood-burning fireplaces to smart thermostats, from candlelight to LEDs. Many advancements arrived through trial and error, and sometimes at great human cost. The densely packed houses of Çatalhöyük, for instance, used flat roofs as streets, with roof openings doubling as chimneys and entrances accessed by ladders—a design that likely bred respiratory illnesses, frequent falls, and fractured bones. As much as human dwellings showcase our genius for adaptation, they also reveal our knack for creating the very risks they were meant to prevent.

The walls we built to keep nature out also created boundaries between people—inevitably fueling envy, suspicion, and inequality. In the earliest settlements, there was little differentiation among dwellings. But as settlements grew into cities, wealth inequality became visible. In Ur, one of the first cities in Mesopotamia, wealthy residents lived in durable homes made of courses of fired brick, while commoners occupied sun-dried mud brick structures prone to decay. Some had no secure shelter at all. Permanent settlement may have safeguarded the weak from the wild, yet its benefits were unevenly distributed.

Millennia later, the pattern persists. Luxury towers rise while people without shelter sleep in their shadows, as the gap between wages and housing costs widens. Even in wealthy nations, housing insecurity undermines health and well-being, particularly for vulnerable groups like children, who suffer developmental setbacks. Studies consistently show that stable housing improves quality of life, reduces healthcare costs, and lowers rates of intimate-partner violence.[1]

And yet, even when architects set out to improve how we live, well-meaning efforts sometimes perpetuate social problems. In the 1920s, the modernist Frankfurt Kitchen introduced a streamlined workspace based on principles of scientific management and time-and-motion efficiency. Though intended to liberate women from domestic drudgery, its compact design—optimized for a single user—often left them working in isolation, with little space for conversation or supervising children. Rather than challenging traditional gender roles, it may have quietly entrenched them.

Our homes and neighborhoods also impact our health—influencing how we move, breathe, and sleep. Even seemingly comfortable homes can harbor hidden hazards. In car-centric suburbs, daily walks give way to long commutes behind the wheel, contributing to rising rates of diabetes, heart disease, and obesity. While our hunter-gatherer ancestors often walked on the order of 16,000 to 17,000 steps per day, the average American today takes about 4,000 to 5,000 steps. Studies indicate that people living in car-dependent areas face a significantly higher risk of developing type 2 diabetes and obesity.[2] Obesity, in turn, can reduce life expectancy by years, in severe cases comparable to the effects of lifelong smoking.[3]

Dense apartment living can present its own challenges, such as limited natural light, which can negatively affect mental health[4]—though apartment living can also foster social connection between neighbors.[5] And those who live in a house with stairs may live longer and healthier lives, benefiting from the daily cardiovascular exercise of climbing them.[6] Indoor air quality poses another challenge, especially with nearly airtight modern construction. Common building materials release volatile organic compounds, while poor ventilation allows pollutants to build up. Outside, those picture-perfect lawns surrounding suburban homes often rely on pesticides and herbicides such as 2,4-Dichlorophenoxyacetic acid that not only can contaminate groundwater but are so toxic that they pose serious risks to children and pets.[7]

Most people now spend the majority of their lives inside their residences. Americans devote about 90 percent of their time to interior spaces, two-thirds of that at home. Inside, design choices impact well-being. Natural light influences mood and sleep patterns,[8] while clutter can elevate anxiety and dull focus.[9] Views of nature or even simple natural elements have been shown to reduce stress and enhance cognitive function.[10] Yet homes may also shape our inner lives in subtler, more poetic ways. "Thanks to the house, a great many of our memories are housed," philosopher Gaston Bachelard observed, "and if the house is a bit elaborate, if it has a cellar and a garret, nooks and corridors, our memories have refuges that are all the more clearly delineated."[11]

"We shape our buildings; thereafter they shape us," Winston Churchill once famously said when advocating to rebuild the bomb-damaged House of Commons to its original design. He believed its layout—two opposing banks of benches—was responsible for the two-party system and the very nature of British parliamentary democracy.

What holds for the House of Commons holds for the home as well. Dwelling is not merely a physical structure but a way of being—both noun and verb—woven into the fabric of human culture. Our homes are not just where we live. They are how we live.

Crafting Our Niche

It was our capacity to dwell that gave us a unique evolutionary advantage. While Darwin focused primarily on how species adapt to fit their environment, modern researchers emphasize that some animals form significant two-way relationships with their surroundings. Humans belong to this group—we engage in what researchers call "niche construction." Like beavers building dams, we create environments that often afford us advantages. These "ecosystem engineers" pass down construction behaviors through generations.

Some animal-made niches rival even the ingenuity of our own creations. Mound-building termites in Australia are renowned for their monumental towers, sometimes reaching about 800 times their body length—the equivalent of skyscrapers taller than any built by humans.[12] They have even developed temperature control systems. Inside, these insects maintain constant temperatures through intricate systems of vents and flues, even as desert temperatures swing dramatically between day and night.[13] Similarly, bees create precise hexagonal honeycomb patterns. This shape makes efficient use of space, eliminating gaps that would occur with circular cells. It uses less wax than triangles or squares would require to enclose the same area while still providing structural strength—a design so efficient that humans now use it in engineering applications. These remarkable structures, however, emerged over millennia as insects whose genes produced more efficient structures had greater reproductive success, passing their genetic traits to subsequent generations.

Humans, by contrast, accelerate architectural innovation through our ability to make tools, think abstractly, and cooperate intentionally. We leverage geometry, mathematics, and engineering to solve new problems within single lifetimes. We create scalable social networks that allow us to transmit new ideas and coordinate construction projects through planned collaboration rather than genetic instinct. Our earliest homes used simple round forms, as circles and ovals distribute the weight of the roof more evenly and round pits were straightforward to excavate. But we soon developed rectangular structures as our needs evolved, because right angles simplify expansion and partitioning into multiple rooms. We later clustered homes into blocks and orthogonal grids, creating ever-larger cities. We mastered arches and vaults, forged steel, and engineered vertical structures that scrape the sky. No species has ever reshaped its environment so swiftly or completely.

Yet this power comes at a cost. Species that construct niches inevitably alter the ecosystems around them. Just as beavers build dams that transform entire watersheds into lakes of their own making, our ability to modify our environment has fundamentally altered Earth's ecosystems. In our relentless expansion and pursuit of ever-greater comfort, we invented machines that moved mountains and paved vast road networks, and built climate control systems that burn through enormous amounts of energy.

Today, the built environment accounts for almost 40 percent of global carbon emissions, much of it from constructing, heating, and cooling residential buildings.[14] And the problem is growing. By 2050, urban populations will increase by 2.5 billion, with cities housing over two-thirds of humanity. To meet this demand, we will need to build roughly the equivalent of a new New York City every month for the next three decades.[15] Meanwhile, as the middle class in emerging economies is expected to double over the next decade, we may see a rise in consumerism mirroring Western patterns, further stoking demand for more floor space. In the US, even as household size halved, floor space per capita doubled from 400 to 800 square feet between 1891 and 2010[16]—contributing to a tenfold increase in total housing volume.

Our homes make up much of our built environment, driving economic activity and demand for land, infrastructure, and resources. This bond is etched into language itself: both "economy" and "ecology" spring from the Greek *oikos*, which means "house" or "household." The ancient Greeks coined the term *oikonomia* (economy) as the management of the household, reflecting the house as society's basic economic unit. Centuries later, German biologist Ernst Haeckel introduced *Ökologie* (ecology), to refer to the study of organisms in their habitats, their "houses."

Perhaps even cities arose from the house. Archaeologists once believed the first cities, such as Uruk in Mesopotamia, sprang from the centralized power of temples and palaces. But archaeological finds at the earlier site of Tell Brak suggest another path: incremental growth, household by household, forming neighborhoods that collectively housed tens of thousands before any dominant civic structure emerged. This is what archaeologists call a "proto-city," a large, densely occupied settlement with urban traits but with little or no early evidence of centralized authority. Like the "swarm intelligence" behind the complex structures built by termites, these larger settlements may have scaled up through the cumulative interactions of many independent households rather than through the top-down direction of political elites. Even when monumental buildings appeared later, they often mimicked domestic architecture. In Mesopotamia, many temples were essentially enlarged houses.

Today, the way we build shapes the planet more than ever before. From the clearing of forests for materials to the carbon footprint of buildings, our housing choices are transforming the environment. In our continuing pursuit to build ever more comfortable homes, we now face climate change and related challenges that threaten the very comfort we sought to create.

From Huts to High-Rises

How did our homes evolve from simple huts made of animal skins and bones to "smart" sensor-equipped buildings? What technological breakthroughs, societal shifts, and cultural currents sparked new ways of dwelling? And how has the evolution of our homes shaped humanity in return—reconfiguring our cities and neighborhoods, raising standards of comfort, and establishing social norms around privacy and domesticity? This book probes these questions, ultimately asking: How did the remarkable story of dwellings redefine our lives and the planet—and how might we build more sustainably in the future?

Dwelling on Earth traces the long, captivating evolution of human habitation and its entangled relationship with the environment. The story of the home is inseparable from the story of humanity itself, unfolding alongside our societal evolution. From brush huts to high-tech habitats, our dwellings have not only shaped how we live but also transformed our world.

For much of history, residential architecture was largely overlooked by architectural historians and archaeologists, who favored monumental temples and palaces. When ancient homes did enter the scholarly spotlight, conclusions were sometimes distorted by outdated science or cultural presumptions. Take the case of the Peking Man discovered in a cave at Dragon Bone Hill near Beijing, dated to about 400,000 years ago. Early excavators proclaimed the site the home of the first caveman—and supposedly a cannibal, based on bite marks found on bones. Decades later, high-resolution microscopes and modern forensic techniques overturned the tale. The marks match those of gigantic hyenas, suggesting the cave was their den, where they dragged in and gnawed human remains.[17]

These interpretive problems had deep roots. One example is the eighteenth-century "primitive hut" theory of architecture, proposed by French priest Marc-Antoine Laugier, who imagined the first homes as sloped roofs supported by wooden columns—a form that conveniently mirrored classical Greek architecture.[18] Until recently, the oval-shaped huts at Terra Amata in Nice, France, were considered the earliest purpose-built homes based on rings of stones found in a beach alcove—a conclusion perhaps skewed by the desire to declare a definitive "first" home. However, new archaeological evidence using micromorphology, which studies soil slices under polarized light, now indicates these rings were not human-built foundations, but likely resulted from naturally occurring stream flows.[19] Nevertheless, the oval hut reconstructions live on, lingering in textbooks and museum displays.

Today, a range of cutting-edge tools enriches our understanding of early homes. DNA analysis reveals familial relationships and migration patterns among ancient residents. Satellite imagery detects settlements where none were expected. Pollen analysis reconstructs ancient climatic conditions. These and other methods provide new insights into early dwellings and settlements.

Yet even with such tools at our disposal, this book does not attempt to provide a complete global history of every dwelling type. Instead, it traces four major transformations: the Agricultural Revolution, the Urban Revolution, the Industrial Revolution, and the ongoing Sustainability Transition. The first three marked transformations from which there was almost no turning back, establishing new levels of complexity, enabling unprecedented forms of settlement, and fundamentally altering how humans could live. The fourth, however, is different—it compels us to choose how we dwell without destroying what sustains us. We'll explore key innovations and how homes evolved through these turning points, from the first vertical apartment blocks of ancient Rome built by unscrupulous speculators to the early terraced row houses in Liverpool created by forward-thinking industrialists.

Before agriculture, dwellings were temporary—grassy beds, huts made of reeds and animal hides—and most vanished without a trace.

But around 12,000 years ago, the Agricultural Revolution allowed us to invest more deeply in permanent settlements. Communities like the Natufians in modern-day Israel and Palestine built circular dwellings of stone and mud as they domesticated plants and animals. Similar round pit houses emerged independently around the globe—solutions to the same problems, arrived at separately.

However, with permanence came peril. Settled communities placed themselves in the path of natural disasters. Floods, droughts, and hurricanes posed considerable risks to their well-being. Communities also significantly modified their natural environments—clearing forests for farms, fuel, and building materials, which exposed topsoil to wind and rain, washing away fertile earth needed for crops. In doing so, they inadvertently contributed to the very "natural" disasters they feared. In many cases, these environmental missteps set the stage for collapse—a harsh reminder of the responsibilities that came with settled living.

The Urban Revolution, roughly six thousand years ago, gave birth to the city and new living spaces. As the demands of irrigation and agriculture favored extended family households, homes began to expand. Circular huts gave way to rectangular forms, far easier to expand and cluster in growing settlements.

With increased settlement size came greater social, economic, and political complexity—and homes evolved in tandem. A growing division of labor gave rise to professional builders. Growing populations and social specialization spurred innovative dwelling types, including row houses and even multistory apartment buildings.

Remarkably, several of these urban forms—such as the atrium house and the organized street grid—emerged independently in different parts of the world, in cultures with no direct contact. In ancient Rome, breakthroughs in materials like concrete made it possible to construct vertical apartment buildings, housing large numbers of urban residents. These unprecedented housing forms enabled more people to live in closer proximity, fostering new kinds of interaction.

Did settled life make us happier? While agricultural settlement is often viewed as inevitable progress, some anthropologists highlight the advantages of nomadic lifestyles. They cite the example of the nomadic !Kung people of the Kalahari, who spend only roughly 40 percent of their time securing food, dedicating the remainder to socializing, dancing, and other pursuits.[20] By contrast, settled life often brought increased labor demands—from dawn-to-dusk farming to endless home maintenance.

Even as the cities of the classical world grew, nomadic people persisted, offering a different model entirely. In the fifth century BC, the ancient Greek historian Herodotus described the nomadic peoples on the Eurasian steppe: "Having neither cities nor forts, and carrying their dwellings with them wherever they go: accustomed, moreover, one and all of them, to shoot from horseback; and living not by husbandry but on their cattle, their wagons the only houses that they possess, how can they fail of being unconquerable, and unassailable even?"[21] These societies had mastered animal domestication but chose not to cultivate crops. As historian Spiro Kostof noted, "They had no use for settled permanence except as their last resting place."[22]

And yet the agglomeration of urban populations brought undeniable advantages. Larger scales of social organization fueled economic productivity and wealth creation—a pattern that continues from ancient cities to modern metropolises.[23] While early productivity manifested in temples and elite housing, today we measure it in GDP. Urban concentration consistently drives innovation.[24] In the

United States, large cities produce about twice as many patents per person as smaller ones.[25] Cities became the engines of civilization.

But even these had limits. Preindustrial cities faced hard constraints to growth. Inadequate sanitation and insufficient agricultural output restricted their population. These barriers would not be broken until the Industrial Revolution, which introduced new energy sources and more efficient means of production—enabling urban growth on an unprecedented scale.

The Industrial Revolution reshaped residential architecture and cities as a whole. Steam trains enabled suburban expansion, while breakthroughs in steel production, construction equipment, and elevators revolutionized building height in cities like Chicago and New York. Meanwhile, a growing bourgeoisie redefined domestic life around the nuclear family—evident in seventeenth-century Dutch row houses, where, to the shock of foreign guests, visitors were expected to remove their shoes.

But industrialization came with a darker side. In many cities, the working class lived in overcrowded, unsanitary tenements. Polluted air, contaminated water, and squalid housing conditions made cities deadly environments, where mortality rates outpaced births. In response to these grim realities, reformers pioneered early planning reforms and regulations that led to better housing initiatives, exemplified by the terraced rows in Liverpool. The construction of modern sewage systems and clean water infrastructure eventually vastly improved urban life.

The twentieth century witnessed a bold modernist movement of urban living that reimagined the home as an efficient machine. This approach manifested in neatly organized rows of apartment blocks and tall towers set in parks. While some cities like Singapore and Hong Kong embraced vertical urbanism, elsewhere, particularly in the United States, domestic life increasingly migrated to automobile-oriented suburban developments.

As we prepare to build many more homes in the twenty-first century, we face new challenges. Today, our homes confront growing environmental threats, from rising temperatures to floods and wildfires. In response, architects are being called on to design more resilient and sustainable dwellings. These range from entire floating neighborhoods to structures made from bio-based materials like mass timber—large engineered-wood panels strong enough to stand in for concrete.

Simultaneously, emerging technologies are transforming how we build and live. Where Mesopotamians once painstakingly molded clay bricks by hand, robotic arms now extrude concrete with precision. Digital design and automated manufacturing such as 3D printing are revolutionizing how we build, even enabling the design of prototypes for Martian habitats. Artificial intelligence is already beginning to generate home designs and manage domestic systems.

Yet amid this wave of innovation, we're also rediscovering the wisdom of time-tested preindustrial traditions. Passive heating and cooling, natural ventilation, and bio-based materials are making a return—not as nostalgic gestures, but as proven solutions. In many respects, our ancestors may have built more sustainably. Mesopotamian cities largely disappeared into the earth. Ours, by contrast, may be remembered by future archaeologists for their concrete debris.

As we confront the intertwined challenges of climate change and rapid urbanization, the long history of dwelling becomes more than a source of insight. It offers a foundation for reimagining how we live. This book traces that history to understand how we arrived at this moment, and to explore what it will take to build more sustainably.

Homes for Tomorrow

As a professor of architecture and urban planning, I've been fortunate to witness an extraordinary diversity of global housing solutions. My journey has taken me from the informal settlements of southern China to Manhattan's supertall skyscrapers, from Hong Kong's meticulously planned public housing estates to the Netherlands' experimental floating homes. Along the way, I've seen how seemingly technical policies—from zoning resolutions to building codes, even landscaping requirements—significantly shape the way we live. In the United States, for instance, regulations meant to keep neighborhoods orderly have inadvertently nudged out "missing middle" housing—such as row houses, duplexes, and apartment buildings that bridge the gap between single-family homes and large apartment blocks. They have also limited mixed-use blocks where apartments sit above corner cafés or neighborhood shops. The result? Fewer affordable, walkable choices in many communities. In Singapore, by contrast, urban planning policies have deliberately cultivated tall buildings that weave greenery into the skyline, proving how intentional policy design can achieve both density and livability.

As a practicing architect, I've watched the profession transform from hand-drawn blueprints to algorithm-driven modeling and AI-assisted renderings. Construction methods, too, have evolved. Brick walls once laid by hand can now arrive as factory-made panels or be installed by robotic arms. Drones monitor progress from above while robotic dogs patrol sites from the ground. Alongside these technical advances, our profession has championed more sustainable buildings, from advocating for stricter energy codes to embracing renewable materials like cross-laminated timber and bio-based finishes.

As a resident, my own experience of home began in a Dutch town. I grew up in a narrow row house, almost identical to its neighbors, each with its own modest backyard. No one had air-conditioning—we didn't need it. Thick brick walls, external shading, and cross ventilation kept interiors cool. The wide sidewalks fostered a sense of community. Most neighbors knew each other. As a child, I could bike safely to school and play in the street.

When I began my studies in Delft, I moved into student housing that was part of a bold experiment in 1970s architecture. Architects had reimagined the conventional layout, centering each floor around a communal kitchen. Most roommates took turns cooking for one another. There were no formal rules requiring this arrangement. The layout encouraged it. It nurtured collaboration and community. To our surprise, one roommate became the town's youngest mayor.

In Barcelona, I lived in a compact apartment in the old town. Despite the limited space, I was steps from shops, cafes, and public transit. Paris offered a similar lifestyle, with its Haussmann-era walk-up courtyard buildings. In New York, I lived in elevator buildings. Hong Kong immersed me in its vertical labyrinth of skyscrapers and "pencil towers." Apartments were small but utilized every square inch through sliding walls, foldout furniture, and built-in storage tucked into every nook.

These cities share an important quality. Most daily activities are within a fifteen-minute walk or bike ride. They are examples of what planners now call the "15-minute city." This experience taught me that quality of life isn't necessarily tied to the size of one's home but to the richness of the walkable surroundings.

My path later led me back to suburban life—to a midcentury modern villa in California, a townhouse in Virginia, and a century-old Colonial Revival house in a New Jersey railroad town. Each move brought new daily routines. In Manhattan, movement was built into everyday life, from walking to stores to catching the subway. In the New Jersey suburbs, staying active often requires a gym membership.

In the chapters ahead, we will explore the larger story of human habitation—from the first fired bricks of Mesopotamia to the modular 3D-printed homes of tomorrow. We'll examine engineering feats that made cities possible, and social experiments that redefined domestic life. We'll uncover innovations we now take for granted—like how the humble corridor reconfigured privacy. We will explore movements shaped by cultural and economic shifts, from Bauhaus to Brutalism.

While we will examine the physical structure of buildings, we will also consider the social structures they create. Each housing type has the ability to shape urban landscapes, daily experiences, and interactions across different walks of life. Even seemingly innocuous design choices can influence social dynamics. As Amos Rapoport observed in *House Form and Culture*, the placement of American dining counters—like the arrangement of chairs in psychotherapy sessions or courtroom layouts—is "remarkably indicative of the roles of the people involved."[26]

Throughout history, the concept and form of home have continually evolved. Unlike the Darwinian evolution of species shaped by natural selection, architecture evolves through artificial selection—driven by human intention. It is up to us to actively shape our built environment. We didn't accept rock shelters as our final dwelling place. We built our way from mud huts to towers of steel and glass—not by chance, but by choice, and through the same cooperative intelligence that first forged our settlements to meet shared challenges. If we could once raise Gothic cathedrals stone by stone, we can certainly reimagine the homes we build today.

Today, we can create homes that do less harm to the planet. Addressing carbon emissions in the built environment is inherently complicated, involving trade-offs across materials, operations, infrastructure, and transportation. But due to advances in digital design, performance simulation, and life-cycle modeling, we now have the tools to understand and optimize these interactions with unprecedented precision. The technology exists. What remains is the collective will to act.

In our quest to build better homes, it's tempting to focus on the newest technologies—solar panels, smart thermostats, superinsulation. But progress won't come from buildings alone. It depends equally on what happens beyond the property line: the design of streets and the shape of neighborhoods. These decisions often lie outside the architect's control, shaped instead by planners and policymakers. And yet, they have an enormous influence. Architects can design exceptional houses. However, they cannot overcome zoning laws that mandate excessive parking or the absence of safe sidewalks and crossings.

Growing up in the Netherlands quickly teaches you that landscapes are made, not given. Hardly a square inch remains untouched. One-fifth of the country is polder—land wrested from sea and river. You realize that the ground beneath your feet is engineered. If we can conjure land from water, surely we can reshape the land we have with equal ingenuity.

As a phrase attributed to Buckminster Fuller puts it, "We are called to be architects of the future, not its victims." We are not prisoners to our surroundings, because we are their authors. The path forward begins with reimagining how we dwell. For dwelling is more than walls and roofs. It's about who we are, how we relate to one another, and how we care for the Earth that remains our only home.

ONE

A Permanent Place

Fire and Shelter

In 1753, the Jesuit priest Marc-Antoine Laugier described the origin of dwelling by imagining a lone "savage" troubled by nature's extremes. This "primitive man," seeking refuge from scorching heat and torrential rain, initially fled to a cave but found it too dark and filled with "foul air." Upon leaving the cave, he embarks on a mission. "Resolved to make good by his ingenuity the careless neglect of nature," Laugier writes, "he wants to make himself a dwelling."[1]

As Laugier's story continues, the man wanders through a forest, stumbles upon fallen branches, and has an epiphany. "He chooses four of the strongest, raises them upright and arranges them in a square." With surprising engineering intuition, he lays four more branches across their tops to create a frame. He then crowns it with a pitched triangle, making a roof truss, and covers it "with leaves so closely packed that neither sun nor rain can penetrate. Thus man is housed."

This tale of instant architecture became the foundation of Laugier's influential theory, championing the simplicity of a "primitive hut," a pitched roof supported by columns, over the theatrical flourishes of High Baroque architecture. While the story shaped architectural thinking for generations, it is far from the historical reality. Rather than a single stroke of genius, the story of human habitation is one of gradual evolution, unfolding over millions of years through the collaborative acts of countless generations. And this story begins not with *Homo sapiens* but with our distant ancestors.

This history begins in the trees, roughly 14 to 18 million years ago, according to evolutionary biologists, when our great ape ancestors likely developed sleeping platforms.[2] They would bend and weave together branches, twigs, and leaves, creating what we might call the first beds. Building these rudimentary and temporary platforms—something modern gorillas, orangutans, and chimpanzees still do—would have offered protection from predators and blood-sucking insects. Perhaps they offered escape from ground-level humidity as well.[3]

But the real transformation came when our hominin predecessors, the forebears of Neanderthals and *Homo sapiens*, broke from this pattern. While apes continued to build fresh nests each night, abandoning them in the morning, our hominin ancestors began experimenting with something surprisingly revolutionary: permanence.[4]

One of the earliest traces of this practice was found in Olduvai Gorge, Tanzania, dating back to around two million years ago. Archaeologists discovered stone artifacts associated with early hominin species. Most importantly, these were clustered in specific locations. This suggests our ancestors were creating the first "places," sites they would return to again and again.

Why bother establishing a favored place at all? Unlike most primates, who consume what they find on the spot, early hominins began carrying food back to a central place to share. Such behavior would have improved the odds of reproduction. "The extraordinarily long period of juvenile dependency necessitates high levels of cooperation and resource sharing by both parents, by other children, and sometimes by other members of the society," evolutionary anthropologists Steven Kuhn and Mary Stiner observe.[5] "It takes a village to raise a child, but it also takes a long time."

Regardless of intent, this seemingly simple change—the creation of places to return to—marked one of the most significant transformations in human evolution. Unlike the solitary nests of apes, these early campsites became the first community spaces in human history.

Here, our ancestors did more than rest—they slept, shared food, crafted tools, and passed down knowledge. As several anthropologists have noted, these sites became "arenas for social learning that had not existed previously."[6] This new social environment may have even helped shape our brains, particularly the neocortex—the region responsible for advanced cognitive functions such as emotional control and planning.[7] This new lifestyle not only set human habitation apart from that of apes, it may have redefined who we were.

This would also have accelerated one of our signature strengths: our ability to make tools, positioning us, as several archaeologists describe, as "ultrasocial engineers."[8] The earliest known trace of this engineering impulse surfaces at Kalambo Falls, Zambia. There, excavators discovered two interlocking timbers dated to roughly 476,000 years ago—evidence that, as the researchers describe it, offers "a glimpse of a capacity to create a built environment" long before *Homo sapiens*.[9]

The next major revolution came with the habitual use of fire, beginning around 400,000 years ago. Fire changed human habitation in ways our ancestors could hardly have imagined. It kept predators at bay, illuminated the darkness, provided warmth, and unlocked new food sources, making previously inedible items like grains digestible. This transformed our relationship with time, cutting the time spent chewing raw foods and extending our days beyond sunset.

Around the same period, our ancestors began to more frequently occupy rock shelters and caves. Fire made the inhospitable conditions of caves more bearable, as caverns were often cold, dark, damp, and home to other residents like lions, bears, and hyenas, which had to be displaced. With fire, these places stayed occupied longer.[10] But fire did more than make campsites and caves more comfortable.

"Home is where the hearth is" goes the saying, and in prehistoric times, the hearth was truly the center of the home. Our ancestors gathered around fires to share food, tell stories, and strengthen social ties. As archaeologists Desmond Clark and Jack Harris observed, fire "helped to weld early hominid groups into the coherent family units that are characteristic of human society."[11]

Rock-shelter, Abrigo de Navalmaíllo, Spain, ca. 73,000 BC.[12]

These more permanent places likely changed our trajectory. They provided safe havens, helping to protect the young and vulnerable and extending the lifespan of the physically compromised.[13] Previously, a bone fracture would have meant certain death. Now, there was hope for recovery.

In some ways, a permanent place made survival easier. But it also required more advanced social skills. This could have affected our evolution. Natural selection could have increasingly favored those better at cooperation, communication, and conflict resolution. The use of fire for cooking reduced the size of our teeth, leaving them smaller than those of other animals. Some archaeologists have proposed that dwelling may have changed our brains. It established a feedback loop: Humans were creating homes, and homes were shaping humans. This process may have influenced the development of future generations in a nonlinear way. As Kuhn and Stiner observed, "More and more, hominins were coevolving with the world that they modified."

These early settlements proved attractive to other hominins, drawing them in with the promise of food, resources, and companionship. Yet this closeness came at a cost. Exposure to smoke from open fires harmed lungs. Meanwhile, the close proximity of people hastened the transmission of mycobacterial diseases through coughing.[14] Tuberculosis, for instance, is estimated to have caused about a billion deaths across history, more than all famines and wars combined.[15]

Managing fire brought other challenges as well. Early humans had to master the delicate balance between warmth and smoke inhalation. Recent studies of sites like Lazaret Cave, occupied approximately 170,000 years ago, reveal advanced spatial thinking. Hearths were strategically placed in "sweet spots" that maximized heat and light while allowing smoke to escape.[16] Too deep in the cave meant safety from predators but poor ventilation. Too near the entrance meant better air but exposure to cold and danger. This spatial problem-solving reflects not only an awareness of these practical challenges but also an ability to overcome them.

Meanwhile, the control of fire enabled our ancestors to venture into regions like northern Europe during periods when nearly 30 percent of the continent lay under ice, dramatically expanding our territory. It also marked humanity's first major impact on the Earth. Long before industrial emissions, our ancestors wielded flames as environmental engineering tools. They managed burn zones that promoted fruit- and nut-bearing plants in the postfire regrowth vegetation.[17] Fire became a powerful hunting aid, exposing the nests of small game and driving larger prey into traps. It effectively shrank the "radius of a meal"[18]—the distance humans needed to travel to find enough food. Our ancient use of fire has influenced many ecosystems and spurred the rise of fire-adapted plant species (pyrophytes).

As our ancestors' mastery of fire grew, so did their ingenuity in creating comfort. More than 200,000 years ago, evidence of the first intentionally created bedding appeared in southern African rock shelters.[19] Early *Homo sapiens* carefully constructed beds of broad-leaved grasses to enhance their comfort. They placed them close to the hearth—and, judging from the scorched ends of the grasses, sometimes too close. This arrangement mirrors modern hunter-gatherer camps, where people still gather to sleep around the fire.[20]

Neanderthals displayed architectural capabilities of their own. Around 176,000 years ago, deep within Bruniquel Cave in France, they ventured more than a thousand feet from the entrance. Working by torchlight, they deliberately stacked hundreds of stalagmite pieces into two broad rings, some bearing traces of fire.[21] This wasn't shelter but one of humanity's earliest monuments. The sheer effort required speaks to sophisticated planning and cooperation.

By 100,000 years ago, hominin settlements show evidence of complex spatial organization. The popular image of Neanderthals living deep in caves turns out to be wrong. Archaeologists found they preferred more accessible spaces near cave entrances and under rock shelters. There, they created distinct zones for different activities, including hearths for cooking and areas dedicated to toolmaking and butchering.[22] They even buried their dead beneath the cave floors and engaged in symbol making, adorning stalagmites with abstract designs using red ochre pigments.

When Neanderthals tracked game, they constructed temporary windbreaks from wood and mammoth bones. One striking example comes from La Folie, a 60,000-year-old site in west-central France. In this harsh, cold environment of Ice Age Europe, Neanderthals created what archaeologists believe was a base camp. Preserved post holes suggest a circular wooden structure, likely supporting

Temporary Neanderthal camp "La Folie," near present-day Poitiers, France, ca. 60,000 BC.[23]

brush or hides, serving as a windbreak. Within this 30-foot diameter space, they carried out several activities. They rested, shaped stone tools, and prepared meals. They may have even laid mats to soften the floor.[24]

As the Neanderthals gradually disappeared around 40,000 years ago—partly due to competition with our own species—*Homo sapiens* began taking shelter-building in new directions. In the Dordogne region of France, they occupied rock shelters and decorated them. They made engravings and stained them with red, yellow, and brown ochre, sometimes starting with a preparatory charcoal sketch. Among these earliest artistic expressions were hand stencils, geometric patterns, and animal figures. One of the oldest symbols was probably a representation of the vulva.[25] These endeavors revealed not only the unique symbolic capacity of our species but also an emerging desire to make living spaces distinctly our own.

The limitation of caves, of course, is that they have a predetermined location. However, modern humans also built more impressive temporary shelters in open locations. One example comes from Mezhirich, Ukraine, dating back around 15,000 years ago. Here, a group of Ice Age hunter-gatherers constructed oval and circular huts from 120 to 240 square feet in size. They were built mostly from mammoth bones and are among the earliest examples of architecture. The largest of these structures, weighing approximately 50,000 pounds, would have required ten people over five days to erect.[26] Given the extraordinary effort required to build them, these structures may have held ceremonial or symbolic meaning beyond simple shelter.

The mammoth-bone huts represent a level of architectural skill that sets them apart from the instinctive nest building of our ape ancestors. The builders demonstrated a rudimentary understanding

Bone hut, Mezhirich, Ukraine, ca. 15,000 BC.

of engineering, deliberately placing each bone to exploit its natural geometry. They created a precise oval or circular foundation and arranged leg bones and jaw bones at regular intervals. They positioned the jaws chin down. The leg bones probably upheld a roof, although it is likely that wooden elements would have helped support it as well. The entrance was marked by large upright mammoth tusks. The wall displayed a careful repetition and symmetry using pieces of the vertebral column. Remnants of hearths inside the dwellings indicate the use of bones as fuel. The final effect must have been striking—like igloos made of bone rather than blocks of ice.

Several of these mammoth-bone dwellings have been found across Eastern Europe and Russia. They helped the builders cope with the frigid temperatures near the end of the last Ice Age when ice sheets stretched far into Europe. Archaeologist Steven Mithen describes what these homes might have been like inside: "The floor is soft, carpeted with hides and furs that surround a central ash-filled hearth. Mammoth skulls and leg bones provide furniture; an assortment of leather bags, bone and wooden bowls, antler and stone

Traditional Inuit igloo, Nunavut, Canada.

tools are scattered by the walls and hung from the rafters—a scene of Stone Age domestic clutter."[27]

In a twist of prehistoric irony, our ancestors' hunting skills proved too effective, leading to the extinction of mammoths around 10,000 years ago—and mammoth-bone dwellings with them. However, humans also used other building materials, particularly wood. Yet these more perishable materials present a challenge for modern archaeologists. Wooden structures rarely survive. Even when promising sites are discovered, researchers struggle to interpret them, due to their decay. As archaeologist John Yellen noted, "Paleolithic Pompeiis are unknown."[28] Most of these ancient homes have long since returned to the soil, leaving archaeologists to piece together their stories from fragmentary evidence.

However, on rare occasions nature preserves a snapshot of prehistoric domestic life. One such example was a fisher-hunter-gatherer base camp of six huts on the shore of Israel's Sea of Galilee dating back 23,000 years. These Paleolithic homes survived thanks to a curiously helpful sequence of events: a fire followed by submergence under lake water, which protected them from decay. They might have remained hidden forever, until a recent drought when water was pumped from the lake. Archaeologists found that the site's foragers had crafted small huts from brushwood, weaving them into dome-like structures enclosing a central hearth. Near the perimeter, they covered the floor with thick bunches of grass laid out in a tile-like pattern on top of a solid layer of clay.[29]

Yet even these well-crafted dwellings were not meant to last forever. This pattern of temporary settlement continues among modern hunter-gatherers today, like the !Kung people in the Kalahari Desert. They rarely stay in one place for more than a few months due to the intrusion of insects that inevitably follows human habitation.[30] Nevertheless, in these fleeting shelters we find humanity's first steps toward permanent places in the landscape. What began as simple

Brush hut at Ohalo II, Sea of Galilee, Israel, ca. 21,000 BC.[31]

returns to favored spots evolved into increasingly sophisticated and enduring manipulations of space that would ultimately distinguish us from every other species on Earth.

Digging In

Roughly 20,000 years ago, the last great Ice Age drew to a close. As the world began to warm, the ice sheets, which once cloaked nearly a quarter of the Earth's land, started to recede. Their retreat did more than reshape the terrain. In the Eastern Mediterranean, they created the perfect laboratory for human innovation. Once-barren steppes flourished into lush woodlands teeming with olive, pistachio, and oak trees, alongside fields of wild wheat and barley. Here, humanity would take major strides toward permanent settlement.

The Natufians, a hunter-gatherer culture inhabiting what would become modern-day Israel and Palestine, were the first to seize this opportunity. Around 14,500 years ago, surrounded by abundant almond and pistachio trees and calorie-rich plants, they chose a different path. They stopped following the seasonal migrations of animals and plants. Instead, they decided to make the land work for them. They settled down.

Their solution to permanent housing, the pit house, was both simple and ingenious. By excavating circular or oval depressions in the earth and roofing them over, they created dwellings that were easy to construct and durable. Without the masonry skill to erect freestanding walls, the Natufians used the earth itself to provide natural walls. Better still, these semisubterranean structures offered superior insulation, remaining warm in winter and cool in summer.

The pit house proved so effective that it emerged in other cultures as well. In Eastern Europe, hunter-gatherers first constructed mammoth-bone huts partially buried in circular pits to ward off the

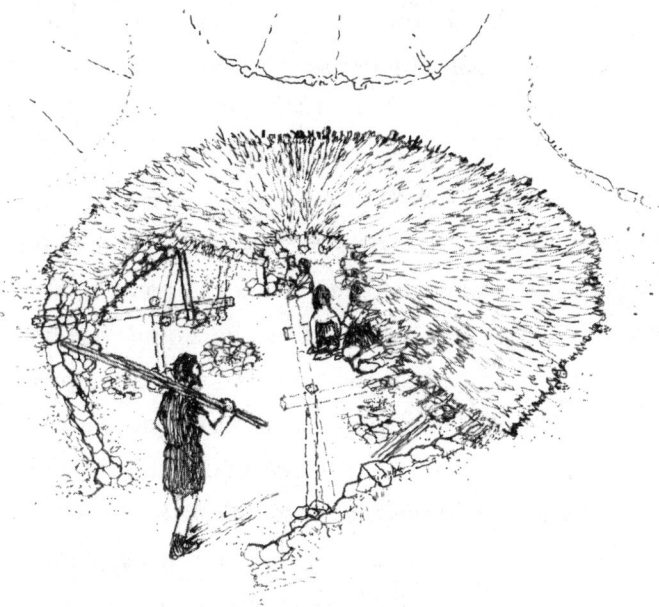

Natufian pit dwellings, 'Ain Mallaha ('Eynan), Israel, ca. 12,500 BC.[32]

cold. The Yellow River Valley of China saw pit houses emerge around 6,500 years ago as shelter from harsh weather. Native Americans in the Sonoran Desert, about 4,000 years ago, also dug oval pits several feet deep for their dwellings to escape the summer heat. While these cultures developed their solutions independently, they all discovered the same solution. The pit house was nearly ideal, requiring minimal resources while being adaptable to almost any climate.

Most archaeologists would agree that the round and oval houses of the Natufians represented the earliest structures to echo our modern notion of a home, marking a key step toward permanent settlement.[33] The Natufians did not just dig a hole and cover it with branches. Instead, they used rocks to stabilize the pit's sides, creating a rudimentary retaining wall. Inside, they built a ring of evenly spaced posts that supported the roof, and anchored the posts with rocks. They likely created a roof from branches or reeds. These homes were modest in size, spanning 10 to 20 feet in diameter. They featured one or several stone hearths.[34]

The circular design of Natufian houses offered several other advantages as well. Round pits were easier to dig than rectangular ones. Round shapes also distributed structural forces more evenly, increasing resistance to wind forces. Unlike their rectangular equivalents, round buildings avoided collapsing corners. Without corners, construction became simpler. The circular design also proved highly efficient, as round shapes enclose maximum space using minimal materials. The presence of a central hearth could warm the interior evenly, ensuring optimal warmth throughout the dwelling. These benefits help explain why round forms dominated early architecture across widely separated cultures from Africa to the Americas.[35]

Perhaps most impressive was the geometric precision of some of the dwellings. One of the excavated remains featured perfectly circular foundations. Elsewhere, researchers found a circular limestone disk tool about eight inches in diameter. Both artifacts exhibit a surprisingly high level of symmetry. This likely reflected the Natufians' deliberate intent to build circular forms.[36] These homes suggest they had planned their buildings in advance, challenging our assumptions about when such deliberate architecture emerged.

Their settlements featured both large and small single-room houses. However, their specific purpose remains uncertain. Curiously, house size showed no correlation with family size or social status—a finding consistent with the absence of evidence of social stratification among the Natufians. As a result, archaeologists suggest the variation in size was tied to function rather than social hierarchy.[37] The larger structures might have functioned as communal spaces or workshops.

For the first time in history, people began living together in such large numbers. Natufians clustered their homes into small hamlets, which supported estimated populations of around 150 individuals. This was a major increase from the typical hunter-gatherer groups of about 15 to 50 people.[38] The Natufians were not full-fledged farmers yet, as they cultivated wild cereals while preserving their hunting practices. Nevertheless, their dwellings represent a major step toward a sedentary existence.

These early villages were likely quite vibrant. Much of life occurred beyond individual dwellings in shared outdoor spaces, such as communal cooking and food preparation. François Valla, one of 'Ain Mallaha's original excavators, argued that life in these communities differed sharply from scattered bands.[39] They likely hosted feasts, ceremonies, and social events. These activities may have been similar to the periodic gatherings of later hunter-gatherer societies, like the seminomadic Inuit in the Arctic, who lived in tents in summer and igloos in winter.

But humanity's first experiment with permanent settlement also attracted unexpected visitors. As the settler populations expanded, so did house mice populations, drawn by the concentrated food waste in villages. House mice emerged around the same time as the first Natufian settlements and quickly outcompeted native wild mice.[40] The ripple effects of this ecological change extended further up the food chain. The abundance of food waste and the mice, in turn, drew wolves closer to human communities. Some scholars suggest that this influx of wolves may have triggered the domestication of dogs—a relationship immortalized in the burial of an elderly Natufian woman, her hand resting gently on a puppy.[41]

In response, the Natufians adapted their structures, modifying the smaller circular buildings between their dwellings—likely granaries—with suspended, sloped floors that deterred rodents and enhanced air circulation to prevent food spoilage.[42] Thus, the Natufians had to adjust to environmental challenges they themselves unintentionally created.

The price of permanence grew steeper with each generation. Fixed settlements introduced water pollution, as accumulated garbage and human waste began to taint their water sources. The constant harvesting of local plants and the overhunting of animals led to gradually diminishing resources. In some cases, it led to local extinctions.

Yet this human-environment dynamic was more nuanced than just exploitation. The Natufians, like other early settlers, pioneered land management practices that reshaped landscapes in both costly and fruitful ways. Through selective harvesting, they unintentionally dispersed seeds. This created new vegetation patterns across their lands. Controlled burning promoted secondary forest growth, drew game animals, and fostered the growth of new plant species. The resulting ash boosted soil nutrients, often increasing local biodiversity and ecological productivity in ways that benefited both human communities and local ecosystems.

Remarkably, evidence reveals that as far back as 12,000 years ago, three-quarters of Earth's land bore subtle marks of human activity.[43] This finding upends our notion of "untouched" and "pristine" nature. The wilderness we now idealize was likely shaped by millennia of interaction between humans and their environment.

However, permanent settlement exposed humans to new vulnerabilities. With fixed dwellings and stored food supplies, communities lost the option to simply pack up and leave. Settlements in river valleys faced flooding, while those in drier areas were vulnerable to drought. Villages in woodlands risked wildfires. Resource depletion added pressure as intensive hunting and gathering began to outstrip natural regeneration. The Natufians found themselves in an increasingly adversarial relationship with nature, both subject to its forces and unintentionally worsening the frequency and severity of disruptive environmental events. These challenges occasionally delivered stark reminders about the increased vulnerability and responsibility tied to their fixed abodes.

These risks intensified with growing populations. Permanent settlement allowed for larger families. With a stable home base, parents could more easily care for multiple children without the strain of continuous movement. This reduced the need to space births widely. The growing economic value of children in early farming and foraging activities likely spurred population growth as well.[44] But larger families strained food supplies. Archaeological evidence from gazelle bones indicates that the Natufians mostly hunted larger males.[45] This would have likely shrunk gazelle populations and meat yields over time. They also overharvested wild plants, reducing their capacity to regenerate.

Around 10,500 BC, the climate suddenly plunged back toward Ice-Age conditions—a brief cold spell known as the Younger Dryas. It likely struck a fatal blow to the Natufians' sedentary life. They abandoned their villages and reverted to nomadism. Nevertheless, they still established smaller, semipermanent camps to exploit seasonal resources.

While their 2,000-year experiment in settled life ended, it was far from a failure. The Natufians pioneered innovations from durable pit houses to sophisticated granaries. Their hard-earned lessons helped pave the way for their descendants to transition from foragers to farmers and continue the trajectory toward permanent human habitation.

Breaking the Circle

One of the few places to witness the evolution from hunter-gatherer encampments to agricultural settlements is Beidha in southern Jordan. Unlike its famous neighbor Petra, whose striking tomb facades carved into red rocks draw crowds and feature in movies like *Indiana Jones and the Last Crusade*, Beidha offers little spectacle. It appears unremarkable—just ancient stone foundations. But what Beidha lacks in grandeur, it makes up for in historical significance. The site provides a key to understanding how so many of us came to inhabit rectangular buildings today.

Beidha was a seasonal encampment around 11,000 BC established by the Natufians, who used the site as a base for hunting activities. It was then abandoned, perhaps due to depleting resources and a cooling climate. Around 9600 BC, after enduring a thousand-year drought, temperatures rose. This dramatic change to warmer and wetter weather likely prompted a new society, descended from the Natufians, to try their luck at permanent settlements.

Perhaps realizing that wild crops would eventually be depleted with continued harvesting, these people began cultivating them. They grew rye, wheat, and barley in the fertile alluvial valley soils. Knowing that solely hunting wild gazelles was no longer sustainable due to overhunting, they started to domesticate sheep and goats. They became farmers.

This was the beginning of the Neolithic period, or the New Stone Age (from the ancient Greek *neos* meaning "new" and *lithos* meaning "stone"). The shift to agriculture enabled these early settlers to produce surplus food and invest more heavily in their dwellings. But by settling in permanent locations to manage their crops, they also had to safeguard them from others who might, quite literally, pick the fruits of their labor. As the architectural historian Spiro Kostof noted, "A fixed place under the sky—that is the Neolithic legacy."[46]

This culture is known to archaeologists as the Pre-Pottery Neolithic people. This name highlights their lack of pottery-making technology, such as the ability to fire clay. Yet what they lacked in ceramic skills, they made up for in their buildings. Returning to villages the Natufians had previously abandoned, these people began using more durable materials like stone and experimenting with innovative construction methods. One of these was the invention of mud bricks.

Mud bricks were one of humanity's first widely used building materials. Mud was available in many parts of the world, but brick making was labor-intensive. It required that villagers laboriously dig clay from the valley floor. They then often kneaded it with straw for greater resilience. They molded this mixture into oblong forms, leaving them to sun-dry for a few weeks. Once hardened, the villagers stacked them and bonded them with mud mortar to raise walls. These mud walls also offered some welcome insulation from both heat and cold. All these efforts demonstrate their dedication to permanent settlement.

Their methods proved successful. The Pre-Pottery Neolithic people expanded across the Middle East. By 8000 BC, agropastoral villages thrived throughout the Levant in the eastern Mediterranean, from the highland regions above the Euphrates River in Syria northward into Anatolia. Some of these villages boasted hundreds of well-constructed houses.[47] One of the smaller settlements was Beidha.

At Beidha, the villagers herded goats, sowed barley and wheat, and also hunted game and foraged nuts.[48] In the beginning, they built pit houses with sunken floors, stone foundations, and wooden posts supporting roofs. But around 6650 BC, their homes were destroyed by fire.

From those ashes rose a new beginning. Departing from the old semisubterranean pit dwellings, they built aboveground designs. They erected walls of mud bricks and sandstone slabs and topped them with flat roofs. They covered floors in plaster and even decorated some with black paint or burnished black-and-red patterns.[49]

Most importantly, their buildings were no longer round but rectangular.

Erecting rectangular houses demanded advanced building techniques, such as joining perpendicular walls at ninety-degree angles. But it gave them significant benefits. These homes could be more easily divided into multiple rooms, each space tailored to a specific purpose. They could more easily be expanded, with additional rooms built adjacent to existing ones. Flat roofs also provided new oppor-

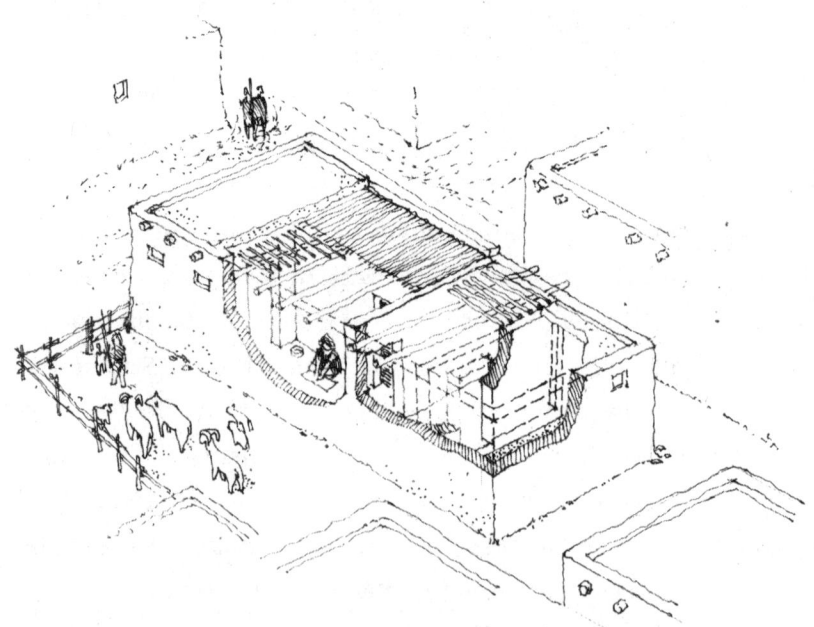

Five-room mud brick house, Abu Hureyra, Syria, ca. 6500 BC.

tunities, such as the potential for upward expansion and rooftop private outdoor space. The shift to rectangular buildings fostered denser communities by allowing for more tightly knit, organized settlements.

Over time, Beidha's population doubled to a few hundred people. Residents built larger houses with up to five rooms, replacing the single-room homes of their earlier pit dwellings. Where circular homes could house one or two individuals, the rectangular multiroom structures could accommodate entire extended families. As agriculture led to an increase in village populations and social complexity, the rectangular plan offered a more practical dwelling arrangement.

This wasn't unique to Beidha. Across the Levant, a pattern emerged. As communities developed their farming and herding skills, they would shift from building circular dwellings to rectangular ones. For instance, Jericho, located in today's West Bank, began as a settlement of circular pit dwellings established by the Natufians. The Pre-Pottery Neolithic people initially continued this tradition of circular pit homes. By 9600 BC, the inhabitants had constructed a wall partially enclosing their village, perhaps to protect from floods, making it the first known fortified town.[50] Their crowning achievement was the Tower of Jericho, a 28-foot-tall round stone structure considered humanity's first work of monumental architecture. It may have had a ceremonial purpose, maybe as a landmark to draw outsiders into their communal way of life.[51]

Around 7000 BC, Jericho became one of the largest villages of its time, housing possibly up to 3,000 individuals. The village architecture of rectangular homes built from mud bricks reflected this. Even the bricks evolved. Where initially bricks had flat bottoms and rounded tops, they became perfectly cuboid, allowing better stacking and creating more stable construction.[52]

This transition from round to rectangular dwellings happened not only in the Near East, but in agricultural societies worldwide, from Mesoamerica to Asia.[53] People arrived at rectangular building independently, suggesting it was a widely favored solution as communities became better farmers. Archaeologist Kent Flannery[54] noted how food storage played an important role in this transition. He found that in early villages with circular or oval-shaped huts, storage facilities typically stood out in the open. This pointed to food being shared communally. This practice resembles the egalitarian culture still observed by hunter-gatherers today, which reduces individual risk as environmental conditions change.[55] But the rise of rectangular homes with multiple rooms brought a major change. Increasingly, one room within the dwelling itself was specifically dedicated to storage. As agricultural societies advanced, the rectilinear house gave households a greater autonomy in managing surplus resources.

This architectural shift came along with a change in social dynamics. As Flannery emphasized, it changed the risk and reward equation for households. When storage was communal, individual households had little incentive to maximize resources for themselves, since everything was likely shared. Private storage changed this. Suddenly, houses within the village had an incentive to compete, each family striving to maximize resources for their own household. At the same time, as early farming villages expanded, it was likely that fewer families were closely related by blood. This could have made them increasingly less inclined to share resources with their neighbors.

One researcher noted that communities with privatized storage had a more "closed" site layout. They featured "either widely spaced household units or closed-in eating and storage areas, in order to avoid the jealousy and conflict which might arise from one household visibly having more than another."[56]

Yet paradoxically, the very walls hiding indoor activities may have intensified jealousy as well. As anthropologist Peter Wilson argued, the presence of walls fundamentally altered our ancestors' visual attention, reshaping their drives and emotions. Hunter-gatherers could carry only what they could move, but once people settled in dwellings, they could accumulate, conceal, and display food, wealth, and status. This shift toward village life, Wilson suggests, was as transformational as when our distant ancestors descended from living in trees to living on the ground, which freed our hands from grasping. Villagers, he argued, became "domesticated people," psychologically and socially distinct from those in roaming bands.[57]

Meanwhile, the number of farmers was growing, outperforming hunter-gatherer societies. By cultivating crops and domesticating animals, agricultural communities could produce food more reliably and efficiently than through foraging alone. This sustained growing populations and more complex societies. Archaeologist Gordon Childe, who coined the term "Neolithic Revolution," or Agricultural Revolution, estimated that in aboriginal America, unimproved land could sustain a population ranging from about .05 to .1 person per square mile. In contrast, Neolithic societies on the Pacific Islands today can sustain populations of approximately thirty or more people per square mile.[58] The transition from a hunter-gatherer lifestyle to an agricultural one dramatically expanded the Earth's "human carrying capacity," the maximum number of people that could be supported.

Given these advantages, it should be no surprise that the agricultural transition ultimately unfolded independently in at least eleven different regions worldwide.[59] This revolutionary shift began about

10,000 to 12,000 years ago, spanning from the cultivation of rice in East Asia to the domestication of squash in the Americas. As agricultural knowledge spread, in regions like the Mediterranean, humans selected and cultivated hundreds of varieties of crops, from olives to grapes.[60] Farming produced the surplus food that enabled more populous, specialized, and socially complex societies—though some might argue it was a double-edged sword.

Farming led to intensified resource exploitation and fierce competition for scarce resources within defined territories.[61] Close contact with domesticated animals and wild pests, such as rodents, increased the incidence of zoonotic diseases like influenza. Dense, sedentary populations, with their higher rates of contact, created perfect conditions for the spread of diseases like measles and smallpox. Farmers and their settlements contributed to deforestation, soil erosion, and water pollution. At times, the very practices that enabled growth also sowed the seeds of their own destruction. Even Beidha was eventually abandoned, perhaps due to the depletion of grazing lands, firewood, and fertile soil.[62]

When I visited Beidha, it was difficult to imagine it was once a much greener place, with grasslands and trees. Today it is an arid desert. As the climate grew more arid over time, the once fertile land became less capable of supporting agriculture. People abandoned village life.

My stay at a Bedouin camp in Wadi Rum a few hours away provided a stark contrast. This otherworldly red desert—immortalized as alien terrain in films like *Star Wars* and *Dune*—at first seems a barren wasteland. Yet the Bedouins, with their goat- and camel-wool tents, seem well adapted to desert life. Their nomadic life in tents, radically different from agricultural communities in houses, shows that settled life is not the only way.

While the transition to rectangular buildings may have been an important step in human development, it wasn't the only path—or an irreversible one. Some societies, after embracing rectangular structures with private storage, returned to circular dwellings and shared storage, perhaps to share the burden of risk in changing economic conditions. And though permanent settlements are the norm for most of us, nomadic and seminomadic traditions persist today.

Many Bedouins clearly prefer it that way. Life in tents immerses them in the sweeping desert landscape and the unpolluted night sky. An archaeologist once observed how Bedouins have a fierce disdain for city life, citing a "mystical hatred of the roof" and a "religious revulsion to the house."[63] Their rejection of rigid walls echoes the ancient Rechabites who, as Jeremiah chronicled, swore, "We do not drink wine." And commanded: "You must never build houses, sow seed or plant vineyards; . . . [you] must always live in tents. Then you will live a long time."[64] And so, not all succumbed to the comforts—and constraints—of rectilinear life.

When Homes Touch

"On a cold November day in 1958, just before nightfall," British archaeologist James Mellaart recalled, he finally "reached the double mound of Çatal Hüyük."[65] He had first spotted the mound, "a third of a mile in length," while exploring the Konya plain of the Anatolian plateau in 1952. But, as he admitted, "dysentery and lack of transport prevented its more formal discovery."

Arriving with a team of archaeologists, he found: "Much . . . was covered by turf and ruin-weed (*Peganum harmala*) but where the prevailing south-westerly winds had scoured its surface bare there were unmistakable traces of mud-brick buildings, burned red in a conflagration contrasting with patches of grey ash, broken bones, potsherds and obsidian tools and weapons. To our surprise these were found not only at the bottom of the mound, but they continued right up to the top, some 15 metres above the level of the plain."

Thus began the "discovery" of Çatalhöyük—though locals had long been aware of it. The settlement grew as an important supplier of obsidian, a volcanic rock prized for crafting blades. Occupied for over two millennia, it likely peaked at about 800 people in 6500 BC, far below earlier estimates of several thousands.[66] Nevertheless, it was one of the largest Neolithic villages of the time.

The village was essentially a massive honeycomb of cuboid houses pressed against each other without ground-level streets. Çatalhöyük was unlike anything seen since. Perhaps its closest modern parallel is found in dense informal settlements such as Rio de

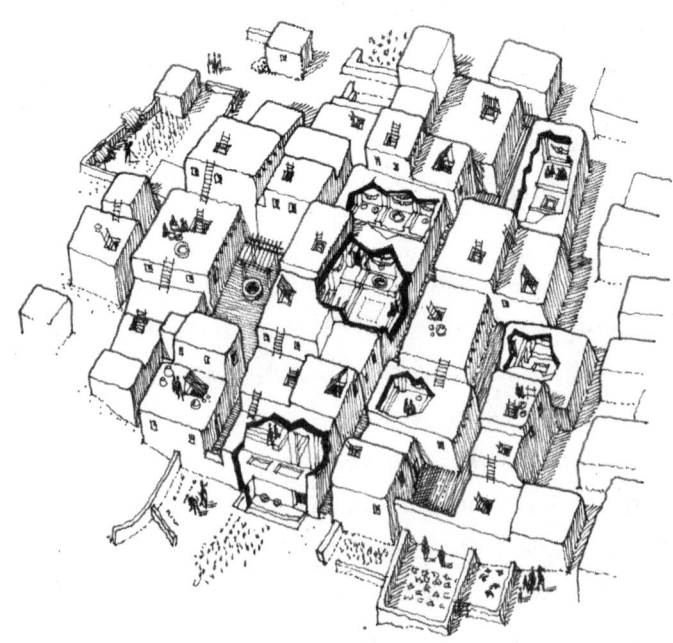

Village of Çatalhöyük, Turkey, ca. 6700 BC.[67]

Janeiro's favelas, where houses are packed so closely that they seem a continuous mass.

The wheel had not yet been invented, so streets were not necessary for wheeled transport. Instead, residents descended into their homes not through front doors but through roof hatches using wooden ladders. This arrangement may have offered some advantages, such as defense. Large windows and doors would have made the interior too hot. And similar to Middle Eastern cities today, these rooftops were active living spaces. Some roofs even had ovens. However, entering homes by ladder would have made life challenging, especially for the elderly and pregnant women.

The sight of Çatalhöyük, with people living in adjacent boxes, would have likely stunned the hunter-gatherers of the time. They might have encountered more people in a single day than they would have seen in their entire lifetime. Their camps were open and transparent. But Çatalhöyük was a maze of enclosed spaces. Activities that had been public were now hidden behind walls.

The appeal of living in Çatalhöyük in terms of quality of life was not immediately obvious, aside from participation in the obsidian trade. Most houses had no windows and only had roof openings. These openings doubled as access into the dwelling and smokestacks for hearths located beneath them, filling interiors with smoke. The word "window" itself, derived from Old Norse *vindauga* ("wind eye"), speaks to this early form of ventilation. Yet this rudimentary arrangement brought health hazards. Skeletal remains showed the buildup of sooty black deposits on the inside of rib cages of older residents, probably a consequence of life in smoke-filled homes.[68]

The village also struggled with hygiene. When a family vacated a home, it often became a dump for waste, including human and animal feces.[69] Infectious diseases spread easily in such unsanitary conditions, with up to a third of human bones showing signs of infected lesions.[70]

But villagers did not just have to endure bad smells.[71] Çatalhöyük's homes required constant upkeep. Built largely from mud brick, the houses were vulnerable to rain. Mud brick deteriorates quickly when wet. Lacking proper drainage or strong foundations, homes demanded frequent repair or rebuilding.

Residents invested significant labor in maintenance. They replastered walls and sleeping platforms with white clay, gypsum, or lime to keep their interiors fresh and clean.[72] This maintenance process may have occurred up to three times a year. Some houses had been replastered about 450 times,[73] lasting up to a hundred years. Builders then leveled entire homes and constructed new ones on top of the old foundations. Some structures had been rebuilt up to six times. Over generations, this practice caused the settlement to rise ever higher, eventually reaching sixty-six feet—roughly the height of a modern six-story building.

Villagers may have been willing to endure these challenges not only for economic reasons but also because they were deeply attached to their homes: Wall paintings were found in almost every house and often included elaborate symbols.

Residents divided their homes into two distinct zones. One was a small room centered around a hearth. It may have functioned as a kitchen area, judging by the ovens and clay bins for storing food found there.

But it was the main room that made Çatalhöyük famous. This room, typically cleaner than the other, had sleeping platforms. The walls and the platforms were covered with paintings, some bearing up to forty layers of plaster and paint. These murals offer windows into their worldview. Some images were morbid, showing vultures pecking at human corpses. Others featured abstract geometric designs, like a nine-foot mural possibly depicting a leopard skin. Many murals depicted wild animals and hunting scenes, even as the villagers increasingly domesticated animals, perhaps to evoke memories of the past.

Most dramatic were the protruding bull horn decorations, or *bucrania*, often set into the wall. Some were placed on small columns inside the room. They were often covered with plaster and painted with ochre red. In one example, three sets of bull horns were stacked one above the other on a wall, with a large human figurine above, its legs splayed wide. The walls also featured platforms with animal skulls, beaks, teeth, and tusks. The residents seemed to choose, above all, the pointier animal remains.

All of this may have been quite shocking to an outsider. Archaeologist Steven Mithen likened it to a "monstrous scene of bulls bursting from the wall. There are three of them at about waist-height—white heads striped with black and red, from which sprout enormous pointed horns.... Around the bulls the walls are painted with bold geometric designs—sharp, oppressive images above handprints in red and black." [74]

Other symbolic components were found throughout the home and the village. Small figurines, often quickly made and discarded, were thought to be part of daily spiritual practices, akin to prayers. In other villages, archaeologists have also found decapitated animal figures that seem to have been ritualistically "killed."[75]

Residents may have also been attached to their abodes because, unlike today, home was also a burial site. Ancestors were buried in fetal positions beneath the platforms. Some bodies were exhumed, their skulls possibly removed for use in ceremonies. These were placed in wall niches, almost as if they were watching over their descendants.

Anthropologist Ian Hodder, who spent decades excavating the site, identified a special category of dwellings. He called them "History Houses."[76] These featured more symbolism and more burials, one holding as many as sixty-two bodies. Though these houses likely held special religious significance, they showed no signs of greater wealth or storage capacity. This suggests a society where religious status did not bring material advantage. The archaeological evidence also hints at a relative, if gruesome, gender equality: Both male and female skulls were used.[77] Men and women also had similar levels of darkened lungs, suggesting they spent equal time at home.

Importantly, these history houses had longer lifespans than other buildings. "Houses with many burials tend to be long lasting,"[78] observed Hodder. He argued that "making history" was essential in agricultural communities where labor had delayed payoffs. In contrast to the immediate return of foraging, farming required a "greater sense of temporal depth, history, and memory."[79] Hodder notes, "The emergence of greater temporal depth was a necessary condition for dense settled life, the delayed returns of intensive subsistence systems." The repeated rebuilding of homes, the burials, and the elaborate symbolism—all played out within the fabric of domestic life—maintained a shared sense of historical community.

Yet this ambitious experiment in communal living eventually faced significant challenges. Demand for wooden building materials led to extensive deforestation around Çatalhöyük. As trees vanished, residents had to travel farther for resources, adding new burdens to their daily work. The stresses of village life may have taken a toll as well. Evidence of interpersonal violence is found in the skulls of residents—of ninety-three skulls examined, twenty-five showed healed fractures, mostly among women, often from blows to the back of the head with round objects. Given that most of the head injuries occurred during the period of highest population density, some believe elevated stress and conflict may have been due to overcrowding.[80]

By 6000 BC, Çatalhöyük was abandoned. It was part of a broader collapse of Neolithic settlements across the region. From Israel to Palestine, farming villages were deserted. People likely scattered into smaller hamlets. While changing climate patterns, including a drop in temperatures, played a role, the inhabitants themselves contributed significantly to the downfall of their villages. Deforestation, overcultivation, and overgrazing depleted the soil's fertility. The pollution from human and animal waste further strained the ecosystems they were living in.[81]

At 'Ain Ghazal in the Jordan Valley, the houses themselves contributed to the village's decline. Villagers upgraded their homes by plastering floors with lime, which made them more water-resistant. Some builders spread the lime plaster as high as six inches up walls, posts, and hearths. But producing lime required burning limestone, heating it to between 750 and 850 degrees Celsius and accelerating deforestation. Trees vanished within a three-kilometer radius of 'Ain Ghazal.[82] Without the stabilizing tree roots, the soil eroded during periods of rainfall and became less fertile. With the soil already exhausted from overcultivation, crop yields shrank and the village was abandoned. Although other factors such as water pollution from human waste likely also played a role, the reliance on plaster technology influenced its downfall.[83]

As archaeologists Nigel Goring-Morris and Anna Belfer-Cohen observed, permanent settlement during this time became increasingly unsustainable: "The whole fragile Neolithic network collapsed in upon itself." By contrast, "the long duration of earlier mobile hunter-gatherer adaptations had enabled the 'fine-tuning' balance between people, the environment, and the resources necessary to avoid overexploitation."[84]

As our ancestors experimented with agriculture, housing, and construction techniques, they created larger and more permanent habitats. In the process, they faced new challenges. They lacked sewers and safe drinking water. They lacked reliable agriculture to support growing populations. Without workable solutions to these challenges of collective life—not realized until the Early Bronze Age—these villages hit a ceiling. Today, Çatalhöyük is a mound in the Turkish landscape, although one recognized by UNESCO as "a site of great importance for our understanding of the first steps toward 'civilization.'"[85]

When our ancestors transitioned from nomadic to settled life, they entered a new "indoor" phase of human existence. The walls they built reshaped not only their physical and mental world but also their relationship with nature. The problems they faced, from resource depletion to environmental degradation, echo those we struggle with today. As landscape architect Anne Whiston Spirn noted, "Modern urban problems are no different, in essence, from those that plagued ancient cities, except in degree, in the toxicity and persistence of new contaminants, and the extent of the earth that is now urbanized."[86]

The issue of home maintenance persists as well. As an owner of a mere hundred-year-old home, I find myself painting basement floors, clearing French drains, and repairing endless small failures. With a drill in hand to hang a family photo, I sense an odd parallel between those ancient residents who carved niches in their walls for ceremonial skulls. They worried about deteriorating mud brick. I worry about asbestos in insulation and lead in old paint. The tools and decorations have changed, but our desire to make our mark on these walls remains deeply human—even if there are hidden dangers in living a settled life.

TWO

Cities of Mud

The Extended House

"In those ancient days . . . the lord of broad wisdom, Enki, the master of destinies . . . founded dwelling places; he took in his hand waters to encourage and create good seed; he laid out side by side the Tigris and the Euphrates, and caused them to bring water from the mountains; he scoured out the smaller streams, and positioned the other watercourses. . . . Enki made spacious sheepfolds and cattle-pens, and provided shepherds and herdsmen; he founded cities and settlements throughout the earth, and made the black-headed [Sumerians] multiply."[1]

In "Debate Between Bird and Fish," a Sumerian essay dating back to the third millennium BC, it was Enki, the god of water, who created the world by laying out the great rivers. This belief reflects the reality of life in Mesopotamia. For it was in this "land between rivers"—for that is what *Mesopotamia* means in ancient Greek—that a new chapter in human history began.

Around 6000 BC, as farming villages in present-day Jordan, Israel, and Palestine were being abandoned, a new wave of settlement emerged in the foothills of Northern Mesopotamia. The twin waterways of the Euphrates and Tigris, born in the highlands of eastern Turkey and stretching to the Persian Gulf, provided the water, reeds, and clay that would build their world. These rivers—one fast flowing and unpredictable, the other broad and steady—would become both a lifeline and a challenge to the people who settled their banks.

The settlement of Tell Hassuna stood along the Tigris River. It was part of the Hassuna culture—one of the earliest farming societies in Northern Mesopotamia, centered in what is now northern Iraq. Villagers built small homes for nuclear families, consisting of just a few rooms. Excavators in 1943 found "the walls were built of lumps of mud of various sizes in a manner approximating the local modern practice. Smaller lumps were used to fill the gaps, and the faces were smoothed."[2] These rudimentary buildings were likely topped with low-pitched roofs made of branches and covered in mud.

Packed-mud house, Tell Hassuna, Northern Iraq, ca. 5500 BC.[3]

However, as agriculture intensified over the centuries, the villagers added rooms to their homes, seemingly at random. Their homes grew into sprawling complexes of fifteen to twenty rooms. Drawing on broader patterns, archaeologist Kent Flannery observed that this was the "next stage of village development, the replacement of nuclear households by extended family households."[4] This likely resulted from the demands of early farming: "The combination of two tasks—cereal agriculture and the grazing of herd animals—requires a division of labor beyond the capacity of a nuclear family." Success required an extended family of fifteen to twenty people to manage fields, tend herds, and diversify into activities such as craft making.

Over time, the villagers expanded their houses into complexes of grouped homes arranged around large open courtyards. This enabled them to enclose flocks at night. These homes, according to the excavators, "show the first clear signs of planning."[5]

Eventually, the fifteen- to twenty-room complexes began to appear in regularized forms. Previously, houses had a larger main room with one or more smaller side rooms. But the internal organization of the new complexes now introduced three distinct types of rooms. The larger rooms of 150 square feet or more were likely used as central gathering areas for communal activities. Elongated rooms of around 100 square feet served as sleeping or working areas. And square-shaped rooms of approximately 20 square feet were probably used for storage.[6] Residents were now intentionally building structures with specialized rooms for the extended family from the start.

This transformation from improvised to planned construction has been described as the "florescence of architecture."[7] With their larger homes incorporating various room types, the inhabitants of Tell Hassuna contributed to a broader trend toward increased social and economic complexity. The new houses were also more efficient, allowing for population densities of up to an estimated 160 people per acre—a figure that rivals some of the most densely populated areas in the world today. Archaeologist Kent Flannery noted, "It is clear that planned, extended family households can produce much higher densities."[8]

But as the residents built up their village, they had to contend with the tensions of their growing settlement. The people of the Hassuna culture used stamped seals to impress clay, probably to mark ownership and safeguard property. The 1943 discovery of 2,400 clay balls hints at a darker side of this new societal development. They were quite likely used as sling missiles, either for hunting or defending what had been built.

Slightly later in time and a few hundred miles downstream toward the south, the people of Tell es-Sawwan faced a different challenge. They belonged to the Samarra culture, an early farming society in what is now north-central Iraq, about seventy miles north of modern-day Baghdad. Located below the 200-millimeter rainfall line, where annual rainfall drops below eight inches, Tell es-Sawwan lacked sufficient water for stable agriculture.

The farmers dug small ditches to channel the Tigris floods to their fields, allowing them to cultivate barley, wheat, and linseed. This mastery over water would come to define Mesopotamian civilization. It increased food security and population density in otherwise marginal lands, while the labor-intensive demands of water management spurred greater social complexity and stratification.[9]

The residents also had to innovate in construction. Unlike in the north, they did not have access to stone and wood. Without forests or quarries, they had no choice but to exploit the abundant clay in the region's alluvial plains. They built their homes with mud bricks—the primary building material of Southern Mesopotamia.

Mud bricks improved upon earlier packed-earth techniques,

which demanded skilled workers and precise attention to make sure the foundations and walls were consistently wide enough. The bricks, in contrast, allowed for simplified, more standardized construction. And they could be more easily transported, whereas packed mud relied on the material being available closer to the site.

However, the river clay was often too sandy. So the residents needed to refine the river clay's consistency. They mixed it with chopped straw, creating a composite material, much like how rebar reinforces modern concrete. Straw and mud together create a substance stronger than either by itself. Dried mud is good at withstanding squeezing. Straw is good at preventing tearing. Combined, they balance each other's weaknesses. Straw alone crumbles when you squeeze it, and dried mud pulverizes when you tear it apart. To further reduce brittleness, they also added dung, which, like straw, helped bind the mud particles together, making it less prone to cracking.[10]

They then pressed this mixture into molds that were open at both ends. After letting them bake for a few weeks, they had long cigar-shaped bricks, roughly the size of a loaf of bread. Builders arranged them in precise patterns, like the header-and-stretcher fashion—alternating layers of bricks laid with their short ends (headers) and long sides (stretchers) parallel to the wall's surface. Finally, they sealed them with clay plaster, creating thick, strong walls that better resisted cracking and crumbling.

As simple as it sounds, it was a labor-intensive process. Producing the straw alone demanded a significant amount of land. A mere hundred bricks would have required at least 130 pounds of straw, the yield of roughly a third of an acre.[11] A single house would have required several acres of cultivated land.

The Samarrans carefully planned their homes as well. The buildings were uniquely recognizable by an enfilade: a sequence of aligned doorways along a central axis. This arrangement created a direct line of sight through the building. It offered an imposing view as well as a more efficient means of movement within the home. It was, in effect, a precursor to the modern corridor.

Villagers arranged their houses in clusters, with courtyards between the buildings. These accommodated ovens and granaries, suggesting a collective approach to resource management and irrigation.[12] By around 5900 BC, Tell es-Sawwan was surrounded by a deep ditch and a buttressed wall. Throughout Samarran villages, clay jars were found with gypsum lids and seal impressions, marking ownership. These developments, along with the presence of clay balls possibly used as sling missiles, indicate a growing anxiety over property protection—and possibly a fear of outsiders pillaging the toils of their irrigated fields.

Farther south near the head of the Persian Gulf, the Ubaid people took their architecture one step further. Their beginnings overlap with the Samarra culture around the sixth millennium BC but endured much longer—until about 3800 BC. At the time, the gulf's shoreline extended far inland, deep into what is now southern Iraq. As archaeologist Leonard Woolley vividly describes it, the Ubaid came to a land of marshes, "dense with reeds and opening out here and there into lagoons or clear channels. . . . It was a country rich enough in promise to make a certain amount of hardship well worthwhile."[13]

In these marshy southern reaches of Mesopotamia, reeds became an abundant and adaptable building material. Lacking access to timber or stone, the Ubaid built simple reed huts. They even built larger structures entirely from reed. These consisted of reed bundles, some up to three feet thick, bent into arches. Reed mats covered these arches to create long tunnel-shaped buildings.

These structures left little trace in the archaeological record, apart from depictions on Mesopotamian cylinder seals. Yet similar vernacular forms exist in Iraqi wetlands today. One such example is the *mudhif*—a long, arched guesthouse used by the Marsh Arabs.[14] Their contemporary reed canoes also look surprisingly like a model canoe found in a later Mesopotamian royal cemetery.[15]

"Now a Mudhif you can't picture until you have seen it," wrote the English traveler Gertrude Bell in 1920. "It is constructed of reeds, reed mats spread over reed bundles, arching over and meeting at the top, so that the whole is a perfectly regular and exquisitely constructed yellow tunnel, 50 yards long.... the whole lighted by fire and a couple of small lamps, and the end of the Mudhif fading away into a golden gloom. Glorious."[16]

While poorer inhabitants likely dwelled in marshland reed huts, the Ubaid people also built more substantial permanent dwellings than the cultures before them. Some were as large as two thousand square feet and were built from molded mud bricks. These were orga-

Traditional reed house (*mudhif*), Southern Iraq.

nized around a central hall flanked by smaller rooms on each side, known as the tripartite design. Ubaid builders may have inherited the house plan from the Samarrans and possibly expanded the enfilade into a broad central hall, though this remains uncertain.

The tripartite design created a hierarchy of spaces. The deeper one moved through successive rooms, the more intimate they became. Private areas like storage spaces and bedrooms required passage through multiple chambers. Meanwhile, the central hall served as a versatile space, lending the building a monumental quality.

As Ubaid settlements grew in scale, social hierarchy became visible in the built environment. At Tell Gawra around 4400 BC, a few larger houses dominated access to communal granaries.[17] They were often visible from afar, serving as focal points.[18] These "prestige

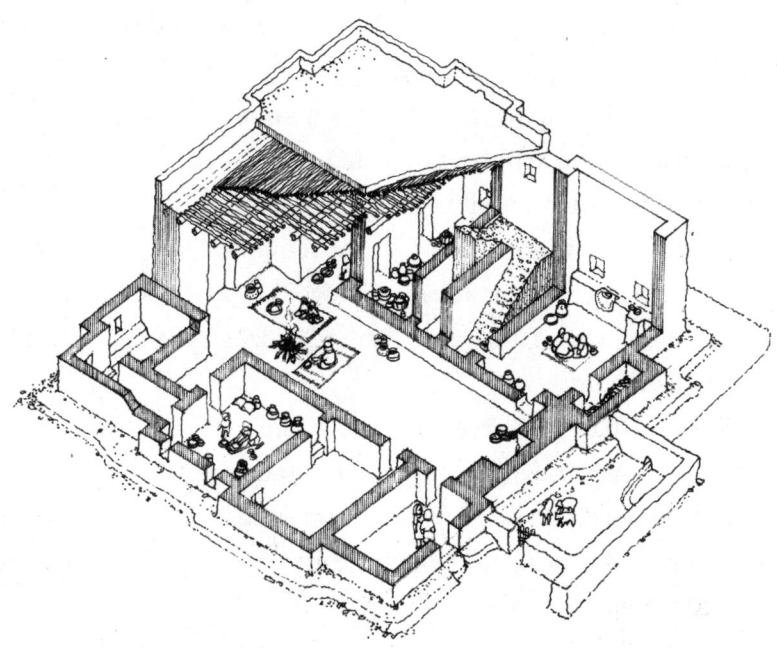

Tripartite house, Tell Madhur, Iraq, ca. 4500 BC.[19]

houses," typical of larger Ubaid villages, may have distributed food to other houses, or they could have had a spiritual or political purpose. Across ancient societies, leaders often operated from their homes, and their homes were typically larger to accommodate social gatherings.[20] This tripartite design, with its central communal area, was ideal for these domestic and civic purposes.

The tripartite house design also influenced religious architecture. In fact, it appears more frequently in what are believed to be public or ceremonial buildings than in domestic ones. Early temples adopted this layout of a central hall lined by smaller side rooms. Builders further distinguished these buildings with features such as niche-and-buttress facades that created striped visual effects and dynamic shadows. As archaeologist Pascal Butterlin observed, the house became "a symbolic unit that could be domestic, prestigious, or religious."[21] It offered a versatile spatial form, adaptable to shifting social, spiritual, and political roles.

Some Ubaid temples may have even adhered to standardized measurements. One scholar proposed the existence of an "Ubaid cubit," a standard unit measuring approximately twenty-eight inches. He concluded that this was used at the Temple VI in Eridu (around 4000 BC), suggesting an advanced level of abstract planning.[22] However, there is no evidence of a standardized system across the broader Ubaid world.

Still, the Ubaid cultural footprint stretched from the Persian Gulf to northern Syria, bringing cultural norms with them. One of their most important legacies was the tripartite house. "The formula proved remarkably durable," noted Butterlin.[23] He argued it became an important element of social organization. "The intensive use of tripartite buildings probably permitted the emergence of chiefdoms and states in a proto-urban context." It was, he concluded, "a true archetype... frequently related to the birth of the first cities." After thousands of years of building homes in Mesopotamia, in these Ubaid tripartite houses of mud brick, we may finally see the early outlines of future urban civilization.

The Ubaid builders' tripartite design accomplished something architects still strive for today: a thoughtful balance between communal and private space. Modern homes continue to follow this logic. They have larger shared living areas and smaller private rooms—and an intuitive flow connecting them. It almost certainly did not spring from a single source of invention. The Ubaid solution, like many others across time and place, reflects a universal logic of habitation—born from the practical realities of how people live together. In the end, there are only so many ways to shape space around the patterns of daily life.

The Ubaid homes also offer lessons in sustainable architecture. While today's energy-efficient buildings rely on composites, laminates, and synthetic insulators, Ubaid builders created relatively durable homes from only earth and sun. Their thick mud brick walls, typically eighteen to twenty-four inches wide, helped regulate indoor temperatures by absorbing heat throughout the warm day and releasing it during the cooler night. And where most of our construction material ends up in landfills, these ancient homes returned, in time, to the soil they rose from. They gradually accumulated into layered mounds—known as tells—that today form the archaeological signature of the region.

In our era of increasing environmental concerns, these elegant, low-tech solutions deserve renewed attention. Nevertheless, the Mesopotamians had environmental problems of their own. The irrigation channels that gave life to their fields slowly filled with silt, demanding constant maintenance. Inhabitants were caught in a perpetual struggle with the very force that had allowed their civilization to flourish: the water flowing from the rivers. It was a constant reminder of the delicate balance they had struck with nature.

Proto-cities

In 1937, mystery writer Agatha Christie accompanied her archaeologist husband Max Mallowan on various digs in Syria. She had first met him seven years earlier at an excavation site. Over the following decades, she joined him on numerous expeditions across the region, cleaning and cataloging artifacts, and even developing film. As she described later in a poem, "A-Sitting on a Tell," she met an archaeologist amid the trenches of a dig. While he passionately extolled the nuances of measuring prehistoric pots, her mind wandered to plotting murders—imagining ways to "kill a millionaire," and stash the body in a "Frigidaire."[24]

Little did Christie know that she was witnessing the discovery of an intriguing mystery—one that would change the origin story of urbanism. During this time, Mallowan made what would prove to be one of his most fortunate discoveries. In Syria, he was the first to excavate a site known as Tell Brak. There, he found an ancient temple filled with enigmatic figurines with distinctive eye motifs. Tell Brak, along with Khirbat al-Fakhar, would fundamentally challenge our understanding of how early cities began.

For millennia, the pattern of village life in Mesopotamia had followed a predictable cycle: When a settlement grew too large, when tensions arose between families or resources grew scarce, it would split like a cell dividing. One group would move away to establish a new settlement. But around 4000 BC, Tell Brak and Khirbat al-Fakhar departed from this pattern. Instead of splitting apart, they grew. Households clustered together in several neighborhood groups separated by open spaces. Each cluster functioned almost like a traditional village, but now these village-like units were part of something larger. Their scale was immense. Khirbat al-Fakhar sprawled across 750 acres, equal to five hundred football fields. Tell Brak was about 130 acres, still larger than other settlements.

These settlements were remarkable for their structure as well. Instead of a dense, cohesive urban core, they resembled a patchwork of household clusters interspersed with open spaces.[25] All of this defied conventional ideas of urbanism. They were too expansive to be called a village. At the same time, they could not be called cities, since they showed no signs of central authority. They had no grand palaces, no soaring temples rising above the skyline. Scholars would come to refer to them as "proto-cities."

This discovery upended the story of urbanization, as traditionally told. Scholars long believed that cities began from the minds of powerful rulers or the necessities of complex irrigation systems. But the evidence from Tell Brak and Khirbat al-Fakhar offers a fascinating alternative: Some cities could have emerged organically, shaped by the collective actions of countless households rather than the decrees of a central authority.[26] Complexity here was not imposed from above but grew from below.

This was no isolated phenomenon. Around the same time, ancient Trypillia settlements in present-day Ukraine exhibited similar traits. These settlements spanned up to 300 hectares, yet they lacked monumental buildings and evidence of centralized power structures. The parallel emergence of such settlements suggests a shared pattern of urban development across different regions, pointing to a broader decentralized model of early urbanization.[27]

What drove people to create these unprecedented communities

in Mesopotamia? One clue lies in a piece of volcanic glass. Obsidian, prized for its ability to be made into sharp tools, was likely the economic engine. Imported from hundreds of miles away, this precious resource attracted people from far and wide. Each household became a workshop, which contributed to a network of decentralized production and trade. Organizing such exchanges required communication, coordination, and trust—which put these communities on a path toward growing complexity, a path toward urbanism.

Yet with this growth came entirely new social challenges. Without centralized institutions to enforce order, residents needed to develop novel ways to manage conflict.

Archaeological evidence reveals that these communities were not quite egalitarian. At Tell Brak, the distribution of animal remains tells a story of social stratification. Pig remains—a cheaper source of meat—were found at the periphery, suggesting that poorer migrants lived in the outer clusters, much like the informal settlements that ring many megacities in the developing world today.[28]

One peculiar aspect of the Mesopotamian proto-cities was the open spaces between clusters of households. These areas may have served as garden plots, like those in ancient Mesoamerican cities. Or they could have been buffers between groups to reduce conflict.[29] By maintaining physical separation, rather than living together in a single dense urban core, the inhabitants of Khirbat al-Fakhar and Tell Brak may have found a way to mitigate the social tensions associated with growing population density.

This evidence points to a new tentative conclusion. Some cities may have formed from a self-organizing process, emerging from the interactions of many independent agents rather than being directed by political elites. The pattern bears a resemblance to what biologists call "emergence"—as with termite mounds. These structures form without a leader directing the process, driven instead by individuals following simple rules—like following trails laid down by others, exchanging information, and building according to instinct.

Households likely didn't set out to form large settlements from the beginning.[30] Instead, the settlement was the organic result of their collective motivations—which may have included feeding dependents, expanding households, and preserving autonomy. As archaeologist Jason Ur, who has studied these proto-cities in Mesopotamia, noted: "Urbanism does not appear to have originated with a single, powerful ruler or political entity. Instead, it was the organic outgrowth of many groups coming together."[31]

The stories of Tell Brak and Khirbat al-Fakhar reveal two possible trajectories for these proto-cities. Between 4000 and 3800 BC, Tell Brak rapidly expanded, possibly housing up to 20,000 people within 300 acres.[32,33] Since nearby settlements were abandoned, it may be that migration drove this expansion. As the population increased, the settlement transformed its structure. Unlike traditional cities that expanded outward from a center, its suburbs grew inward, merging with the central core. The outskirts became specialized zones for various functions. There was an industrial area equipped with bread ovens and pottery kilns. Another area was essentially a massive two- to three-hectare trash mound. This suggested that the inhabitants pushed such less-desirable activities to the periphery, as happens in modern cities.[34]

But Tell Brak's growth reached natural constraints. Northern Mesopotamian settlements relied on cultivating a growing hinterland, leaving traces that persist to this day—over six thousand kilometers of "hollow ways," the sunken paths formed by humans and livestock walking through agricultural fields.[35] Yet dry farming in

Northern Mesopotamia had its limits, bounded by the land's productive capacity and the practical distance over which food could be transported. The more the settlement grew, the longer the farmers' commutes. These challenges capped the population at around 20,000 inhabitants.[36] Once a settlement reached this ceiling, it became increasingly vulnerable to environmental pressures. Fluctuations in rainfall or periodic droughts could lead to food shortages and social unrest.

As Tell Brak grew, its society became increasingly complex and hierarchical. Archaeologists have uncovered over one thousand clay seals used to secure jars and baskets or mark ownership of goods and raw materials. These artifacts reveal deepening social divisions within the community—potential sources of social stress.[37] Indeed, the challenges we associate with modern urban life were present from humanity's first experiments with urban living: from industrial hazards to long commutes and social inequities.

These tensions probably erupted into violence. Archaeologists discovered mass graves on the edge of Tell Brak containing skeletal remains with clear signs of trauma, especially blunt-force fractures to several skulls, indicating deliberate killings. The demographic profile of the victims—including women and children—suggests these graves may have been the result of internal conflict, rather than attacks by foreign invaders. The presence of animal remains buried alongside the human victims suggests the killings may have been followed by a feast or ritual.[38]

The response to these growing challenges represented a turning point. As Tell Brak expanded, it built two impressive monumental buildings. First came a structure known as the Red Building, with walls up to six feet thick of distinctive red mud bricks. It stood near the industrial area and likely served as an early administrative center, overseeing production. By now, Tell Brak had firmly adopted centralized institutions.

But it was the second structure—the Eye Temple that Max Mallowan first discovered—that revealed something new about early urban society. The temple's design followed the same tripartite layout as a typical house but on a much larger scale. The builders had taken the familiar form of domestic architecture and transformed it, expanding the central hall into a sacred space and elevating the building on an artificial platform. "Archaeologists call it a 'temple,'" explains Jason Ur, "but to the people of Brak, it was another household—this time the household of a god."[39]

This architectural choice was not accidental. It reflected deeply held beliefs that the divine realm was organized in families, and human society—especially its most important institutions—was modeled on this divine template. So naturally, the gods would dwell in houses and require the same provisions as people. Palaces and temples across Mesopotamia retained house-like forms. In fact, the terms for temple or palace in later Sumerian literally translated to "big house." This shows that the house played a major role in shaping larger collectives and providing the structure for the first institutions. It became a template for organizing society at every scale, from family dwellings to divine spaces.

The temple's most distinctive feature—the thousands of "eye idols" found within—offers a window into the soul of early urban society. Made from clay or stone, they were simple enough that anyone could make them. There were so many of them that they appear to be a form of religious expression available to everyone, regardless of status. The ritual associated with the eye idols may have helped bind together an increasingly complex urban community.[40] While their purpose remains a mystery, with no clear parallels except at Khirbat al-Fakhar, they speak to the role of shared symbols in urban life.

Their allure endures. At the Metropolitan Museum of Art, I stood before a display case of eye idols, each about the size of my palm. These idols felt quite intimate. A pair of oversized eyes tops their trapezoid-shaped bodies, making a profile similar to Mickey Mouse ears. Some larger idols featured smaller child figures carved onto their bodies, evoking parent-child relationships. Other idols had multiple sets of eyes. These wide owl-like eyes may have symbolized attentiveness to the gods, which was a recurring theme in later Mesopotamian art.

The remarkable resilience of these early urban settlements appears to have rested on more than just economics. Religion and shared belief systems likely anchored these communities as well.

With their oversized eyes and single unbroken eyebrow—a feature considered attractive in later Mesopotamia—the eye idols may have offered their users a common purpose. While most idols were found within the Eye Temple, many appeared in domestic spaces—perhaps as protective symbols, extending the divine presence into the intimate sphere of home.

We may never understand their true meaning. Yet the role of shared symbols endures. At the museum, I watched many visitors drifting to the gift shop to investigate designer pottery and fridge magnets depicting ancient art. These souvenirs may represent a similar desire for belonging—to carry home pieces of something greater than ourselves.

In time, this marvel of bottom-up urbanism gave way to a new order. By 3800 BC, Khirbat al-Fakhar was abandoned, its inhabitants relocating to Tell Hamoukar, a new site about a mile to the north. Archaeological evidence of over 1,200 clay projectiles suggests the city's fall. Around 3500 BC, Hamoukar's mud brick walls likely crumbled under assault, as attackers unleashed thousands of these sling "bullets." Perhaps it was the southern Uruk civilization, which was beginning to extend its influence into the region.[41] After breaching the walls, the invaders set the city ablaze.

Tell Brak's fate was different. The city survived, but only as a colony of Uruk. Its distinctive culture faded away, and the production of eye idols ceased. A new urban age had begun. As the center of civilization shifted toward the south, the decentralized household-driven model that had defined Tell Brak gave way to a new urban form—one that would face challenges of its own.

The Courtyard House

In one of the earliest myths told by the Sumerians, "Inana and Enki," the goddess Inana challenges the god Enki to a drinking contest. She emerged victorious with the *mes,* divine decrees symbolizing the core elements of Sumerian civilization. "Holy Inana received the craft of the carpenter, the craft of the coppersmith, the craft of the scribe, the craft of the smith, the craft of the leather-worker, the craft of the fuller, the craft of the builder, the craft of the reed-worker,"[42] the ancient myth recounts. However, these divine gifts, which enabled the functioning of their cities, were not all purely beneficial. Alongside civilization's advances, Inana also received "deceit" and "the plundering of cities" and "making lamentations." Bearing these powerful gifts, Inana returns triumphant to Uruk, the city under her protection, where she is greeted with a grand feast.

This myth captures the essential duality that would define early urban life, when humans first gathered in large numbers. On one hand, extraordinary innovations. On the other, formidable challenges. It was in Uruk where this new urban form of human dwelling would first take shape: the city, forever transforming humanity's relationship with the environment and with each other.

Uruk emerged around the fifth millennium BC on the fertile banks of the Euphrates River in Southern Mesopotamia, about 250 kilometers south of modern-day Baghdad. Natural barriers like the Zagros Mountains to the east and the Arabian Desert to the west provided the Sumerians with relative isolation, at least until horses were increasingly used in warfare. But they had to contend with an unforgiving environment. The scorching summers and arid climate spurred them to innovate. By harnessing the annual floods of the Euphrates and Tigris Rivers through a vast network of canals, they transformed barren salt flats and marshes into fertile fields of barley, dates, figs, and chickpeas.

The irrigation system catalyzed a transformation in society. Building and maintaining canals required coordinated labor, technical planning, and centralized oversight. Dams were constructed to regulate water flow. Whether bureaucracy emerged to manage irrigation or irrigation expanded under a rising elite remains debated. Regardless, by the fourth millennium BC, state-level governance had formed—likely driven by the demands of infrastructure and the growing trade in vital and luxury goods.

Uruk benefited from significant technological advances. The wheel enabled oxen to pull three times their usual load. Plows boosted agricultural productivity. Boats waterproofed with natural tar, or bitumen, could move heavier cargo. By 3600 BC, Uruk had grown to 250 hectares. It had become the largest and most influential settlement of the region. With monumental temples and a centralized administration, it merited the title of "city." Around 3000 BC, at its peak, it housed as many as 50,000 people—enough to fill a modern-day arena. With this large population, Uruk benefited from economies of scale, reducing labor costs and amassing larger military forces to defend its granaries, often relying on slave labor.[43]

Much of Uruk's domestic life remains elusive. Archaeological excavations often favored temples and palaces, leaving limited evidence of what ordinary homes looked like. The city's earliest layers lie buried under more than eighty feet of later occupation, with only 0.1 percent of the lowest levels excavated.[44] Yet Uruk's colonies, particularly Habuba Kabira, reveal how the earliest city dwellers adapted to urban life.

Habuba Kabira was established around 3500 BC about 800 miles upstream from the mother city. Many of the houses centered on open courtyards, departing from earlier Ubaid dwellings, which were organized around enclosed halls. Several elite residences featured both courtyards and halls. These halls likely served as reception areas and reflected a growing emphasis on privacy within domestic spaces.[45] This made them similar to the later *liwan*—a long room traditionally used for greeting guests in certain Middle Eastern homes. Some believed that this was a natural progression from the Ubaid house. As archaeologist Michael Roaf noted, "The tripartite house of the Ubaid period became a courtyard house, with a reception room along one side of the courtyard."[46]

The courtyard, meanwhile, helped bring light and fresh air into the building's interior without compromising security, avoiding the need for windows in the building's exterior walls. Though buildings had courtyards before, the courtyard house became increasingly prevalent, shaping Middle Eastern architecture for millennia.

These homes tell a story of increasing sophistication. The use of sun-dried bricks of standardized sizes suggests a degree of mass production. The roofs were likely flat, made from reed mats laid over beams and coated with mud. Pivot stones at wall openings point to early door mechanisms, allowing doors to swing, long before modern hinges. Terra-cotta pipes beneath mud floors point to early forms of drainage.

Habuba Kabira's layout represented a departure from earlier Neolithic villages, which lacked planned streets, like Çatalhöyük, where houses abutted each other in one continuous mass. Instead, Habuba Kabira had a hierarchy of streets. Straight main roads likely went the full length of the settlement, while narrower lanes led to residential areas. It even featured an early attempt to manage stormwater. A few streets had drains lined with stone slabs and terra-cotta pipes that connected the town's drainage to the surrounding countryside.[47] Other Sumerian cities may have had similar systems.[48] And although these systems did not extend into homes, Uruk itself may have housed one of the world's earliest toilets—a deep cylinder-shaped pit inside a small room in a religious building dating back to around 3200 BC.[49]

The skyline of Uruk embodied a new urban order. In the Eanna District, the brick temple complex of Inanna featured thousands of clay cones whose painted, flattened ends—set into wet plaster in zigzag and diamond-shaped patterns, imitating textiles and mats—formed one of the world's first mosaics. Another district featured the White Temple, dedicated to the sky god Anu, rising forty feet above the city on its massive platform. They were a constant reminder of divine power.

But perhaps Uruk's greatest legacy came from the humble materials of everyday life: clay and reeds.[50] Before writing emerged, people used clay tokens to calculate and account for goods in increasingly complex economies. These tokens eventually gave rise to simple pictographs as the volume and variety of goods outstripped the capacity of the token system. These then evolved into the more abstract *cuneiform*, after the Latin term for "wedge," named for the distinctive wedge-shaped marks made by pressing reeds into soft clay.

This invention revolutionized human civilization. Writing enabled not only complex urban administration but also the preservation of knowledge, stories, and ideas across generations. While some tablets were intentionally fired to make them permanent, most remained unbaked and were even reused, meaning vast amounts of early writing have vanished. Yet some remarkable examples endure. One of the earliest surviving tablets, dating to around 3100 BC, offers administrative records for brewing beer, complete with pictographs of a building, a chimney, and an ear of barley in a jar.[51] Urbanization had ushered in a new era of human progress—beer included.

Writing, monumental architecture, specialized labor, political organizations, dense populations—all these were part of a dramatic transformation in human societies that Gordon Childe termed as the "Urban Revolution." He saw this occurring independently across the ancient world, from the Indus Valley to Egypt and China. With urbanization came a fundamental shift in human relationships. Historian Lewis Mumford likened cities to pressure cookers: "As with a gas, the very pressure of the molecules within that limited space produced more social collisions and interactions within a generation than would have occurred in many centuries if still isolated in their native habitats, without boundaries."[52] Architectural historian Spiro Kostof described this as "energized crowding"[53]—the essence of cities, where proximity to others led to greater opportunities, connections, and innovations.

The concentration of thousands of people in cities also created unprecedented environmental challenges, straining water and agricultural systems and sometimes contributing to their decline. During the late Uruk period, around 3200 to 3100 BC, the region likely experienced increased aridity. The marshes gradually receded. Subsistence agriculture became increasingly difficult. Initially, this crisis may have driven people toward urban centers, where large-scale reserves acted as a buffer against unpredictable crop yields.

However, these people then found themselves subject to political regimes. Uruk seemingly experienced escalating internal and external violence during this period. Seals depict prisoners, with their hands tied behind their backs, kneeling before spear-wielding soldiers. Artifacts such as mace-heads, slingshot balls, and arrowheads point to violent confrontations. Meanwhile, urban existence in Uruk may have teetered precariously on the edge.[54]

By 3000 BC, Uruk's influence ended. Colonies such as Habuba Kabira were abandoned. Artifacts from the Uruk culture, once found as far away as central Iran and Egypt's Nile Delta, stopped appearing, suggesting the city's trade networks collapsed. The causes of this decline remain a mystery. They could be internal tension resulting from environmental stress, intrusions by people from Eastern Anatolia and Transcaucasia, or an influx of Semitic-speaking people from the west.[55]

Uruk's influence declined, but many of the architectural solutions found in its settlements lived on. One of the most enduring strategies was the courtyard house, which would go on to define urban form across North Africa to the Indus Valley. It offered a practical solution: thick mud-brick walls that moderated temperature swings through thermal mass. The courtyards brought light and air into the home while preserving privacy. Even the narrow streets, hardly wide enough for a single donkey cart, had their role. They cast shade and channeled cooling breezes, creating favorable microclimates throughout the city.[56]

CITIES OF MUD

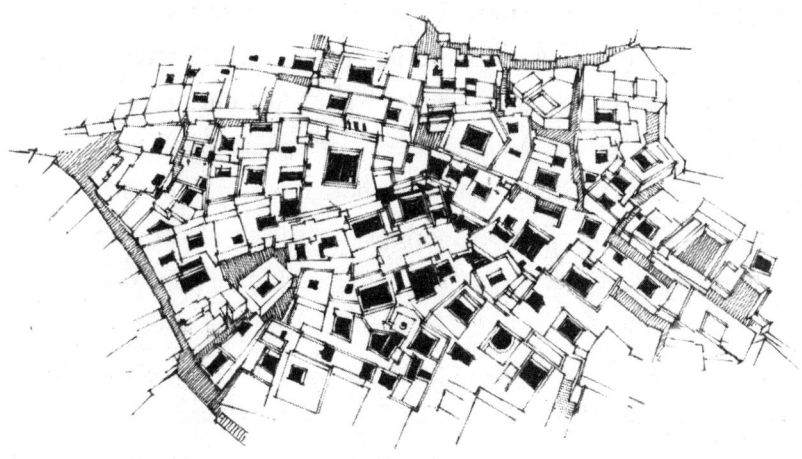

Traditional courtyard houses, Marrakech, Morocco.

These were not unique inventions of Uruk but shared adaptive responses to life in warm environments. They emerged independently across regions facing similar conditions. The courtyard house still offers comfort in hot weather today, from the *siheyuan* of Beijing to the *riads* of Fez. In these early settlements, we find not only the building blocks of urban life but also an architecture in dialogue with the earth and the sun.

Clay into Rock

A text from 2152 BC describes Gudea, a Sumerian ruler, in a temple's brick-laying ceremony: "Gudea put the blessed water in the frame of the brick mould.... He set up the appropriate brick stamp so that (the inscribed side) was upwards.... He raised the impeccable carrying-basket and set it before the mould. Gudea put the clay in the mould, he acted precisely as prescribed, and behold he succeeded in making a most beautiful brick for the house.... He struck the brick mould: the brick emerged into the daylight. He looked with complete satisfaction at the stamp (impression) on the clay.... raised the brick out of the frame of the mould: he carried the brick—a lovely tiara... which reached up to heaven—and went among his people."[57]

Nearly four millennia later, we still mark the beginning of construction projects with ceremony, although with golden shovels and photo opportunities. Yet these modern rituals pale in comparison to the profound significance that brickmaking held for the ancient Mesopotamians. Rulers like Gudea often depicted themselves carrying a basket of clay on their head, containing the first brick. They inscribed bricks with their names. They boasted about the number of bricks used in their works. So important were bricks that there was a brick god, Kulla, who was invoked during the laying of the first brick. In a society unable to use stone for building, creating bricks was nothing less than manufacturing artificial rock—a godlike act of transforming mud into the building blocks of civilization.

The story of the brick is, in many ways, the story of human dwelling itself. They are part of humanity's journey from temporary shelters of straw and wood to more permanent structures of brick and stone. In Mesopotamia, this evolution of bricks would reshape not only houses but also the fabric of human society—though it came at a cost.

By the middle of the third millennium BC, an unprecedented urban revolution was sweeping across Southern Mesopotamia. The once-sparse landscape had blossomed into a network of thriving cities, each spanning hundreds of hectares. The promise of opportunity drew villagers by the thousands, until an astounding 80 percent of the population lived in urban centers larger than forty hectares.[58] More than simple cities, these were city-states, complete with suburbs, satellite villages, and agricultural hinterlands, all governed by dynastic kings and temple elites.

But this urban explosion created an urgent challenge: how to house such dense populations safely and permanently. Houses were often not built safely, sometimes leading to collapse. So serious was this risk that the world's first building code, the Code of Hammurabi (circa 1750 BC), addressed it with chilling clarity. "If a builder constructs a house for a man but does not make it conform to specifications so that a wall then buckles, that builder shall make that wall sound using his silver."[59]

But cases could be far more severe. "If a builder constructs a house for a man, but does not make his work sound, and the house that he constructs collapses and causes the death of the householder, that builder shall be killed. If it should cause the death of a son of the householder, they shall kill a son of that builder."

One problem lay with sun-dried brick. The traditional sun-dried mud bricks that had served village builders for generations proved dangerously inadequate for urban life. When exposed to moisture, these bricks could deteriorate and disintegrate[60]—sometimes catastrophically. This is why builders frequently plastered sun-dried brick walls with fresh mud or gypsum to shield them from moisture and erosion, often reapplying it several times a year. Over time, they knocked down entire structures and rebuilt new ones atop earlier foundations. Life in early Mesopotamian settlements was defined by constant upkeep.

Several Mesopotamian cities show evidence of devastating floods, which would have destroyed most homes. Around 3500 BC, the city of Ur experienced a flood leaving up to eight feet of silt, leading excavator Leonard Woolley to believe it was evidence of the "Great Flood." While this is debated since it was more likely a local event, ancient Mesopotamians understood the limitations of their sun-dried brick homes. So they found a new solution. They began baking bricks. The Bible later echoes a similar turning point in Genesis, when humanity, after the Great Flood, resolves to rebuild: "They said to each other, 'Come, let's make bricks and bake them thoroughly.' They used brick instead of stone."[61]

Fired brick offered a more durable solution to the problem of moisture. By heating bricks to around 900°C to 1,000°C, a process called vitrification begins, where some of the silica and alumina in the clay fuse together, making the brick harder and more like a ceramic material. This firing removes chemically bound water and significantly reduces the porosity found in sun-dried bricks. However, Mesopotamian kilns rarely reached full vitrification. Nevertheless, the resulting bricks were still much more durable than sun-dried ones.

But fired bricks were a luxury, requiring both fuel and skilled labor. Economic records show that transporting 370 burnt bricks to a construction site cost one silver shekel—roughly 8.4 grams of silver.[62] These expenses restricted their use to urban centers with the resources and artisans to produce them.

The impact of this innovation was clearly visible in Ur. While ceramics and bricks had been fired since the fourth millennium BC, it was in this port city—where the Euphrates once met the sea—that fired bricks became increasingly common. During the Third Dynasty of Ur (2112–2004 BC), a period later called the Sumerian Renaissance, the city became the capital of an empire known for its major building projects. Appropriately, one of the most iconic depictions of King Ur-Nammu, an early ruler who founded the Third Dynasty, shows him carrying a basket of mud on his head, symbolizing the laying of the first brick.[63]

By the height of Ur's power, fired bricks had become symbols of urban prosperity. They were increasingly used in private buildings—

especially in courtyards, bathrooms, and wall footings prone to water damage. Baked bricks were laid at the base of walls as damp courses, to protect against moisture from rain and groundwater. This seemingly modest innovation greatly enhanced durability. While the sun-dried bricks above have mostly eroded, the fired bricks remain.

There were other techniques for managing moisture as well. A typical house featured an entry vestibule, "sometimes provided with a water-jar and a drain for the washing of the feet of those entering,"[64] imagined the excavator Leonard Woolley. It led into a courtyard paved with brick, with a carefully constructed drain at its center. Not yet able to make long pipes, builders stacked interlocking baked clay rings—an early plumbing method also used in their first toilets. These rings had holes along the sides to let water escape. Builders surrounded them with broken pottery to act like a filter, preventing clogging. This made it conceptually similar to a modern perforated drainpipe surrounded by gravel, like a French drain. As Woolley described, "a round pipe, 20 or 30 feet long, made of terracotta rings set one above the other; there were holes in the sides of the rings and round them there was a packing of broken pottery which kept the earth from blocking the holes."

This central placement of the drain was used to move water away from the building's walls. Such was the importance of proper drainage that an ancient text warned: "If the water in the court runs to the back, expense will be continual; if the water in the court runs to the middle of the court, that man will have wealth."[65]

Mesopotamians also used bitumen, a sticky, waterproof material that was a naturally occurring tar found along the Tigris and Euphrates Rivers. They used it to waterproof their boats and their homes as well. Bitumen helped seal floors and also served as a mortar to bind bricks. Since it was stronger than mud mortar, it was especially useful for lower courses. Bitumen was likely also applied to coat roofs—similar to the use of asphalt roofs today.

To create flat waterproof roofs, Sumerian builders layered beams, reed mats, mud, and bitumen plaster. Even the *Epic of Gilgamesh*, the world's oldest known work of fiction, nods to the eternal challenge of roof maintenance, cursing a sacred prostitute with a leaky roof: "The roof of your house, no builder shall plaster!"[66]

The widespread use of bricks, however, did put its limitations on domestic architecture. Mud bricks are strong under compression—like handling downward pressure from gravity. That makes them appropriate for walls. However, they are weak in tension and can crack or fail under the tensile forces that develop when spanning an opening, such as a window or doorway. Brick lintels had to be short, limiting window sizes. Therefore, homes faced the challenge of dark interiors.

Mesopotamian builders eventually got around this by using bricks to build arches, which primarily work under compression. This allowed them to span larger spaces with bricks alone, but this is not something they did for dwellings. Builders likely used timber beams to span window openings or support roofs.[67] However, wood was scarce in ancient Mesopotamia.

And it was their lack of wood that likely prevented multistory buildings. Several houses at Ur show remnants of staircases, and the brick walls were often quite thick. This led some to suggest they had a second story, while others propose they simply provided access to the roof. Roof space was almost certainly used—especially in dense cities where street-level space was limited. However, full multistory construction would have been prohibitively expensive. A second floor in a courtyard house would require additional timber not only for stairs but also for balconies to support upper-level access.

Archaeologist William Hafford proposed that many homes may have featured a "hybrid second story":[68] partially enclosed rooms or shelters on the roof, perhaps made of reeds or brick, which expanded living space without the cost of full vertical construction. Most Sumerian houses likely had flat roofs, made possible by the minimal rainfall in the region. These rooftops served multiple purposes, including sleeping, drying laundry, or winnowing grain—just as they still do in many Middle Eastern villages today.

Another design element that made efficient use of the dry climate was the courtyard. Since courtyards required no roofing, they enabled larger, more complex buildings than would have been possible with enclosed rooms alone.[69] At the same time, they enabled light and ventilation deep into building interiors. This efficient open-air form spread from homes to palaces, temples, and administrative complexes. Such parallels between domestic and sacred architecture may have reflected the builders' beliefs in anthropomorphic gods sharing humanlike needs.

It was in these types of important public projects, from temples to palaces, that fired bricks were most prominently used. These structures needed to stand the test of time. And the monarchs saw themselves as builders. Unlike later Neo-Assyrian rulers who often glorified battlefield victories, earlier kings commonly boasted of building projects, such as temples and city walls. They expressed their royal power through major construction projects. They liked to associate themselves with brick—or rather, fired brick.

One such example comes from Uruk's legendary five-mile wall, estimated to have been built with millions of bricks.[70] According to the *Epic of Gilgamesh*, the wall is famously attributed to Gilgamesh, the semi-mythical king. Alongside recounting the monster-slaying exploits of the hero and his quest for eternal life, the epic's narrator pauses several times to celebrate Gilgamesh's architectural legacy: "Survey its foundations, examine the brickwork! Were its bricks not fired in an oven?"[71] Yet the very prevalence of city walls during this period also signals an era marked by tension, from competition among rival city-states as well as increasing external threats.

The process of brick production may even have propelled advances in mathematics and measurement. Bricks are among the earliest surviving artifacts to carry written records of length, area, volume, capacity, and weight—making them unique in the history of premodern metrology.[72] Reeds also played a critical role in standardizing units: One Sumerian length measurement was literally called "the reed," and bundles of reeds were used as informal volumetric standards. Later Babylonian tablets reflected how mathematics helped solve practical construction needs. One fragment poses problems that wouldn't seem out of place on today's standardized tests: "The [area of the] house is 5 *sar*. For a height of 2½ *nindan*, how many bricks should I get made?"[73]

The Mesopotamians continually experimented with brick forms. Initially, the Samarra culture used cigar-shaped versions. Later, the Uruk period saw standardized rectangular or square ones, similar to modern types known as Reimchen bricks. By the early third millennium BC, a new variety emerged: plano-convex bricks, with flat bottoms and domed tops like a loaf of bread. Though more difficult to stack and requiring greater amounts of mortar, these bricks allowed for creative construction techniques. Builders sometimes arranged them in distinctive patterns, such as herringbone. Over time, however, practicality prevailed, and rectangular and square bricks once again became the norm.

In Ur, the use of fired bricks became increasingly extravagant. Some homes featured fired brick walls up to two meters high—far more than necessary to act as a damp course at the building's base.[74] Since walls were likely plastered, this excess would have been invisible to the eye—making it an odd social indicator of wealth.

Yet these architectural innovations came at a cost. The process of baking bricks and constructing monumental buildings required a vast amount of timber, placing pressure on the region's forests. Imported timber was expensive, so it was mostly used for public buildings. Wood became so scarce that homeowners would take their doors with them when moving—a practice noted in historical texts discussing house sales.[75]

Local woods like poplar only yielded short beams. To feed the demands for public buildings, Mesopotamians sourced materials from afar. Ships transported cedar, prized for palaces, from Turkey and Lebanon, as well as oak from Arabia.[76] The *Epic of Gilgamesh* even recounts how the hero and his ally, Enkidu, ventured to the famed Cedar Forest, wielding an axe, to slay its guardian and fell its trees. By 2800 BC, the once-abundant Lebanese cedar forests in the eastern ranges were largely depleted.[77]

The widespread deforestation of Southern Mesopotamia set off a cascade of environmental consequences that would linger for millennia. Without tree cover to anchor the soil, erosion intensified. Seasonal floods from mountain snowmelt saturated fields, and as the water evaporated, salts accumulated in the soil. This creeping salinization—still a challenge for farmers in Iraq today—gradually undermined agricultural productivity. Over time, many farmers abandoned their fields and returned to pastoral nomadism. These twin pressures of deforestation and soil degradation likely played a role in the decline of Sumerian civilization by 2000 BC[78]—though its collapse may have also resulted from administrative overreach or external threats.

The very innovations that had enabled magnificent cities ultimately contributed to their downfall. The Mesopotamians degraded their environment, leaving scars still visible in the arid landscapes today. The lower stretches of the Euphrates and Tigris, once cloaked in palm and poplar, now lie barren as stretches of desert. In some areas, the soil has become so saline that modern attempts to make sun-dried bricks result in bricks with "minimal resistance to fracture,"[79] and are "no longer considered suitable" for construction.

Urban life came with other challenges as well. Dense cities accelerated the spread of airborne diseases and infections from poor sanitation. And there are no records indicating that Mesopotamian kings, unlike later rulers, prioritized paved streets, clean water, or public latrines.[80] Irrigation canals supplied water, but they were distant from homes, forcing city dwellers to contend on their own with the daily struggle of securing fresh water and disposing of their waste.

The convergence of these problems—environmental degradation, urban diseases, and agricultural decline—left the city-states increasingly vulnerable. Nomadic groups, the Guti and the Martu, exploited Sumer's weaknesses, launching raids that destabilized the region. The Sumerians' contempt for these tribes echoes in their writings: "The Martu who know no grain. The Martu who know no house nor town, the boors of the mountains."[81] In a desperate bid to defend their already strained agricultural resources, the Sumerians envisioned a 170-mile wall between the two rivers. But it was too late. Grain prices increased sixtyfold, leading to severe famine in the city of Ur. A major blow came in 2004 BC, when the Elamites, inhabitants of the Zagros Mountains, besieged and burned the starving city.

Yet the city endured. While its political dominance waned, it rose again within a few decades as a significant center up until the Old Babylonian period—though it never again served as the seat of a royal dynasty. Many consider it Abraham's birthplace, giving it significance in Judaism, Christianity, and Islam.

The ancient Mesopotamians had written the opening chapter of urban civilization. They implemented architectural innovations like courtyard buildings and fired bricks that laid the groundwork for city life. They forged new urban blueprints that, unwittingly, would shape our built environments thousands of years later. And yet, for all their advancements, they still clung to traditions from their Neolithic ancestors, such as burying the dead under the floors of their homes.

Ur's compact, walkable layout—where homes, workplaces, and temples stood within easy reach—foreshadowed today's concept of the "15-minute city."[82] Like ancient Ur, modern cities still sprawl into suburbs beyond their cores.[83] And in some ways, little has changed: Brickmaking still involves mixing clay, shaping it in molds, and firing it in kilns. And nearly four thousand years later, we continue to inaugurate building projects with rituals. Though today's hard hats and oversized scissors hardly rival the deep resonance brickmaking once held for the ancient Mesopotamians.

Today the region is mostly inhabited by herders and farmers and dotted with tells. These earthen mounds stand as monuments to both societal innovation and environmental degradation. The decline of Mesopotamian cities highlights the complicated balance between environmental stewardship and our ongoing quest to enhance our buildings. It poses a challenge still relevant today: how to reap nature's bounty without destroying the source.

Nothing captures this tragic fall more powerfully than the "Lament for Ur," which voices the despair and tragedy of the Sumerian people as their once-thriving city fell into ruin. "O brick-built [Ur], the lament is bitter, the lament made for you. O city, your name exists but you have been destroyed. I shall cry 'Alas, my city.' My houses of the outer city were destroyed—I shall cry 'Alas, my houses.' My houses of the inner city were destroyed—I shall cry 'Alas, my houses.'"[84] Shortly afterward, Sumerian became a dead language, marking the close of humanity's first great urban experiment.

THREE

Order and Ornament

The House of Many Spaces

Socrates, an unlikely architectural critic, once turned his mind to the ideal home. "If a man is to have the sort of house that he needs, ought he to contrive to make it as pleasant and convenient as possible to live in? . . . Isn't it pleasant to have a house which is cool in summer and warm in winter?"[1] When this was admitted, he continued. "Well, in houses that have a south aspect, in winter the sun shines into the [porticoes], while in summer it passes over our heads and over the roof and casts shade." Writing in the fifth century BC, Xenophon documented how Socrates described the benefits of a southern overhang, articulating the essence of passive solar design—principles that remain relevant today. The philosopher emphasized that such a design "offers at all seasons the most agreeable retreat."

Even Aristotle, a century later, reinforced the importance of southern orientation, noting that "for well-being and health, again, the homestead should be airy in summer, and sunny in winter. A homestead possessing these qualities would be longer than it is deep; and its main front would face the south."[2] So obvious was this knowledge to the ancient Greeks that the playwright Aeschylus mocked those ignorant of it, describing "primitive man" as having "neither knowledge of houses built of bricks and turned to face the sun . . . but [dwelling] beneath the ground like swarming ants, in sunless caves."[3]

In ancient Greece, philosophers gave serious thought not only to politics or ethics but to housing. They considered the home's adaptability to the environment and its relation to the position of the sun. They reimagined its integration into the city. They even defined its relation to society as a whole. As Greek society grew more complex, houses evolved from simple spaces into dwellings with increasingly specialized rooms. This marked a new step in the history of habitation, as architecture began to mirror the expanding intricacies of daily life.

The house that came to symbolize this evolution was the Greek courtyard house. It rose to prominence following a dark chapter in history known as the Bronze Age Collapse around 1200 BC. This period saw invasions, internal rebellions, climate change, and disruption of trade, leading to the de-urbanization of the Eastern Mediterranean and Near East. But by the eighth century BC, a resurgence began. Iron plows and crop rotation improved food production. Political stability and expanding trade gave rise to a new era of city-states. Athens rose as one of the most powerful cities, establishing the world's first democracy and building the Parthenon.

One of the best windows into Greek domestic life of this period comes from Olynthus, located on the Chalkidiki Peninsula near modern-day Thessaloniki. During the rise of Greek cities in the fifth century BC, when Athens and Sparta vied for dominance, King Perdiccas II of Macedonia sought to consolidate his power. He encouraged unification of the Chalkidiki cities. According to the historian Thucydides, "Perdiccas at the same time persuaded the Chalcidians to abandon and pull down their cities on the sea-coast and settle inland at Olynthus, making there a single strong city.... And so they proceeded to dismantle their cities, move inland, and prepare for war."[4]

As settlers moved to the city, it adopted a rational grid plan to efficiently divide the land. Houses in these new areas of Olynthus were strikingly uniform, especially on the North Hill, now known for the Olynthian House style. The average house was quite substantial, with its ground floor alone measuring more than three thousand square feet—about three times larger than the average European home today. What was unique about this house type was its open courtyard surrounded by a *pastas*, or a roofed colonnade. It protected the interior from direct sunlight while at the same time allowing for cooling breezes. The columns were made from wood and set on

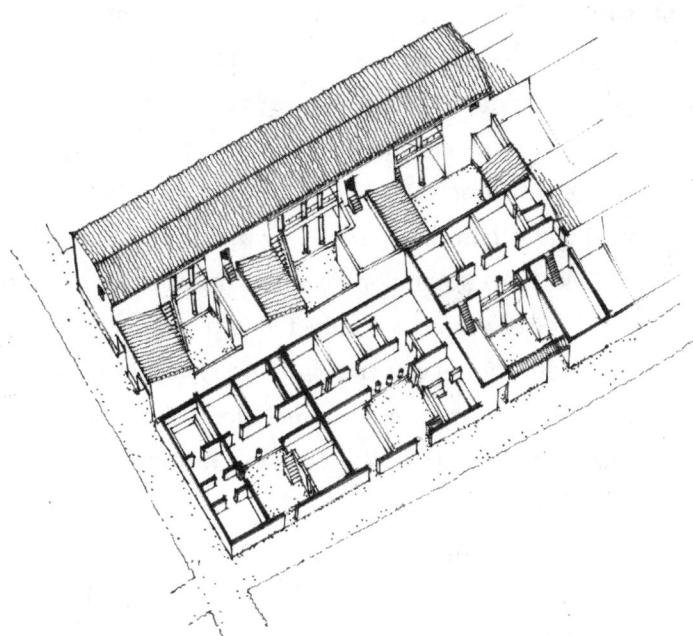

Pastas houses, Olynthus, North Hill Section, Greece, 432–348 BC.

stone bases, which provided a foundation and helped protect against ground moisture.

The pitched wooden structures supporting the roofs became increasingly important as more houses adopted terra-cotta tiles. Once reserved for temples, terra-cotta roofing increasingly spread to private homes by the fifth century BC—a sign of technological advancement and social aspiration. The overlapping tiles provided a balance between the lightness of thatch and the durability of heavy stone tiles. These roofs were waterproof and more fire-resistant, and they conferred prestige.[5] Their production required specialized molds, kilns, and skilled labor to manufacture at scale—some were stamped with the branded marks of their makers.

The courtyards in Olynthus were often located in the southern portion of the house. This was no accident. The Greeks understood the sun's seasonal angles and positioned them to draw in winter sunlight while shading the interior from the harsh summer sun. This understanding may have been driven by the scarcity—and expense—of wood in Greece, due to deforestation from shipbuilding and manufacturing beginning in the seventh century BC.

The typical Olynthian house had a recurring set of rooms used for domestic tasks like cooking or weaving. This included a primary room, sometimes with a hearth, connected to two smaller chambers. One of these smaller rooms was the "flue"—a space for lighting fires and waste disposal. Some houses even included a terra-cotta bathtub set on a mortar floor. Together, these spaces formed what scholars call the "oikos unit."

Importantly, the Greek term *oikos* meant both household and the house itself. They saw it as a fundamental unit of the city and city-state (*polis*). As Aristotle said, "Every polis is composed of oikoi."[6]

This was largely because the house served as a hub of economic activities and production. The word "economy" derives from *oikos*, meaning "management of the household." At Olynthus, for instance, archaeologists found olive crushers, grape-crushing floors, grinding stones, and many loom weights inside houses.

Women were in charge of the household, performing duties like weaving textiles, while men were responsible for affairs outside the house. Philosopher Xenophon, in *Oeconomicus*, describes an Athenian speaking about his fifteen-year-old bride: "It seems to me that God adapted women's nature to indoor and man's to outdoor work. . . . As Nature has entrusted woman with guarding the household supplies, and a timid nature is no disadvantage in such a job, it has endowed women with more fear than man."[7] Yet, despite their work, many Greek women lived under the legal guardianship of men, with no political voice, limited legal rights, and little access to public life.

Literary sources suggest that within the house there existed gender-specific spaces. One such space was the *gynaikonitis* (meaning "of women"), or women's quarters. In Aristophanes's comedy *Thesmophoriazusae*, a woman complains about jealous husbands: "We are incessantly watched, we are shut up behind bolts and bars in the *gynaikonitis*, and dogs are kept to frighten off the adulterers."[8]

The *andron* (meaning "of men") was a square chamber measuring roughly 200 square feet, designed for entertaining guests. It included several couches arranged for symposia, the male-only drinking gatherings familiar from Athenian literature. These rooms were among the most elaborately decorated, with colorfully painted walls and floors featuring colored mortar or plaster and vibrant mosaics made from pebbles arranged in geometric patterns. Since house sizes were generally similar, wealth was expressed through decoration—such as the famous Bellerophon mosaic found on an *andron* floor at Olynthus, depicting the mythological hero riding Pegasus and fighting the Chimera.

Each *andron* typically contained sofas for the host and his guests to recline on while enjoying meals served on small tables. Wine, always diluted with water, was the beverage of choice—although that did little to discourage overindulgence. As the comic poet Eubulus captured, through the voice of Dionysus: "Three bowls only do I mix for the temperate—one to health... the second to love and pleasure, the third to sleep. When this is drunk up wise guests go home. The fourth... belongs to violence, the fifth to uproar, the sixth to drunken revel, the seventh to black eyes... the tenth to madness and the hurling of furniture."[9]

Yet, artifacts found across rooms suggest these gendered spaces were more fluid than male authors imply.[10] Rooms like the *andron* and the *gynaikonitis* may have accommodated both genders depending on the occasion. In *On the Murder of Eratosthenes,* the Greek speechwriter Lysias describes the male defendant living in the upper-level *gynaikonitis*, while his wife, after childbirth, stayed in the ground-level *andron* to "avoid the risk of descending by the stairs."[11]

Greek houses were likely multifunctional. As the Greek statesman Aeschines noted, "It is not the lodgings and the houses which give their names to the men who have lived in them, but it is the tenants who give to the places the names of their own pursuits. Where, for example, several men hire one house and occupy it, dividing it between them, we call it an 'apartment house,' but where one man only dwells, a 'house.' And if perchance a physician moves into one of these shops on the street, it is called a 'surgery.' But if he moves out and a smith moves into this same shop, it is called a 'smithy'; if a fuller, a 'laundry'; if a carpenter, a 'carpenter's shop'; and if a pimp and his harlots, from the trade itself it gets the name of 'brothel.'"[12]

Privacy was paramount in Greek domestic architecture. Homes had unassuming, mostly windowless exteriors built from stone rubble masonry and mud brick, often plastered over. Entryways were subtly designed to deter unwanted visitors. Many areas were off-limits, with the *andron* being the only space open to outsiders.

According to the historian Plutarch, most doors had a knocker: "without knocking at the door, it is great rudeness to enter another's house."[13] Likely a metal ring affixed to the door,[14] it was intended to protect against awkward encounters: "A stranger coming in unawares, the mistress or daughter of the family might be surprised, busy or undressed, or a servant be seen under correction, or the maids be overheard in the heat of their scolding."

What truly set Olynthus apart, however, was its neighborhood planning. Urban planning became an increasing consideration for the Greeks. Even Aristotle once listed the duties of city administrators, ranging from building inspections to more macabre responsibilities: "They prevent the construction of buildings encroaching on and balconies overhanging the roads, of overhead conduits with an overflow into the road, and of windows opening outward on to the road; and they remove for burial the bodies of persons who die on the roads."[15]

Olynthus North Hill had an orthogonal grid layout, forming rectangular blocks of six to ten houses. Narrow alleys neatly bisected the blocks down the middle, facilitating the drainage of rainwater. Avenues and streets were paved and oriented north-south and east-west.

This grid was not without precedent. Earlier gridded cities included the pyramid town of El Kahun in Egypt and Mohenjo-

Daro in the Indus Valley. Similar patterns emerged independently across the world, from the Mayan gridded city of Nixtun-Ch'ich' to the ancient Chinese city of Anyang. This widespread adoption led one researcher to suggest that the grid had been established "long ago" as "a generic urban solution, independently achieved by many peoples."[16]

What distinguished the Greek approach was how this grid concept became an integral part of a broader political philosophy and functional planning. According to Aristotle, during the fifth century BC, Hippodamus of Miletus, often hailed as the "father of urban planning," proposed a gridded city that reflected his social theory, where the city was divided into three classes—artisans, soldiers, and farmers—and the equal lots within each area suggested a measure of equality within each class.

In some ways, the grid became a tangible manifestation of humanity's pursuit to master nature. At Olynthus, this commitment to straight lines persisted despite the challenging hills. The uniform grid provided organizational clarity and guaranteed a predictable urban blueprint, streamlining space allocation for public roads and houses.

The city's layout with its intentional placement of similar courtyard homes replicated across every block followed the principle of modularity. There seemed to be a conscious consideration of how the smallest unit—the room—related to the shape of the entire city, much like individual cells assembling into the tissues and organs of a living organism. Rooms formed houses, houses combined to make blocks, blocks made up a neighborhood, and together these neighborhoods constituted the city as a whole. This modular approach to urban design, where individual residential units like the courtyard house formed larger ordered systems, appeared across distant civi-

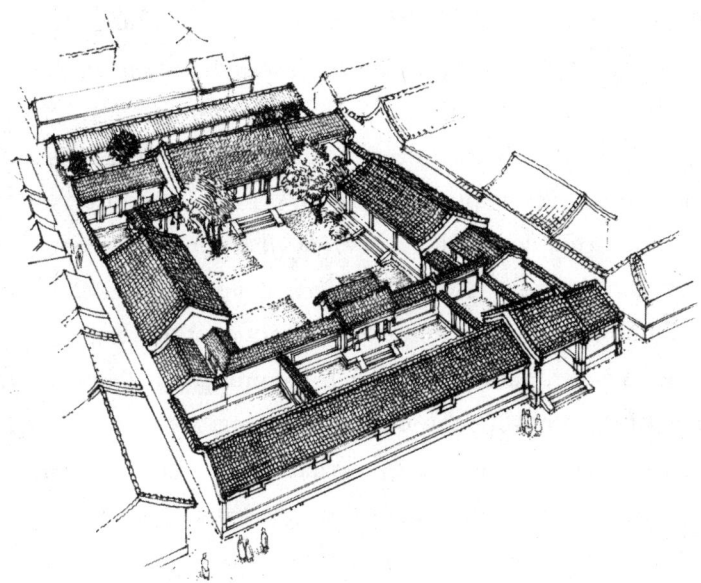

Classic Beijing courtyard house (*siheyuan*), ca. 1300–1900 AD.

lizations. For instance, it finds a strong parallel in the arrangement of Chinese *siheyuan* (courtyard houses) within their gridded cities.

Some suggest this interconnectedness resonated with the Stoic belief of *oikeiôsis*. This term, derived from *oikos*, refers to a process of belonging—like being "at home" with something. To illustrate this, the Stoic Hieracles drew concentric circles in the sand, from the smallest circle of the individual to the family, fellow citizens, the country's people, and humankind. This interconnectedness embraces a cosmopolitan ideal, emphasizing shared identity— although one from which slaves, pervasive in ancient Greece, were excluded. Today, urban designers continue to draw upon modularity to create well-planned cities, emphasizing the relationship of individual buildings to the broader urban fabric.

Yet for all its architectural achievements, Olynthus couldn't escape its tragic fate. When the city eventually aligned with Athens out of fear of Macedon's growing power, it incurred the wrath of Philip of Macedon in 348 BC. He not only plundered the city but also sold its inhabitants into slavery. These devastating acts led to the exceptional preservation of Olynthus's homes and interiors. Many of the Greek architectural ideas seen at Olynthus would later influence other cities in the classical world, particularly in the Mediterranean.

Combining practical needs with philosophical ideals, Olynthus serves as a reminder of how urban planning can shape society.[17] Its innovations, from neighborhood planning to solar design, still feel strikingly modern. As solar energy historian John Perlin notes, "Olynthus is proof that planning for the use of solar heat was possible on a large urban scale in antiquity."[18]

While we often celebrate ancient Greece for its literature and philosophy, we should not ignore its more practical legacy in these ruins on the flat-top hills of northern Greece—proof that sometimes, the best textbook for modern urban design is written in the foundations of the past.

Marble and Mosaics

As philosopher Seneca walked the streets of ancient Rome, he must have been agitated by the gleaming marble columns and shimmering mosaic-covered walls of private homes. "A thatched roof once covered free men," he declared, "under marble and gold dwells slavery."[19] Yet even as he wrote these words, wealthy Romans were transforming their homes into ever more elaborate displays of prosperity—Seneca included, as he himself owned several luxurious villas.

The tension between luxury and virtue that so troubled Seneca lay at the heart of what made the Roman home, or *domus*, so distinctive. Every architectural choice carried meaning. Marble was a statement about power, deliberately echoing the architecture of temples and public monuments. A narrow passage at the home's entry was calculated theater, heightening the dramatic contrast with the spacious atrium beyond.

The Roman atrium home represented a leap in residential sophistication. While the Celts lived in rudimentary mud huts, affluent Romans enjoyed the luxury of their domestic conveniences. They drank water delivered through aqueducts and enjoyed amenities that were far ahead of their time, such as indoor plumbing. Within their homes, they luxuriated in lavish gardens and dining rooms with marble floors, sculptures, and wall paintings. Their conception of luxury homes was not too different from ours today—except that, long before they had domesticated cats (the word "domestic" itself derives from *domus*), they kept weasels and snakes to catch mice.[20]

The luxurious homes of Rome, of course, weren't built in a day. Around 900 BC, Roman abodes were humble huts built with wattle and daub. These were wooden frame structures filled in with twigs and branches daubed with mud mixed with straw and manure to make it stronger. These thatched-roof huts were perhaps the kind Seneca nostalgically alluded to. But by the close of the sixth century BC, the Romans had transitioned to the domus, an urban residence with several rooms, uncut stone walls, and a terra-cotta roof. Meanwhile, the elite lived in elaborate palaces built from cut stone with many rooms. Nevertheless, poorer citizens continued to live in mud huts—a built expression of growing class divisions.[21]

The rise of the domus as a symbol of luxury paralleled the ascent of the empire itself. As Rome expanded and conquered territories, it absorbed architectural ideas along with them. This began with the Etruscans, master builders known for their use of the arch and vault. By the fifth century BC, Romans had adopted the Etruscan-style atrium home, with rooms arranged around a central open courtyard.

From the street, visitors entered through a dim passage that opened into a luminous atrium, which served as a public reception area.[22] At the heart of the atrium was the *impluvium*—a sunken basin that collected rainwater, a technique inherited from the Etruscans. This feature not only provided water stored in cisterns but also beautified the space by reflecting the sky.

By 100 BC, the Roman domus increasingly borrowed from Greek designs to incorporate a *peristyle*—a colonnaded courtyard. In grander homes, the atrium became the public-facing area near the front of the house. Meanwhile, the peristyle garden became the

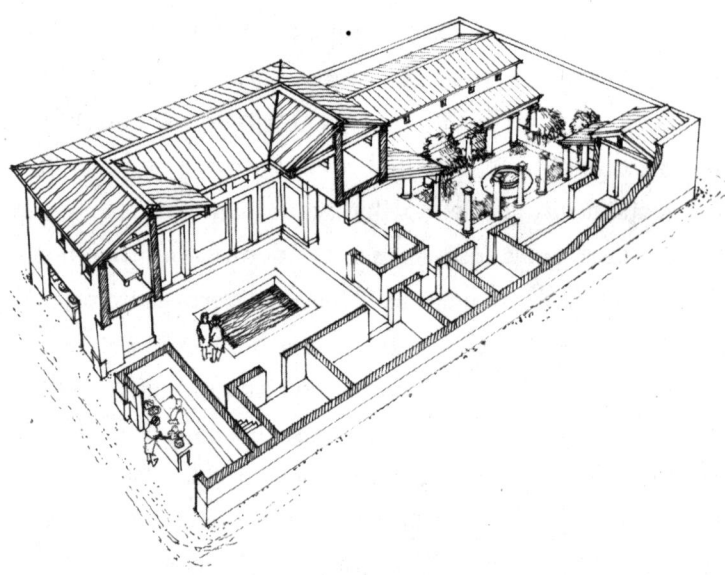

Roman house (domus), Roman Empire, ca. 100 BC–200 AD.[23]

heart of family life at the rear of the house, with access to the kitchen and dining room. Wealthier residences may have also had an upper story, used for sleeping quarters and storage.

The commercial aspect of the domus set it apart from the villa, its bucolic counterpart nestled in the Roman countryside. Many domus residences were fronted with one or two *tabernae*, storefronts used to sell agricultural produce or food. Although these *tabernae* were structurally part of the building, they typically had no direct internal access and functioned independently, managed by *tabernarii*—urban freedmen operating under the patronage of the domus owner.

Inside the domus, the *tablinum*, or study, functioned as the paterfamilias's office. It was strategically located at the juncture between the more public and private parts of the house, allowing the paterfamilias to see all the way to the street when sitting at his desk and keep an eye on all comings and goings. The house also contained squarish rooms called *cubicula*—versatile spaces used mainly as bedrooms but also occasionally as discreet meeting spots. Interestingly, the term *cubiculum* is the etymological root for the modern workplace's partitioned space, or office *cubicle*.

The domus played a major role within Rome's patron-client system. Patrons received daily visits from lower-ranking clients seeking favors and protection in exchange for loyalty. These visits must have also been subtle inspections—opportunities to affirm the patron's status, through the display of wealth and taste.

This social dynamic likely fueled the architectural spectacle of the domus. Floors were often paved with marble or colorful mosaics. Walls featured frescoes or stucco molds imitating marble paneling or columns. In some cases, even when actual marble was used elsewhere in the house, walls were painted to mimic marble.[24] Some

Romans, like Seneca, considered such opulence excessive, because marble was traditionally reserved for temples and public buildings.

One space particularly designed to impress guests was the *triclinium,* named after its "three couches," borrowed from the Greek custom of reclined dining. This space often adjoined the atrium and was sometimes fronted by a fountain. It was lavishly decorated with artwork, mosaics, draperies, and occasionally even shell-encrusted plasterwork. Poets, musicians, or even acrobats performed in between courses.

To some degree, the main rooms were arranged following deliberate proportions. In *De Architectura,* the first surviving treatise on architecture, Roman architect Vitruvius argued that buildings should mirror the harmonious proportions of nature, such as the human body. "Since nature has designed the human body so that its members are duly proportioned to the frame as a whole," he wrote, "the ancients had good reason for their rule—that in perfect buildings, the different members must be in exact symmetrical relations to the whole general scheme."[25] He noted, "Dining rooms ought to be twice as long as they are wide," and peristyles "should be one-third longer than they are deep."

Like their Greek predecessors, Roman architects often oriented their buildings to take advantage of shade and solar gain. Similar to Hellenistic houses, the domus looked inward into courtyards and colonnades, which promoted ventilation and daylight. Vitruvius even prescribed seasonal orientations: "Winter dining rooms and bathrooms should have a southwestern exposure."

Remarkably modern in his thinking, Vitruvius stressed climate-responsive design across the empire's vast geography: "One type of house seems appropriate for Egypt, another for Spain... one still different for Rome. This is because one part of the earth is directly under the sun's course, another is far from it.... Designs for houses ought to conform similarly to the diversities of the climate." For Vitruvius, architecture demanded more than technical skill—it required knowledge of astronomy, geometry, history, and even music. An architect, he argued, "should be a good writer, a skillful draftsman, versed in geometry and optics, expert at figures, acquainted with history, informed on the principles of natural and moral philosophy, somewhat of a musician, not ignorant of the sciences both of law and physic."

Romans wealthy enough to own a domus could often afford the additional cost to connect to their local water supply. This water was sourced from locations as far as forty-four miles away, transported via aqueducts to central distribution points or cisterns. From there, it was distributed in lead pipes to different neighborhoods. Over time, Rome built eleven aqueducts spanning over three hundred miles. The city even had its own water commissioner, including Sextus Julius Frontinus, who once boasted, "With such an array of indispensable structures carrying so many waters, compare, if you will, the idle Pyramids or the useless, though famous works of the Greeks!"[26]

The water inflow into a private home was controlled by a bronze valve, and its standardized diameter—determining flow rate—set the fee owed to the city. Rome's water system was revolutionary, supplying an estimated one thousand liters per person per day, double that of modern Rome. Yet while the wealthy enjoyed bathhouses and vast amounts of private water, common citizens fetched significantly less from public fountains, though a still generous sixty-seven liters per day.[27]

Despite this abundant supply, many domus lacked proper sanitation. If private toilets existed, they were little more than cesspits, often placed disturbingly close to kitchens. The stench alone would have ruined an appetite. The problem worsened with upper-floor toilets, where waste frequently leaked from loose-fitting terra-cotta downpipes, saturating rooms with filth and stink.[28]

One reason many homes avoided connecting to the city's sewer system—beyond the cost—may have been the lack of traps. Unlike modern plumbing, where U-shaped water traps block sewer gases from entering buildings, Roman sewers offered no such protection. Even Rome's famed *Cloaca Maxima*—the "Greatest Sewer"—was designed to channel rainwater, not human waste, which was typically dumped onto the street or recycled as fertilizer.

Romans may also have been wary of creatures swimming upstream through the sewer pipes into their homes. Roman author Aelian describes such an invasion, recounting how an octopus "swam up through a subterranean sewer . . . and emerged in a house on the shore where some Iberian merchants had their cargo. . . . It threw its tentacles around the earthenware vessels and with its grip broke them and feasted on the pickled fish."[29]

Beyond managing water, Roman homes integrated several heating and cooling strategies. Water in the *impluvium* cooled the surrounding air through evaporation. A few Roman homes even had ceramic pipes embedded inside walls, circulating cold water from aqueducts. This effectively created an early cooling system. Other homes featured private thermal baths with *hypocaust* systems—hollow chambers beneath floors and inside walls.[30] Heated by an oven's fire, the air would rise through these spaces and thus keep the rooms at a constant temperature. Borrowed from the Greeks, this method became common in Roman bathhouses.[31]

Some even had sunrooms enclosed with transparent stone, designed to trap heat. These rooms used early windowpanes made from *lapis specularis* and were called *heliocamini* (solar furnace rooms). The Romans were the first in recorded history to legislate sun rights: the sixth-century Justinian Code protected the "*heliocaminus*'s right to the sun" against obstructions that might cause excessive shadow.

Over time, domus interiors grew more lavish. Libraries, gardens, fountains, and private baths became symbols of elite status. Cicero, the famed Roman orator, encapsulated the sentiment in 46 BC: "If you have a garden in your library, you'll lack nothing."[32]

Pompeii opens a window into these richer dimensions of Roman domestic life. Located near present-day Naples, it was a commercial hub with about 11,000 inhabitants. The rich volcanic soil allowed the surrounding region to flourish agriculturally, supporting grain crops and vineyards.

Virtually every domus in Pompeii had gardens, typically positioned at the rear of the building. These gardens frequently included manicured lawns, fragrant shrubs, and fruit trees.[33] The affluent, however, elevated landscape design to an art form. Their peristyles, or column-framed courtyards, often housed fountains, ponds, statues, and shaded recesses. The rarer and more exotic the plants and statues, the greater the homeowner's prestige. Some Romans used the ponds to breed exotic fish—a fashionable hobby among the elite.

These gardens married aesthetics with practicality. Ornamental species like oleanders and boxwood grew along with fruit-bearing trees such as pomegranates, figs, and cherries. Some plants were grown for their medicinal benefits, such as melissa, which was used to treat insect bites and ease melancholy when brewed as tea. Some walls inside the house often featured garden frescoes depicting exotic natural scenes, almost creating an illusion of endless nature. As Cicero noted, "By means of our hands we struggle to create a second world within the world of nature."[34]

Pompeii's domus had elaborate interiors. Floors featured intricate mosaics, such as the iconic *Cave Canem* ("Beware of the Dog") mosaic at the House of the Tragic Poet. This piece features a chained, ferocious-looking dog—a reminder that Romans kept dogs as both pets and protectors. The spiritual life of the household was evident from the many statues and artifacts representing various deities. They often included a sculpture of Janus, the two-faced god who oversaw beginnings and endings. He presided over doorways and transitions.

Romans surrounded themselves with frescoes. These portrayed everything from scenes of daily life to Hercules's heroic feats and Narcissus gazing longingly at his reflection. Wall painting was such a refined art form that it progressed through four distinct styles between 200 BC and 79 AD: from marble imitation, to architectural trompe-l'oeil, to ornamental fantasy, and finally a sophisticated fusion of all three.[35]

Among the most spectacular homes was the House of the Vettii—one of Pompeii's largest and most lavishly adorned. Its presumed owners, the Vettii brothers, were freedmen who had climbed the social ladder, likely through commerce or wine trading. As a conspicuous display of wealth, the placement of two lockable chests in the grand atrium—the home's public reception space—flaunted valuables being safeguarded in plain sight.

Most striking in this atrium was a fresco of the god Priapus, depicted weighing his disproportionately large phallus on a scale against a bag of coins. The message here was clear: fertility and fortune, displayed with a boldness bordering on ostentatiousness that we today associate with the nouveau riche.

Yet beneath the art lay a disturbing societal reality. Phallic imagery symbolized fertility and affluence. Meanwhile, erotic frescoes often reduced women to mere sexual objects, sometimes even depicting them in scenes of violation. In the House of the Vettii, graffiti scratched onto the walls of a small interior room suggest the space may have functioned as a brothel. These clues reflect broader social inequality and double standards in Roman society.[36] For most of Roman history, women were legally placed under the guardianship of men. Excluded from politics and denied formal education in writing, their voices were rarely recorded, their stories largely untold.

All the inequities and indulgences of Pompeian life were buried in an instant when Mount Vesuvius erupted catastrophically in 79 AD. In a few hours, Pompeii and its inhabitants were smothered under ash. Pliny the Younger, who provided the only eyewitness account, writes, "You could hear the shrieks of women, the wailing of infants, and the shouting of men. Some were calling their parents, others their children or their wives, trying to recognize them by their voices."[37]

The ash, after cooling into soft stone, preserved Pompeii in remarkable detail. Today, plaster casts from the voids in the solidified ash reveal heartbreaking scenes. In a particularly striking one, a mother clutches her child, her face in agony, frozen in time.

The lessons of the domus stand immortalized in stone and ash. Visiting Pompeii is almost time travel; you can linger in the gardens of the House of the Vettii and walk the grooved stone sidewalks that once guided the wheels of carts. To understand the city's fate, climb Mount Vesuvius to experience its state of "active rest." On a windless day, its sulfurous breath can be pungent enough to make visitors gag.

And beyond its extraordinary preservation, the Roman domus continues to shape our built environment. From marble-clad foyers and faux paneling to manicured hedges and elaborate statues, Roman ideals continue to shape how we design homes and gardens.

The domus was not just a shelter—it was an expression of self. Even now, our dwellings declare who we are, who we wish to be—and, in the lush language of lawns and interiors, what we value most.

The Walk-Up

The price of living in Rome must have been substantial. A tombstone from a shared tomb outside Rome bears an inscription termed "The Tenant's Lament" for the ex-slave Ancarenus Nothus. It reads: "My body knows no longer hunger . . . now it is no longer [paying] deposit on the rent, but enjoys for free an eternal lodging."[38]

As people migrated to Rome seeking opportunities, they would have faced daunting housing challenges. Ancarenus Nothus, who belonged to a lower urban class, likely lived in an *insula* (Latin for "island"). *Insulae* were apartment buildings that often occupied entire city blocks and may have risen up to eight stories. Their ground floors typically housed shops, while the upper floors were crammed with *cellae*—single-room units arranged around a central light well.

Long before the Industrial Revolution brought vertical living, the *insulae* pioneered the concept of the walk-up building. Though their origins remain obscure, a historical record of the Roman historian Livy suggests they may have existed as early as the third century BC. He recounted an unusual event, in which "an ox is reported to have climbed up of its own accord to the third story of a house, and then, frightened by the noisy crowd which gathered, it threw itself down."[39]

Architecturally, the *insula* may have borrowed certain features from the domus, such as a colonnaded atrium. Like the domus, its entrance was typically a narrow walkway flanked by stores. But besides these more familiar elements, it also introduced innovations: communal staircases, vaulted arcades, balconies, and multi-

Insula Diana, Ostia, ca. 150 AD.⁴⁰

functional spaces that combined residential, commercial, and even religious uses within a single complex.[41]

The *insulae* became a lucrative business. Marcus Licinius Crassus, a Roman general and notorious real estate mogul, exploited the city's frequent fires and building collapses. According to the first-century biographer Plutarch: "He proceeded to buy slaves who were architects and builders," snapped up fire-damaged buildings from panicked owners at "a trifling price," and then used his slaves to rebuild them and profit.[42] "In this way the largest part of Rome came into his possession," Plutarch noted. Crassus was allegedly the wealthiest man in Rome.

Around the same time, the Roman architect Vitruvius championed vertical living. "With the present importance of the city and the unlimited numbers of its population, it is necessary to increase the number of dwelling-places indefinitely."[43] He recognized that "the case has made it necessary to find relief by making the buildings high." By having "many floors high in the air," he noted, "accommodations within the city walls ... multiplied," and "the Roman people easily find excellent places in which to live." Yet Vitruvius also acknowledged the limitations of traditional building materials. "Brick walls, unless two or three bricks thick, cannot support more than one story."

Structural stability was an ongoing concern. The poet Juvenal lamented: "We live in a city shored up for the most part with gimcrack stays and props: that's how our landlords arrest the collapse of their property, papering over great cracks in the ramshackle fabric, reassuring the tenants they can sleep secure, when all the time the building is poised like a house of cards."[44]

"I prefer to live without fires and midnight panics," Juvenal concluded. "By the time the smoke's got up to your third floor apartment (and you [are] still asleep), your heroic downstairs neighbour is roaring for water and shifting his bits and pieces to safety. If the alarm goes at ground level, the last to fry will be the attic tenant, way up among the nesting pigeons."

Fire was an acute hazard in buildings constructed with light wood frames and filled in with branches daubed with mud. As Vitruvius warned, "As for 'wattle and daub' I could wish that it had never been invented. The more it saves in time and gains in space, the greater and the more general is the disaster that it may cause; for it is made to catch fire, like torches."[45]

Enter Roman concrete. Though lime had been used for centuries as a binding agent, such as by the Egyptians, the Romans transformed it into concrete, a standalone building material. By mixing lime with volcanic ash, sourced near Mount Vesuvius, they created a remarkably strong concrete that could even set underwater. Seneca noted, "The dust at Puteoli becomes stone if it touches water."[46]

This breakthrough allowed Romans to build structures on a scale never before seen. Monumental works like the Colosseum and the Pantheon were made possible—and so too were more resilient, multistory *insulae*. Builders often paired concrete with brick-facing and vaulting techniques,[47] enabling vaulted ground floors providing stability and room for shops and communal spaces.

A turning point came after the Great Fire of Rome in 64 AD, which raged for six days and destroyed nearly two-thirds of the city. In its aftermath, Emperor Nero launched a sweeping reconstruction effort. Imperial reforms eventually introduced new building codes and a height cap of sixty Roman feet (roughly equivalent to our current feet). These regulations were among the earliest height restrictions, though they were probably more often violated than followed.[48]

These new codes mandated fire-resistant materials, such as stone and brick, in *insula* construction.[49] Yet, risks remained. Without steel reinforcement, Roman concrete had its limits. Structures above five stories grew increasingly vulnerable to cracks—and, especially during earthquakes, risked collapse.

At the same time, legal protections for tenants were minimal. One example comes from the correspondence of statesman and philosopher Cicero, who speculated in *insulae*. "Two of my shops have fallen down and the rest are cracking. Not only the tenants but the very mice have migrated," he wrote in his letters. He betrayed no sign of remorse, already eyeing higher rents through reconstruction. "Other people call this a misfortune, I don't call it even a nuisance."[50]

Sanitation was another urban hazard. Tenants used chamber pots, and despite prohibitions, they were often emptied out windows.[51] Later Roman laws addressed the issue: As recorded in the *Digest of Roman Law*, victims struck by falling waste were entitled to medical compensation and wage replacement. Juvenal described the grim reality:

> See how pots strike and dint the sturdy pavement.
> There's death from every window where you move.
> You'd be a fool to venture out to dine,
> oblivious of what goes on above,
> without your having penned that dotted line,
> of your last testament.[52]

The public latrines of Rome, however, while providing a communal solution, had their flaws. Ancient latrines lacked partitions for privacy, with rows of up to twenty seats. The shared *xylospongium*, or sponge on a stick, was the only tool provided for personal cleaning. Users seeking relief had to contend with scurrying rats and the danger of igniting sewer gas rising through the openings.[53] And patrons had to pay for the privilege. Emperor Vespasian, in a move that would later lend his name to public urinals (*vespasiennes* in French), imposed a tax on urine collected from these latrines, which was sold to launderers for its ammonia content—allegedly inspiring the famous Roman saying *pecunia non olet*, or "money doesn't smell."

The upper floors of the *insulae* were notorious for leaky roofs and pests. Then there was the inconvenience of climbing multiple flights of stairs. Poet Martial described the plight of a "rapacious fellow" who climbed up "some two hundred steps" to get to his garret.[54] Unlike modern penthouses in today's elevator buildings, these top floors were the least desirable. Poorer residents occupied the upper story. The author Petronius captured this divide in *Satyricon* when a character tells his wife, "If you are born on a mezzanine, you don't dream of a house."[55]

At their worst, the *insulae* could be likened to warehouses for human storage. One researcher noted "unhappy resemblances" to the *horrea,* the multistory warehouse buildings.[56] Yet for all their flaws, *insulae* marked an achievement in high-density urban living, giving many an opportunity to live in the city.

This was particularly evident in the well-built *insulae* of Ostia, Rome's ancient port city. These gradually replaced domus structures as the dominant building type.[57] With their brick-faced concrete and well-spaced layout, they reflected Nero's postfire building codes.[58] With Ostia's ruins relatively intact, the city opens a rare window into ancient vertical urban life.

On my visit to Ostia, the surviving *insulae* struck me as well-built. For instance, portions of the richly textured brick facade of the four-story Insula of Diana still stand strong today, two thousand years later. The intricate mosaics on some of these buildings signal a level of luxury. Still, these surviving examples may skew perceptions, as structures built with subpar materials would have decayed more readily.

Ostia makes clear that *insulae* were not just tenement buildings. It even has entire upper-middle-class apartment districts. Some upscale versions had a *tablinum,* an office-like reception area commonly found in wealthier domus, overlooking a courtyard.[59] Others had apartments boasting as many as seven rooms.[60] These buildings often had distinctive names, such as Insula Bolani, Insula Vitaliana, and Insula Sertoriana, reflecting prestige[61]—similar to modern apartment buildings today.

These *insulae* afforded their residents access and convenience. In Ostia, about two-thirds had ground-floor stores[62]—a necessity since apartments lacked running water, making home cooking difficult. Many residents would have gotten "takeout" from nearby *thermopolia*, food stalls serving fast fare like sausage-stuffed bread, an ancient version of a hamburger. For laundering togas and tunics, residents turned to nearby cleaners. Some *insulae* even had private baths and shrines. Shopkeepers often lived above their storefronts.

The Insula of Diana, for instance, lies a stone's throw away from the forum, a block from the main street, and directly across from a *thermopolium*, where aromas would have wafted through the open counter. Instead of the quiet and crickets heard today, there would have been the excitement of thousands of people. In their mixed-use form, *insulae* recall nineteenth-century European blocks, such as in Paris and Barcelona. There, shops are located on the ground floor and households reside above—a combination that creates convenience for residents and built-in demand for stores.

But Ostia's prosperity did not last. Roman deforestation for smelting, construction, shipbuilding, and farming triggered soil erosion that silted the harbor. Much of trade then moved to Portus, a deeper man-made harbor built by Claudius. By the third century AD, Ostia's harbor became too shallow for large ships. The changing environment led to stagnant ponds that bred malaria-carrying mosquitoes.[63] Ostia's population declined for centuries.[64] Today, the city lies two miles inland. Its *insulae*—once symbols of urban vitality—became quarries, their bricks repurposed elsewhere.

Nevertheless, the *insulae* of Ostia remain a compelling model of dense, walkable living, with a vibrant street culture. Ancient cities like Ostia, constrained by pedestrian and animal-based transport and housing shortages, built compact, multifunctional cores. Even as their ruins stand in quiet repose, these buildings challenge our assumptions as we confront the issues of urban sprawl. Their history proves that innovation often arises under constraint, and the architecture of the past can inspire the blueprints of the future.

The Dense and the Dispersed

Seeing Rome at its zenith would have been awe-inspiring. With a population close to one million, it was a colossus of a city, ruling an empire of 60 to 70 million people—perhaps a quarter of the global population.[65] The Latin poet Claudian marveled at its reach, writing that "This is the city which, sprung from humble beginnings, has stretched to either pole, and from one small place extended its power so as to be co-terminous with the sun's light."[66] By 400 AD, a public inventory boasted the capital's concentration of 19 aqueducts, 28 libraries, 2 circuses, 423 neighborhoods, 254 bakers, 46 brothels, and 144 public latrines.[67] From this center, Rome served as the heart of an empire interconnected by 29 military highways and a 250,000-mile road network. As Virgil proclaimed, it was an "empire without end."[68]

This sophisticated network dominated most of Europe and beyond, knitting together countless cities—from the frontiers of Scotland to the deserts of North Africa and the plains of Iraq. It served the military, commerce, and, crucially, the city of Rome itself, drawing in its lifeblood from distant regions, such as grain from Egypt. As the saying goes, "All roads lead to Rome."

Yet remarkably, the city of Rome itself occupied only about five square miles, achieving extraordinary density. Many Romans lived in crowded multistory *insulae*. Rather than spreading outward, Rome compacted its life inward, packing more people and activities into its limited footprint. This intensification extended to the countryside: Romans pioneered techniques such as advanced irrigation, fertilization, crop rotation, and terracing.

"We are the absolute masters of what the earth produces," heralded Cicero. "The rivers and the lakes are ours. We sow the seed, and plant the trees. We fertilize the earth by overflowing it. We stop, direct, and turn the rivers: in short, by our hands we endeavor, by our various operations in this world, to make, as it were, another nature."[69]

But Cicero and his contemporaries ignored the law of unintended consequences. Rome's reshaping of the landscape disrupted delicate ecological balances, triggering environmental challenges that would hasten the empire's decline. Chief among these was deforestation. The energy demands of Roman metallurgy alone required the annual harvest of an estimated 26,000 square kilometers of woodland—an area nearly the size of Belgium.[70] Public baths, household heating, and the production of fired bricks—including portable kilns carried by the legions—further intensified wood consumption. Over time, the lush, forested hills of Italy and Greece withered into arid slopes, barely able to support vineyards.[71]

Romans witnessed deforestation throughout the empire, as for instance poet Lucan noted: "Day by day they press the forests to retreat up the mountain and to yield their place for cultivated land."[72] But all of this triggered a cascade of consequences. As the naturalist Pliny the Elder observed in Greece, "harmful torrents often run together when the woods which used to hold and absorb the rains have been stripped from the hills."[73] Rather than addressing the root cause, Rome struggled to fight the symptoms. Soil erosion clogged rivers and silted up harbors,[74] rendering remedial efforts to maintain some port cities like Ostia futile.[75]

Rome's compactness also made it uniquely vulnerable to disease. Deforestation created vast stretches of stagnant, mosquito-infested fields, fueling malaria outbreaks.[76] The Pontine Marshes south of the city were notorious as *loca palustria*, or "fever areas." Roman agriculturalist Varro came close to understanding the cause, warning of "small beasts" that were "too small to be seen," and recommending that houses be built in elevated, well-ventilated places to allow the wind to blow the pests away.[77] While the elite escaped to elevated villas in the summer, the urban poor remained behind—in the close quarters of the *insulae*, where disease spread rapidly.[78,79]

Rome's resilience diminished as its challenges mounted. The first major shock came in 410 AD, when the Visigoths, once allies, turned against the Romans. This culminated in the sack of the Eternal City.

Then nature struck. In 536 AD, a massive volcanic eruption ushered in a Late Antique Little Ice Age, bringing colder temperatures, heavier rains, and waterlogged landscapes ideal for malaria-carrying mosquitoes. A volcanic winter reduced sunlight and crop yields.[80] Not long after, the devastating Plague of Justinian erupted in 541 AD—reappearing in waves over the next two centuries and killing between 25 and 50 million people. Rome's once-prized trade routes became conduits for contagion.

Even before these disasters, life in Rome could be grim. Average life expectancy hovered in the low twenties, with the poorest faring worst.[81] Their bodies, unceremoniously discarded, were often dumped in open pits outside the city walls. Cramped living conditions, inadequate sanitation, and rudimentary medicine created the perfect storm for disease.

This urban reality was shared by ancient cities worldwide. Like others, Rome relied on a constant influx of outsiders to survive.[82] Lower-status individuals, including slaves, soldiers, and servants, struggled to form stable families, leading to low birth rates.[83] Without steady migration from the countryside, the urban population would wither. And as that population declined, maintaining the infrastructure that supported it—roads, aqueducts, and defense walls—became increasingly impossible.

By 1084 AD, Norman forces set the city ablaze in another devastating sack. Rome's population had dwindled to around 20,000 people, becoming a mere shadow of its former glory. The once-prized aqueducts, engineering marvels that had carried water for centuries, fell into disrepair. Most of their waters ceased to flow.

Remarkably, the city endured. However, other ancient cities would not survive. In roughly the same era, almost all of the Classic Maya cities collapsed.[84] During the eighth to tenth centuries AD, at the beginning of the Medieval Warm Period, Maya urban centers in the Central Lowlands faced some of the most severe droughts and temperature fluctuations in their history. Their cities represented a fundamentally different approach to urban life, which would prove more vulnerable to environmental stress. The fate of a metropolis, it seems, was intimately tied to how its people chose to dwell.

Unlike Rome's concentrated design, Maya communities created a landscape of scattered household compounds integrated with garden plots and agricultural fields—what archaeologists call "agrarian urbanism." Cities such as Tikal and Copán were low-density urban centers that blurred the line between city and countryside. This scattered dwelling pattern likely emerged from environmental adaptation. In a tropical forest environment, where there are dry periods and soils are more quickly depleted, decentralized settlements could better exploit local resources.[85]

In many ways, this model achieved remarkable sustainability. The Maya managed to preserve some of the richest biodiversity in the tropics[86]—a striking contrast to the centralized urbanism of semiarid settings, which relied heavily on a narrow set of domesticated species like wheat, barley, cattle, and sheep. Yet their extensive water management systems proved vulnerable to climate instability.

As seasonal weather patterns changed, they disrupted agriculture, eventually leading to urban abandonment. Populations dispersed to peripheral regions.[87]

This pattern of dispersed dwelling would find its grandest expression in the jungles of Cambodia, where Angkor was emerging as a radically different kind of metropolis. Recent lidar (light detection and ranging) surveys reveal that at its peak in the twelfth century AD, Angkor sprawled over 350 square miles—dozens of times larger than Rome at its height. While both cities potentially housed nearly a million people, their patterns of dwelling could not have been more different.

While many Romans lived in dense *insulae* that could rise several stories high, Angkor's commoners lived in scattered homes made of thatch and wood. A Chinese observer noted, "They only use thatch for their roofs, and dare not put up a single tile. Although the sizes of their homes vary according to how wealthy they are, in the end

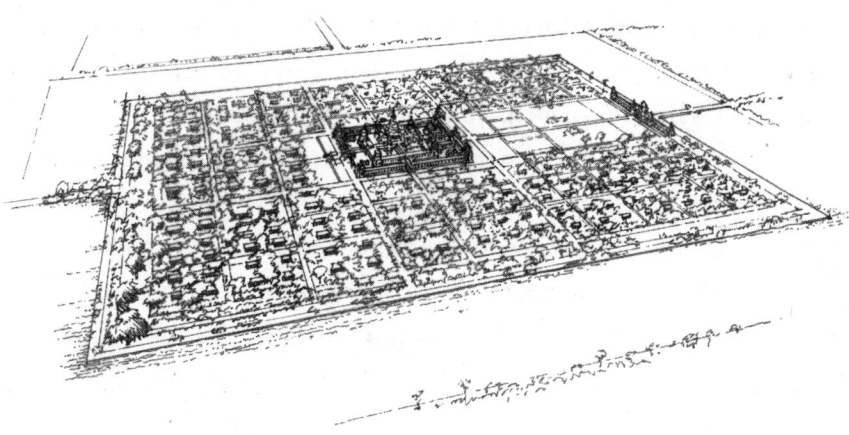

Reconstruction of Angkor's central area, Cambodia, twelfth century AD.[88]

they do not dare emulate the styles of the great houses." Like Rome, Angkor exhibited social inequality—but because of its predominantly wooden construction, virtually no trace of common dwellings survives. Near the massive Tonle Sap Lake, which fluctuated dramatically with the seasons, houses were built on stilts or floated. Communities arranged themselves around communal ponds, while larger reservoirs collected monsoon waters.

Angkor's elaborate water management system—a vast network of canals and reservoirs—enabled year-round cultivation. However, around 1350 AD, the transition to the Little Ice Age brought heightened climatic instability. Alternating droughts and intense monsoons overwhelmed Angkor's finely tuned hydrology. The clearing of vast forestland for rice fields exacerbated the problem.[89] During periods of intense rainfall, coarse river sand washed into the canals, causing siltation.[90] During droughts, new emergency canals diverted water from the hills to the city. But when heavy rains returned, these same canals funneled destructive runoff, damaging the canal infrastructure.[91]

The very complexity of Angkor's engineered landscape—once its strength—became its Achilles' heel.[92] Meanwhile, additional challenges mounted, including political instability. The population fell below the minimum necessary to maintain its complex water management infrastructure. The great city was largely abandoned as people returned to villages, and the jungle reclaimed its domain. The once-mighty Khmer empire was reduced to a regional state.

Archaeologist Roland Fletcher has shown that Angkor's fate was not unique. In *The Limits of Settlement Growth*, he demonstrates how preindustrial low-density cities reached critical thresholds as they expanded, shaping their development—and ultimate fate. Comparing Angkor, Tikal, and Anuradhapura (a similarly sprawling tropical city built by the Sinhalese), Fletcher writes, "The critical thing is that there was absolutely no connection between these three low-density cities, and they were each on a terminal path."[93]

His research concluded that low-density agrarian urbanism "can create gigantism and leads to severe ecological collapse."[94] These sprawling civilizations proved less adaptable than compact cities like Rome.[95] While the great low-density agrarian cities endured for perhaps a millennium, Rome's concentrated form—though battered—survived. Of course, even that longevity pales in comparison to the small mobile camps of hunter-gatherers, which proved to be a sustainable system for 2.5 million years.

"The form our cities take is not neutral," Fletcher concludes. It affects "our social capacity to adjust and survive."[96] Rome's dense vertical housing posed public health challenges but ultimately proved more resilient than dispersed dwelling patterns. When populations declined, its more concentrated urban infrastructure could still function with fewer people. In contrast, the extensive systems of Angkor and the Maya required large populations to remain viable.

I have visited Angkor several times. Standing among the banyan trees that now engulf several of the temples, it is tempting to see this as another case of architectural hubris—a civilization that invested too much in monuments. But if we look beyond the stone temples, across the vast plain now overtaken by forest, a different story emerges. What seems like untouched jungle was once a vast metropolis of dispersed dwellings. Angkor's true achievement—and fatal vulnerability—lay in its infrastructure.

The ancient choice between dense and dispersed urban living was not only a matter of lifestyle and exploiting resources. It was a decision that determined a city's resilience to climate stress. As today's megalopolises sprawl ever outward amid accelerating climate change, Angkor's fate offers a sobering warning. How we dwell, and what we build to support that dwelling, will help determine whether our cities endure, or fall.

FOUR

The Industrial Home

The Canal House

In the heart of northwestern Europe, an unlikely swamp became an ingenious experiment in domestic architecture. The Netherlands occupied a precarious position in a delta where three of Europe's major rivers met the temperamental North Sea. This low-lying region, with its ever-shifting boundaries between water and land battered by relentless North Sea storms, remained sparsely populated for centuries. Yet from this challenging landscape emerged two important concepts at the dawn of the Industrial Revolution: a new approach to family living and a reimagined relationship with the natural environment.

Early explorers noted the people's defining struggle against water. Around 325 BC, Greek explorer Pytheas of Massalia observed of the inhabitants of this marshy region that "more people died in the struggle against water than in the struggle against men."[1] Later, Roman naturalist Pliny the Elder echoed this sentiment, describing the land as "pitiful" and prone to flooding. He noted, "These wretched peoples occupy high ground, or manmade platforms constructed above the level of the highest tide ... they live in huts ... and are like sailors in ships when the waters cover the surrounding land, but when the tide has receded they are like shipwrecked victims."[2]

By the twelfth century, the inhabitants near modern-day Amsterdam—future capital of the Netherlands—began to seize control of their environment. They piled earth to build dikes a few feet high, shielding their village and farmland from floods. They cut channels through peat soil, diverting water toward the river. This transformation of marsh into usable terrain led to the saying "God created the Earth, but the Dutch created the Netherlands."

But this seeming control over nature came with unforeseen consequences. As water was drained, the peatland sank. This in turn required higher dikes and more maintenance—an early harbinger of the environmental dilemmas the Netherlands still faces today. To address the challenge, communities formed "water boards" to manage water collectively. These organizations, predating city governments, levied taxes and assigned farmers to maintain specific stretches of dike.

After the catastrophic All Saints' Flood of 1170, farmers built a bridge across the Amstel River, with locks underneath to control the water. This dam gave the city its name—Amsterdam. Life in this early settlement was modest and industrious: farmers grew barley and rye, fishermen caught eel and carp, and dwellings were simple wooden huts with straw roofs and mud floors. The residents developed a network of canals to manage water and to serve as routes for transport and trade while doubling as a rudimentary sewer system—with the first household chore often involving emptying the family chamber pot into the canal.

The catalyst for Amsterdam's transformation came in 1585, when the Spanish siege of Antwerp drove a wave of wealthy merchants and skilled artisans north. They brought capital, craftsmanship, and global trade connections. They helped make Amsterdam the center of a thriving republic built on commerce and relative freedom from rule by monarchs. The Dutch grew rich through maritime trade, to the envy of neighboring nations.

The city's reputation for liberal culture and tolerance of religious differences became legendary, and Amsterdam became a haven for people of all backgrounds. This distinctive social fabric was, arguably, born from the shared struggle against water, which required everyone to contribute, regardless of their beliefs. As historian Russell Shorto writes, "This—the water, the perils, the bravery, the absurdity of the geographic position, and the development of complex communal organizations to cope with the situation—explains much of Amsterdam's history and provides as well a backdrop to the development of liberalism."[3]

Dutch water management also transformed land ownership, in contrast to the feudal manorial system dominant in medieval Europe. Through the engineering of "polders"—new land reclaimed from marsh and sea by enclosing it with dikes and draining it with windmills—more farmers became landowners. By the sixteenth century, in Holland's peat-rich regions, the vast majority of the land was owned by individual farmers.[4] This independence from feudal authority fostered a spirit of entrepreneurship, paving the way for the emergence of the world's first multinational corporation in Amsterdam, the Dutch East India Company (VOC), in 1602. The VOC pioneered innovations in stock ownership, shipbuilding, cartography, and insurance—though its legacy is tarnished by its deep involvement in slavery and deforestation of colonial lands.

This economic boom coincided with a profound shift in domestic life. The transition from communal feudal households to private single-family homes marked a new chapter in how people lived. Medieval houses were primarily "public," meaning that families, servants, and guests frequently shared living quarters, sleeping in communal rooms. Even Italian Renaissance palazzi offered little privacy, with rooms sometimes featuring four doors, one on each wall.[5] By contrast, the Dutch bourgeoisie, less dependent on servants than their European peers, cultivated smaller, more intimate living spaces. Their new homes, the canal houses, were designed around the nuclear family. As architectural historian Witold Rybczynski has argued, these canal houses helped shape the modern concept of home.[6]

The golden age of canal house construction coincided with the Dutch Republic's peak of urbanization and innovation. In the seventeenth century, the Netherlands was likely the most urbanized society in the world and a hub of industrial ingenuity.[7] Industrial zones like Zaan district near Amsterdam buzzed with hundreds of windmills, powering saws to cut timber, grinding grain, pulping fiber for paper, and grinding pigments for paints.[8] Meanwhile, Amsterdam's population surged from 30,000 in 1585 to 220,000 by 1680.

In response, the city built the Fourth Extension, a bold urban plan executed between 1663 and 1682. It added three great canals—Keizersgracht (Emperor's Canal), Herengracht (Patricians' Canal), and Prinsengracht (Prince's Canal)—defining the city's signature crescent-shaped layout.

Building on swampy ground posed enormous engineering challenges. The low peatland required canal excavation and the installation of locks to manage water levels. Each house's foundation relied on about forty wooden piles—usually made of imported Scandinavian softwood—driven as deep as sixty feet through layers of peat, sand, and clay. The rhythmic work of pile drivers became such a constant feature of city life that it spawned its own genre of folk songs, often with suggestive lyrics: "There he goes, all day long, up and down."[9]

The wooden foundation system posed a unique engineering challenge. To avoid rot, the piles had to remain submerged. But their tops, connecting with the building's masonry, needed dry conditions for the mortar to set. Builders solved this by digging additional ditches to temporarily drain the site, allowing mortar to cure, before submerging the piles. This delicate choreography of water and building epitomized the Dutch spirit for living on the edge of land and sea.

The resulting architecture was remarkable. The canal houses emerged as gabled brick structures, primarily built as merchant homes. Tax policy drove their distinctive form: buildings were as narrow as sixteen feet since taxes were based on frontage width. To compensate, houses were deep and tall, up to seven stories—with steep red-tiled roofs and distinctive gables reaching skyward, reminiscent of the ships' masts dotting the horizon.

The narrow design, while fiscally prudent, demanded architectural ingenuity. The most obvious compromises were the extremely steep staircases—typically without landings—that still challenge the nerve of modern-day tourists. Yet within these constraints, each house retained its individuality. While unified by their shared narrowness, they each had unique frontages with subtle symmetry and pronounced gables. This gave rise to an increasingly diverse array of styles, with stepped, bell, and spout gables. One architect in particular, Philips Vingboons, became renowned for pioneering the widely imitated neck gable and applying classical principles of symmetry to narrow facades.

The facades themselves told stories of their owners through their decorative elements. Gable stones served as both address markers

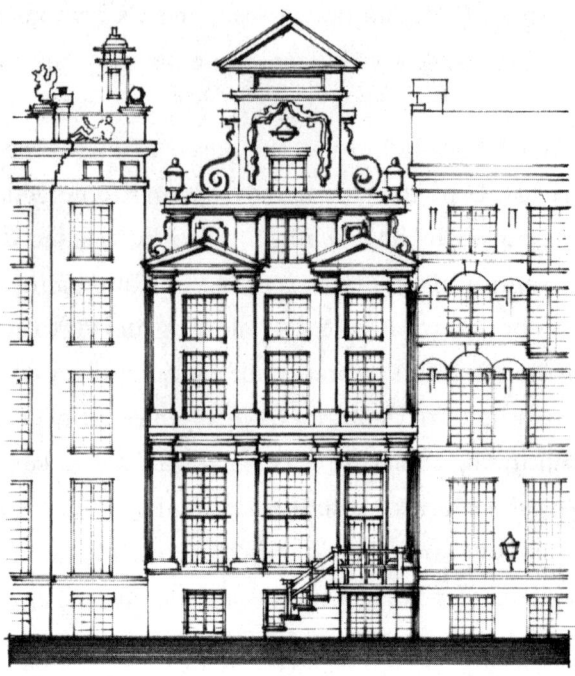

Canal house, 319 Keizersgracht, Amsterdam, Philips Vingboons, architect, 1639.

and advertisements, depicting images that signaled the owner's trade or family name—such as a man reaching into another's mouth, signifying a dentist. The ways in which the homes met the street contributed to a vibrant street life. Stoops and steps connected front doors to the sidewalks, creating semiprivate platforms ideal for sitting, sharing a beer, and people watching—a tradition still embraced by Amsterdammers today.

These buildings balanced domesticity and commerce. They were both homes and warehouses, allowing merchants to store goods when market prices were unfavorable. The ground floor often housed an office, with family living quarters behind it. Upper levels were dedicated to storing goods like spices. The most ingenious feature sat near the roof on the gable: a cantilevered beam with a metal hook. This simple device transformed the building into a hoisting machine—merchants could employ a rope and pulley to lift cargo from their boats through large windows. There, sash windows could remain open at any height, thanks to an innovative counterbalance mechanism of pulleys and counterweights.[10]

Commerce and domestic life shared a roof, but they remained deliberately separate. Corridors and partitioned rooms cultivated a sense of privacy. The vertical arrangement reinforced separation as well. Workshops were often located partially below ground, while the raised ground floor reception area led into the domestic realm.

This attention to spatial organization extended to an almost obsessive devotion to cleanliness. During a seventeenth-century visit to Amsterdam, English diplomat Sir William Temple observed "the strange and curious Cleanliness so general in that City." One particularly vivid anecdote described a "strapping North Holland lass," who, upon noticing a magistrate's dirty shoes, "took him by both Arms, threw him upon her back, carried him cross two Rooms, set him down at the bottom of the Stairs, pull'd off his Shoes, put him on a pair of Slippers that stood there, and all this without saying a word."[11]

An English writer observed how even doorknobs, nails, and hinges were polished to a shine: "Every door seems studded with diamonds."[12] The Dutch, concluded Irish travel writer Thomas Nugent, were "perfect slaves to cleanliness."[13]

The interior spaces of these homes reflected the values of the emerging middle class. One architectural critic later called the seventeenth-century Dutch dwelling "the home of the home," noting how its inhabitants "emptied their purses into domestic space."[14] This investment in domestic comfort is immortalized in Vermeer's paintings, which depict interiors rich with consumer goods that would come to define middle-class life: original artwork, imported vases, fine furniture, and decorative wares.[15] A typical inventory from the sale of a tailor's home listed: "five paintings (worth five guilders in total), three tables, a cradle and a child's chair, assorted books, Delft earthenware and tiles, pewter tankards and plates, a spinning wheel, seven lace curtains, two beds and a sleep bench with mattress, an oak wood chest, linen cabinet, several cushions, two mirrors (one broken), twenty-odd chairs (some of them for work), six sets of bed linen, forty-one napkins and a birdcage."

The kitchen housed an arsenal of specialized equipment: stew pans, cast-iron pots, baking pans, tea kettles, and griddles, arranged against walls of glossy ceramic tiles. Other domestic equipment included items like flatirons and bed-warming pans. While domestic duties traditionally fell to women, many women managed to establish roles for themselves in a male-dominated society, also engaging in business and social activism.

Yet the Dutch struggled to reconcile their newfound wealth with Calvinist values of austerity, a condition historian Simon Schama called an "embarrassment of riches." This tension was visible in the highest ranks: William Temple remarked on "the simplicity and modesty of their magistrates, in their way of living." He marveled that even Vice Admiral de Ruyter, one of the nation's most revered naval commanders, never "dressed in clothes better than the commonest sea-captain . . . and, in his own house, neither was the size, building, furniture, or entertainment, at all exceeding the use of every common merchant and tradesman."[16]

There was, however, one acceptable indulgence: nature. Many homes had rear gardens growing roses, irises, hyacinths, and lilies, a quiet rebellion against Calvinist moralists who frowned upon such horticultural frivolity. Amsterdam's fertile alluvial soil and maritime climate created perfect conditions for cultivating rare plant species. The introduction of tulips from Turkey in the seventeenth century sparked a significant Dutch industry. It even led to the infamous "Tulip Mania," a botanical gold rush that is considered the first recorded speculative bubble.

The Fourth Extension regulations struck a balance between collective harmony and individual expression. Planners mandated buildings to meet the property line, creating aligned rows of canal houses. They ensured continuous garden space within blocks, limiting garden houses and pavilions beyond ninety feet behind the front property line and capping their height at ten feet.[17] But they also encouraged architectural creativity within these constraints, allowing "cornices, ornaments or protruding parts of buildings, used for commodity and beauty." These, as well as balconies, could extend beyond property lines, without incurring tax penalties. Amsterdam's building codes had evolved from reactive medieval regulations into forward-thinking guidelines that actively encouraged architectural innovation.

The new canals were lined with carefully spaced trees—primarily poplars and lindens, chosen for their water-absorbing properties that helped stabilize the marshy ground. British diarist John Evelyn described Amsterdam as "a City in a Wood," noting that "nothing can be more pleasing, especially being so frequently planted and shaded with the beautiful lime-trees, set in rows before every man's house, affording a very ravishing prospect."[18] The city's design enhanced this experience: Its radial concentric layout, with curving ring canals, broke lines of sight and created an experience of suspense and intimacy.

The completed canal rings drew global attention. Peter the Great even took up residence in Amsterdam to study its engineering and urban planning, later applying what he learned to the founding of St. Petersburg, also built on shifting marshland. Today, the canal rings are a UNESCO World Heritage Site, hailed as "a new and entirely artificial 'port city.' . . . [and] a masterpiece of hydraulic engineering, town planning, and a rational programme of construction and bourgeois architecture."[19]

Dutch architectural influence spread globally through maritime trade and colonization. The distinctive step gables found their way as far as New York. Dutch bricks—especially the high-quality yellow klinkers—were a prized export, used both as valuable cargo and as ballast to stabilize ships. The scale was impressive: The ports of Amsterdam alone exported some 30 million bricks in 1668, which found their way to colonial outposts and port cities across Asia, Brazil, and North America.[20] Dutch architectural expertise became equally sought after: Netherlands-trained architects found employment throughout Europe, from German principalities to Scandinavian kingdoms and Russian cities.

But the Golden Age did not last. In 1672, known as the "disaster year," England challenged Dutch naval supremacy and lucrative trade routes. Meanwhile France, backed by two German states, launched a land invasion. Dutch dominance began to fade.

Amsterdam's delicate relationship with nature would also come to haunt it. Today, the canal district faces new threats: subsiding soils, settling foundations, intensifying storms, and rising seas. These challenges are no longer uniquely Dutch. With roughly 1 percent of the world's inhabited land reclaimed from water, Amsterdam offers a sobering preview of what many coastal cities may face in coming decades.

Yet its allure endures. Having lived in the city myself, I've seen how the canal houses remain vibrant, if idiosyncratic, homes—

complete with creaking floors, perilously steep staircases, and the famously uncurtained windows that still startle visitors. But walking beside those tranquil canals—knowing they sit six feet below sea level—is a quiet, persistent reminder of both Dutch ingenuity and the mounting pressure of climate change.

Much like its seventeenth-century canal houses, Amsterdam continues to live in tension with water. The city adapts and innovates, transforming environmental threats into design opportunities—but some warn that, in time, it may have to relinquish parts of the very land it once so boldly reclaimed.

The Workers' Terrace

In 1840, Dr. William Henry Duncan, disturbed by the conditions of his ailing patients, conducted a survey of Liverpool's working-class dwellings. He was shocked, finding overcrowded cellars, unsanitary conditions, and rampant disease. What began as a doctor's report laid the foundation for reforms that would reshape urban housing and public health across industrial Britain.

By the 1840s, Liverpool had the nation's highest death rate, with diseases like tuberculosis ravaging the population. The working class had an average age at death of just nineteen years—the lowest in the country.[21] While the prevailing view blamed the poor for their own misfortune, Duncan's survey revealed that it was their environment that proved deadly: one-fifth of Liverpool's population resided in cellars with dirt floors, no ventilation, and inadequate sanitation, sometimes with as many as sixteen people per room. Disease thrived. In his notes, Duncan even observed a double cellar, "where nearly 30 individuals slept every night" and "a kind of well had been dug in the floor for receiving the offal and filth of the household.... Fever of a malignant type broke out among these unfortunate beings, and in the course of a week or two carried off seven or eight of their number."[22]

Living conditions were horrific. Workers inhabited back-to-back houses, each measuring about twelve by twelve feet. These typically had a kitchen on the ground floor, two bedrooms above, and a cellar dwelling below. Crammed around narrow courts, these homes had densities of up to 700 people per acre[23]—six times that of present-day Manhattan. Sometimes, hundreds shared water from a single standpipe contaminated by nearby overflowing cesspools. Duncan observed, "I found the whole court inundated with fluid filth which had oozed through the walls from two adjoining ash-pits or cesspools.... An intelligent Irishman who lived there told me [that] the stench at night... was enough to 'rise the roof off his skull as he lay in bed.'"[24]

Liverpool's case was extreme, but not unique. Writing about London in his 1845 publication, *The Condition of the Working Class in England*, Friedrich Engels painted an equally horrifying picture: "The streets are generally unpaved, rough, dirty, filled with vegetable and animal refuse, without sewers or gutters, but supplied with foul, stagnant pools.... The filth and tottering ruin surpass all description. Scarcely a whole window-pane can be found, the walls are crumbling, door-posts and window-frames loose and broken, doors of old boards nailed together."[25]

These dire conditions were the result of explosive urbanization. After establishing the world's first intercity railway connecting to Manchester in 1830, Liverpool had become a major port city in the global trade network—a critical link between Britain's industrial heartland and overseas markets. Over the nineteenth century, the city's population surged ninefold as waves of migrants arrived to work on the docks, transforming Liverpool into England's second-largest city.

Yet, Britain had distinct advantages in confronting its urban challenges. Institutions such as the Society of Arts, the Royal Institution, and the Mechanics' Institutes democratized scientific knowledge through public lectures and experiments.[26] This culture of applied science and innovation fostered a fertile environment for urban reform. The same scientific spirit that fueled Britain's Industrial Revolution was now redirected toward solving its urban crisis.

In response, Liverpool pioneered the 1846 Sanitary Act. It appointed William Henry Duncan as the city's and nation's first medical officer. James Newlands assumed the role of first borough engineer. After meticulously studying Liverpool's topography, Newlands designed and implemented an eighty-six-mile network of sewers over eleven years. Ingeniously, it included oval-shaped tunnels to help concentrate the flow even with little liquid, preventing blockages. His innovative design included rear passageways in neighborhoods to facilitate easy access to drains and to garbage for collection.[27] It was the world's first integrated sewage system, later inspiring London during its 1858 Great Stink. By the time of Newlands's retirement in 1871, life expectancy had doubled from 1847 levels.

While these underground improvements transformed public health, an equally important change was taking shape aboveground. The solution to the worker housing problem came from an unlikely source: the terraced house, a building type tracing back to seventeenth-century Britain. The design drew inspiration from Amsterdam's canal houses in its use of shared party walls built to the property line. But unlike the individualistic canal houses, British terraced houses featured uniform facades and consistent heights.

This offered greater efficiency in construction and a more cohesive appearance.

This architectural form combined the repetitive efficiency of row housing with the refined aesthetics of the Italian Renaissance. The concept first emerged in London's Piazza Covent Garden during the 1630s, where five-story row houses borrowed the classical proportion and symmetry promoted by Italian architect Andrea Palladio. By the Georgian period, terraced housing had become synonymous with urban elegance. London's desirable Belgrave Square and Birkenhead's Hamilton Square were lined with rows of terraced houses that created a monumental urban presence. Even the name itself carried prestige. The term "terrace," suggestive of garden terraces, evoked a harmonious appearance.[28]

The strength of the terraced house was its adaptability. Originally the domain of the wealthy, by the mid-nineteenth century the form evolved to house urban workers, propelled by Britain's economic transformation. Between 1780 and 1870, real GDP per person nearly doubled, eventually reaching 70 percent above France and Germany.[29] Meanwhile, building acts in the 1850s and 1860s mandated standards such as minimum room sizes and required rear yards. By 1861, Liverpool had banned the notorious back-to-back houses altogether.[30]

Architect Richard Owens seized this opportunity, building housing specifically for workers. He located his terraces near Liverpool's docks, knowing that dock workers had to be physically present at "stands" every morning in the hopes of being selected by foremen for a day's labor. He partnered with Liverpool's leading land speculator and built these homes speculatively, without prearranged buyers, funded through loans. This encouraged standardization in the form of systematic rows of terraced houses, as this would reduce financial risk.[31]

Owens chose the pragmatic efficiency of the terraced house, further optimizing the building process and doing this at scale. While he meticulously laid out overall plans, he allowed builders the flexibility to detail their work within set standards. His demanding nature and abrasive temperament often came through in his correspondence. In one characteristic letter to a local building official, he wrote: "Dear Sir. You have too many committees and too many Clerks of the Works at your place. The work I saw last Wednesday was done exceedingly well and I have no reason to think but that all the rest is done the same."[32]

Richard Owens's terraced houses marked a significant advancement from the cramped court housing of the early industrial age. Each of Owens's homes offered its own water supply—an unheard-of luxury compared to the communal pumps of the past, where residents queued for water. Modern amenities included flush toilets in the rear yard, a far cry from the era when women had to pay a penny for public toilets—a practice that gave rise to the phrase "going to spend a penny."

The interior layout reflected evolving ideas about domestic life still evident in many houses today. Front rooms, meant for entertaining guests, featured parlors with ornate fireplaces and bay windows. Back rooms housed kitchens and sculleries. These houses were no longer spaces for outside work.

Although Owens catered to various income groups, his most significant achievement lay in raising the standard of working-class homes. One such example was the Welsh Streets neighborhood within the Toxteth area, built to house some of the 20,000 Welsh

Victorian terraced row houses, Voelas Street (part of the Welsh Streets), Richard Owens, architect, Liverpool, 1880s.

builders who migrated to Liverpool for work. By his retirement, Owens had built over 10,000 homes.

These homes reflected the Industrial Revolution, from standardized Welsh slate roofs to their coal-heated interiors. Steam-powered trains revolutionized the transport of building materials. This led to standardized material sizes to facilitate export. For instance, slate came in specific sizes from "Narrow Lady" to "Wide Duchess."

Yet it came at a cost. The widespread use of coal for heating and industry led to air pollution. In London, this gave rise to thick yellowish fogs known as "pea-soupers." These made breathing difficult and obscured much of the city. Poet Elizabeth Barrett Browning, in 1856, described the scene as a "great tawny weltering fog ... as if a sponge had wiped out London."[33] The pollution was so severe that some architects deliberately opted for bright red bricks simply to keep their buildings visible in the smog.[34]

In Liverpool, residents fought a constant battle against the dark smog and ubiquitous soot that covered their terraced homes. Yet they maintained fierce pride in their dwellings, keeping exterior bricks soot-free and doorsteps well-polished. The daily ritual of "doing the step" with a Donkey Stone—a cleaning block originally designed to clean greasy mill steps—produced varying shades from white to brown. In Victorian Liverpool, a gleaming doorstep signaled respectability.[35]

Despite these environmental challenges—whose full health impacts remained largely unknown at the time—the terraced house became a quintessential emblem of British urban life, eventually housing a quarter of the nation's population. Its influence stretched far beyond Britain, traveling with the empire to places like Singapore and Malaysia, where it was adapted to tropical climates. In America, the design inspired Brooklyn's brownstones and San Francisco's Painted Ladies. From the shophouses of Southeast Asia to the row houses of North America, the building type proved versatile enough to suit local climates, materials, and aesthetic tastes. It transitioned through various architectural movements, from the restrained elegance of Georgian design to the ornate embellishments of the Victorian era, while maintaining its core principles of efficient, urban living.

I came to appreciate this legacy firsthand while living in London. My home, shared with a roommate, occupied one floor of a three-story terraced house—a modern adaptation of what was once a single-family home. The flat retained its generous Victorian proportions with high ceilings and large sash windows that flooded the rooms with light. The street outside preserved its historical character, presenting a long row of brick facades—its monotony enlivened by the cadence of punctuating bay windows and recessed front doors.

I later discovered that our house stood on the very block where a young Charles Dickens once lived while his father was imprisoned for debt. From this place, the twelve-year-old Dickens would walk five miles each day to Warren's Blacking Factory, where he labeled jars of shoe polish—experiences that would later inspire his novels.

Two centuries on, London bears little resemblance to the scene Dickens described. "Even in the surrounding country it was a foggy day, but there the fog was grey, whereas in London it was, at about the boundary line, dark yellow, and a little within it brown, and then browner, and then browner, until at the heart of the City ... it was rusty-black."[36] The smog has since cleared, yet the terraced row endures.

Today, it represents principles we now associate with sustainable urban development, such as efficient land use and adaptable spaces. The terraced house represents an ideal middle ground—what urbanists now call "missing middle housing" in North America—offering density without the anonymity of high-rises and privacy without the expansive footprint of detached homes. And while residents no longer need to polish their doorsteps with Donkey Stones to assert moral standing, their homes continue to command it.

The French Flat

In 1869, the *New York Tribune* heralded a new development in Manhattan: "Few people who pass through Broadway are aware that ... there is now in course of erection ... one of the largest and most magnificent hotels on the Western Continent, which, when completed, will throw in the shade the largest hotels in this country—rivaling even the 'Grand Hotel' at Paris in magnificence."[37] This was one of a growing number of hotels catering to families seeking longer-term accommodations, offering a blend of home comforts and hotel services. It marked a growing trend toward a more communal, hotel-style existence—laying the groundwork for the modern apartment building, forever reshaping Manhattan's skyline.

The following year, the eight-story Grand Central Hotel opened its doors. It had an elaborate mansard roof in the style of Napoleon III, 630 rooms, and three elevators, reputedly capable of whisking guests to the top floor in just thirty seconds. The hotel catered not only to travelers but also guests desiring longer stays, single men, and even wealthy families. It offered residents the conveniences of hot-water baths and in-house dining, without the need for servants or domestic equipment of their own. Yet this Parisian-inspired building, and others like it, sparked both curiosity and concern.

Critics feared this new form of communal living would erode the sanctity of family life. One male journalist warned, "Hotel life is agreeable and desirable for masculine celibates. But he is unwise who takes his wife and family there for a permanent home. How many women can trace their first infidelity to the necessarily demoralizing influences of public houses—to loneliness, leisure, need of society, interesting companions, abundance of opportunity, and potent temptation!"[38]

There was also moral anxiety about shifting gender roles, with fears that it allowed women to "stray" from their domestic duties. In 1879, *The New York Times* lamented the rise of "lazy and fashionable women, discovering that their delicate organizations could no longer withstand what they called the drudgery of housekeeping," who now gravitated toward hotel life.[39]

Beyond moral panic, critics feared the erosion of domestic intimacy. Architect Calvert Vaux voiced this worry: "The ceaseless publicity that ensues, the constant change, and the entire absence of all individuality in the everyday domestic arrangements, will always render this method of living distasteful as a permanent thing to the heads of families who have any taste for genuine home comforts."[40]

Yet these hotels also emerged as a practical response to Manhattan's geography and rapid growth. Bounded by water, the island could only expand vertically. The city's transformation into America's premier trade hub was propelled by the 1825 completion of the Erie Canal, which sharply reduced transportation costs between New York and America's interior and drove up land values. The Jeffersonian ideal of independent homeownership became increasingly out of reach. More people became renters, and with soaring rents, New York experienced its first housing crisis in the 1830s.

As the metropolis swelled, its housing problems became impossible to ignore. The proliferation of slums in many parts of the city highlighted the contradictions of a metropolis that, despite its wealth, struggled to adequately house its population.[41] Single-family brownstones were subdivided into units called "floors" and "apartments." Purpose-built structures also emerged: the infamous *railroad flats*. Rooms in these five- to seven-story tenement buildings were arranged in a straight line, like boxcars on a train. This layout forced residents to pass through one room to reach the next. And many of the interior rooms were deprived of windows.

The crisis deepened with waves of immigration, particularly after the Irish Potato Famine in 1845. Between 1820 and 1860, New York City's population grew more than sixfold, surpassing 800,000.[42] As the city struggled to absorb this growth, living conditions in tenements deteriorated, rivaling the worst slums of industrial England. In 1865, *The New York Times* drew a grim comparison, noting that parts of the city resembled Liverpool, "one of the British cities which approaches our terrible death-rate."[43] The article described conditions eerily similar to New York's railroad flats that demanded immediate reform.

But reform efforts repeatedly fell short. The first law mandating windows in rooms was quickly undermined—developers simply installed windows in walls between interior rooms, allowing little light or ventilation. Even the 1879 New York State Tenement House Act, the so-called Old Law, brought minimal improvement. Its mandate for an external window in every habitable room led to the creation of narrow airshafts and the infamous "dumbbell" floor plan. It was so named because, when seen from above, the buildings resembled a dumbbell: broad at the front and rear, pinched in the middle by the airshafts. This design proved unsanitary and hazardous, with waste often thrown into the shafts and fires easily spreading from one floor to the next. Real improvement came only with the 1901 Tenement House Act, the New Law, which mandated indoor toilets and windows facing the outdoors—not interior voids. The result was a new generation of tenements with open courtyards, improved ventilation, and greater space between buildings.

Between the squalor of tenements and the luxury of hotels, a growing middle class sought alternatives. Living in a tenement building would have embarrassed the "middling class" of "book-keepers, artists, editors, clerks, lawyers, copyists, mechanics, and members of other professions and trades who desire privacy."[44] This group, unable to afford single-family homes in Manhattan, faced lengthy daily commutes from more affordable areas. Many, at first, found refuge in boarding houses and residential hotels within the city.

Public perception of communal living gradually improved. In 1853, *Putnam's Magazine* observed, "Society is rapidly tending towards hotel life, and the advantages of a cluster of families living together under one roof are every day becoming more and more apparent." The magazine challenged prevailing assumptions about privacy, noting, "Families can be just as isolated in a hotel as in a separate house.... We ride in public carriages, travel in public steamboats, ships, and railroad cars, and there is no reason why we should not live in public houses?" Surprisingly, the article even claimed that family life in hotels was less "exposed to impertinent observation."

This social concern presented architects with a unique challenge: to design buildings that not only stood apart from the negatively perceived tenements but also appealed to middle-class families accustomed to single-family homes. Their solution was the "apartment house:" a new building type that blended communal living with personal solitude—pioneering the concept of being "alone, together."

Drawing inspiration from European precedents, architects such as Calvert Vaux looked to Paris. Multifamily living wasn't new, dating back to ancient Rome's *insulae* and the servants' quarters in medieval mansions. But the modern apartment had evolved in nineteenth-century Europe along its Haussmannian boulevards. Parisian buildings stacked middle-class apartments in impressive multistory blocks, with size, ornamentation, and tenant wealth generally decreasing on higher floors. Vaux and other American architects adapted the model to create elegant, respectable apartment buildings that matched the aspirations of New York's upwardly mobile residents.

The architectural ambition behind these new multifamily buildings was clear. In *The New York Times*, J. R. Hamilton described a design that diverged from conventional tenements: "The great and fundamental difference... is the *complete separation* which is obtained, and which—with the exception of using one grand general staircase for egress and ingress—enables the families to be as private and distinct from each other as if each possessed a separate street entrance on the same block."[45] The building, he emphasized, bore "no resemblance whatever to what is usually understood here as 'tenement houses.'"

These new designs aimed to re-create the comforts and independence of single-family homes within a multiunit structure. According to Hamilton, "On arriving at either landing the visitor comes to the front door of a first-class residence, which he has to ring a bell for admission, precisely as he would in the street." Once inside, the apartment offered a full domestic suite: "a fine front parlor 16 feet square, four bedrooms, bath-room, water closet, China closet, and other closets in abundance—dining-room, kitchen and all appurtenances—facilities for raising coal (from a separate cellar in the basement) and getting rid of refuse, without the necessity of ascending and descending any stairs."

This vision materialized in 1869, when the first such apartment building rose on East 18th Street in Manhattan. The Stuyvesant Flats, designed by Richard Morris Hunt for developer Rutherford Stuyvesant, stood five stories tall, housing sixteen apartments and four artists' studios. Hunt, trained at the École des Beaux Arts, skillfully reduced the building's scale to fit among existing row houses. He topped it with a mansard roof receding from the front and marked it with a modest entrance of two adjacent and receding doors.

Though the distinction between this "French flat" and tenement buildings was partially a matter of semantics, its enhanced plumbing and in-unit bathrooms improved upon tenement living.[46] As *The New York Tribune* reported in 1869, "It is an attempt to introduce in this city the style of house-building almost universal in Paris, that of including several distinct suites of rooms under a single roof. This is wholly different from the plan of the tenement house."[47]

Early residents discovered several pitfalls. The apartments often had small awkwardly arranged rooms—suitable, as the saying goes, for "the newly wed and the nearly dead."[48] Buildings lacked elevators, corridors were narrow and dim, and poor soundproofing exposed neighbors' activities. Apartment layouts forced guests to pass bedroom doors on their way to the dining room, compromising privacy. Kitchens were inconveniently relegated to the rear of the units to contain cooking smells—a characteristic associated with tenements.[49] Still, these buildings managed to strike a balance between the grandeur of public buildings and the intimacy of private homes. They offered residents a sense of collective identity, along with a pride of their individual apartments.[50]

The experiment proved successful. Stuyvesant Flats achieved full occupancy quickly, ushering in the era of French flats. Soon a wave of technological innovation would further transform apartment living. By 1870, as New York City's population approached one million, two breakthroughs changed urban architecture: steel-frame construction and the safety mechanism for elevators. Steel enabled taller buildings through strong and efficiently built post-and-girder systems. Elisha Otis's invention of a safety brake made once-dangerous elevator rides safe, shattering the stair-climbing constraints of walk-ups. This eventually reversed the social hierarchy of vertical living—upper floors became premium real estate, giving rise to the penthouse and, ultimately, the skyscraper.

The 1880s heralded a new generation of apartment buildings that fully leveraged these technological advances. Elevators allowed them to go taller, but these buildings also expanded outward, sometimes occupying entire city blocks. They had larger communal areas, including vast interior courtyards, central halls, and reception areas. Apartments often included parlors for receiving guests or conducting business—ideally with street views. They had private amenities such as running water, bathtubs, and toilets, in contrast to tenements where facilities remained communal.⁵¹

The Dakota epitomized this evolution. Completed in 1884 on the Upper West Side, it was one of New York's first luxury elevator apartment complexes. Edward Cabot Clark, cofounder of the Singer Manufacturing Company (known for its sewing machines), commissioned architect Henry Janeway Hardenbergh. He designed the eight-story Dakota in a bold German Renaissance style, its elaborate facade, soaring gables, and intricate decoration evoking an almost castle-like grandeur. To address the poor acoustics of earlier buildings, he used solid masonry walls and iron-beamed floors for enhanced sound insulation.⁵²

Yet its aspirations clashed with the constraints of physics: The city's water pressure couldn't reach its upper floors. The solution

Dakota Apartments, Upper West Side, New York City, Henry Janeway Hardenbergh, architect, 1884.

proved elegantly simple. Basement pumps directed water to six tanks in the attic, which then used gravity to distribute water throughout the building. As wooden water tanks crowned more and more rooftops, this system—cost-effective and reliable—became a defining feature of New York's skyline.

But the economic pressures of Manhattan real estate reduced what might have been an inviting courtyard into a cramped communal space. One architect observed that this courtyard fell far short of its potential as "a safe, pleasant and sheltered place, under the eye of a janitor, where tenants can enter, but thieves cannot, and where children can play, out of the street."[53] Instead, it was "a dreary substitute for the most attractive part of Parisian building."

Across the island—and two years before the Dakota welcomed its first residents—Thomas Edison tackled another fundamental constraint of residential life: reliance on gas light. In 1882, his company switched on the first commercial power station, the Pearl Street Station. Electricity delivered a cleaner, safer alternative to gas lamps, reducing fire risks and indoor air pollution. It would soon take residential life into new directions. Electric elevators enabled taller buildings, while electric household appliances enhanced domestic convenience.

Electrification reshaped household dynamics. Electrical appliances—vacuum cleaners, electric irons, stoves, and washing machines—theoretically reduced domestic labor, though in reality they also raised standards of cleanliness. Nevertheless, smaller apartments and the benefits of communal facilities still relieved some of the burden of housework, particularly for women, who were traditionally tasked with managing the home. In parallel, apartment living in Manhattan gave residents easy access to restaurants, theaters, and other cultural attractions, allowing them to participate in urban life and leisure.

THE INDUSTRIAL HOME

By the turn of the century, electricity's widespread adoption had major effects on Manhattan's domestic landscape, reducing the need for household staff—from 188 servants per 1,000 families in 1880 to just 66 per 1,000 by 1920.[54] Electrification significantly enhanced the quality of life in many apartment buildings, but not everyone benefited. Poorer tenements often lagged far behind.

The rise of the apartment building was swift and complete. From just 200 buildings in New York City in 1875, the number surged to over 10,000 by 1910.[55] By 1929, 98 percent of Manhattan's population lived in apartment dwellings.[56] With this shift came social acceptance. Publisher Moses King noted in 1893, "Apartment-life is popular and to a certain extent fashionable. Even society countenances it, and a brownstone front is no longer indispensable to at least moderate social standing."[57]

Manhattan would never be the same. By 1925, New York had overtaken London as the world's most populous city. Its skyline alone stood as a monument to human innovation, its towering structures equipped with elevators and around-the-clock electric lighting that seemed to defy nature. It had become a vertical city.

But this triumph of engineering exacted an environmental toll. The coal-powered plants that enabled vertical living cast a literal shadow. By 1928, the US Public Health Service reported that sunlight in New York City had been reduced by 20 to 50 percent due to pollution from heavy coal combustion used for heat and power.[58] The air was laden with sulfur dioxide and soot, choking the streets below.

Yet today, the apartment buildings that once burned coal now represent the efficiency of shared infrastructure and vertical living. With their shared walls and centralized heating, apartments use less energy for heating and cooling than detached homes. And the very density that was once controversial now supports public transit and bike-sharing systems. These may not be perfect, but they significantly reduce the need for car ownership.

Though the Stuyvesant Flats was eventually demolished, its innovative approach to shared living continues. Today, it is hard to imagine apartment living as controversial—yet I unexpectedly glimpsed those early challenges while living a block from the Stuyvesant's former site, in a postwar elevator building. During a renovation to install recessed lighting, I could hear my upstairs neighbors' footsteps and conversations. It was a sudden reminder of how closely together we lived. When I found that the only sound insulation was a layer of yellowed newspapers, I quickly installed a modern soundproof ceiling—and so, each generation finds new solutions to old problems.

The footsteps faded, but that peculiar urban intimacy remains in the building's common spaces—from fleeting encounters in elevators to the sight of neighbors washing underwear in laundry rooms. These moments embody the paradox of urban life, of strangers bound by proximity, of closeness without familiarity. Modern city dwellers accept these small compromises for the rewards of urban living—restaurants and cultural activities at their doorstep.

Originally a pragmatic response to geographic constraints, this controversial French import has unexpectedly become an example of sustainable urban living. These buildings represent one of our best attempts to live efficiently, shaping not just our skylines but our very sense of what it means to dwell in a modern city. As they rise higher, they continue to negotiate the balance between density and livability, privacy and community—tensions that shape the character of urban life. As cities grow skyward, the question persists: How can people live close enough to create culture, comfortably enough to call it home, and still tread lightly on Earth?

The Railroad Garden

"No great town can long exist without great suburbs," declared landscape architects Frederick Law Olmsted and Calvert Vaux. In their 1868 report for their design of Riverside, located eleven miles outside Chicago, Olmsted and Vaux cited now-debunked scientific findings: "The mere proximity of dwellings which characterizes all strictly urban neighborhoods, is a prolific source of morbid conditions of the body and mind, manifesting themselves chiefly in nervous feebleness or irritability and various functional derangements, relief or exemption from which can be obtained . . . by removal to suburban districts."[59]

These words, penned amid the smog of exploding nineteenth-century cities, captured a broader shift in how Americans envisioned home. The following year, the prairie landscape began its transformation into what would become one of America's most influential garden suburbs. As workers planted thousands of imported trees to give the flat prairie a more forest-like appearance, a new kind of community was taking root.

It was a stark contrast to the multistory apartments in the crowded city. Riverside featured single-family homes set on generous verdant lawns. Streets were lined with trees, some with planted medians. An existing river wound through the neighborhood. Most significantly, it rejected the conventional grid layout of American cities in favor of the philosophy articulated by Olmsted and Vaux: "We recommend the general adoption, in the design of your roads, of gracefully-curved lines, generous spaces, and the absence of sharp corners. The idea being to suggest and imply leisure, contemplativeness and happy tranquility."

The curved roads had no functional necessity whatsoever—the site was mostly flat. However, their purpose was symbolic and experiential: a break from the rigidity of the urban grid. Olmsted and Vaux believed sharp corners and straight lines reflected an "eagerness to press forward, without looking to the right hand or the left." Instead, their plan would be "positively picturesque, and when contrasted with the constantly repeated right angles, straight lines, and flat surfaces which characterize our large modern towns, thoroughly refreshing."

Riverside was among several experiments in urban planning that sought to blend the best of city and country living. A garden suburb like Riverside, Olmsted would later write, would combine the best of both worlds—"sylvan surroundings ... with a considerable share of urban convenience."[60] This ideal in the form of planned garden suburbs would spread globally, inspiring *gartenstädte* in Germany, *città giardini* in Italy, and similar neighborhoods across Europe, reaching as far as India, Australia, and South Africa.

The timing of Riverside's creation coincided with Chicago's meteoric rise as a nexus in America's expanding trade network. The completion of the Erie Canal in 1825 had connected the Great Lakes to the Atlantic, while the railroad boom of the 1850s transformed Chicago into the nation's largest inland transportation hub. This strategic position fueled explosive growth, with the city's population surging from 100,000 in 1860 to half a million by 1880.

By the mid-nineteenth century, many industrial cities were blanketed in dense smog and grimy soot. Emissions from factories, power plants, home furnaces, and coal-burning locomotives were so pervasive, they entered people's homes, staining furniture and corroding metal. This was one of the reasons why affluent urbanites began fleeing to the suburbs.

In the United States, the vision of suburban life was largely shaped by landscape architect Andrew Jackson Downing. In his influential 1850 book, *The Architecture of Country Houses*, he argued: "The battle of life, carried on in cities, gives a sharper edge to the weapon of character, but its temper is for the most part, fixed amid communings with nature and the family."[61] Downing championed the concept of "good houses"—single-family homes that he believed elevated individual morality and upheld the nation's integrity. "When smiling lawns and tasteful cottages begin to embellish the country," he wrote, "we know that order and culture are established."

Downing drew inspiration from the English garden tradition, which rejected the symmetrical, geometric layouts and sculptured trees of French formal gardens like those at Versailles. Instead, it embraced meandering paths, asymmetrical clusters of trees, and irregularly shaped water features. English gardens, though meticulously engineered and maintained, were designed to appear effortlessly "natural." And it was a particular type of nature that it sought to replicate: the serendipitous beauty of the English countryside with its gently rolling hills and clumps of trees. This was the paradox at the heart of what later became known as the "planned picturesque."

At the heart of Downing's reinvention of domestic life lay the lawn.[62] Unlike traditional residential plots of the era, which often featured productive gardens of vegetables and herbs, Downing envisioned homes fronted by carefully maintained expanses of grass—a seeming contradiction between making things feel "natural" and what was actually highly sculpted and manicured perfection. He wanted "grass, not grown into tall meadows, or wild bog tussocks, but softened and refined by the frequent touches of the patient mower, till at last it becomes a perfect wonder of tufted freshness and verdure."[63] He concluded, "In short, the ideal of grass is a *lawn*."

Downing's influence extended beyond landscaping to architecture. He favored homes with picturesque silhouettes—layouts with wings arranged in L shapes or T shapes, creating an engaging profile and adding a distinct feeling to the house's exterior. These more elaborate architectural plans departed from the earlier, more rectangular designs of American residential architecture, which had European colonial influences.

While Downing provided the vision, it was the steam engine that made its implementation possible. Suburbs weren't new—ancient Romans had their own versions of country villas—but they had always been constrained by one fundamental limit: the range of the horse. Now, for the first time in human history, that constraint was about to be shattered. Commuting from greater distances became feasible for those who could afford it, leading to the emergence of affluent suburbs such as Scarsdale near New York and Brookline (where Olmsted lived) near Boston—all developed around railway stations. A new type of community was being born. It would reshape American life for more than a century.

Glendale, Ohio, was one of the first planned garden suburbs in the United States to embody Downing's ideals. The 200-acre subdivision for commuters was laid out in 1851 along the railroad to Cincinnati. One observer noted the novelty of its layout, with streets arranged in "almost every variety of curve known to the mathematician. To the uninitiated this is somewhat confusing, but to the residents it presents no difficulties."[64] The writer further noted that locals were "compensated by the added beauty and the park-like aspect which it renders possible."

Tragically, in 1852, Downing died in a steamboat fire on the Hudson River—a common hazard of the industrial age. But his vision lived on through his protégés. The next year, his partner, Alexander Jackson Davis, developed the influential garden suburb of Llewellyn Park in New Jersey, along the new Morris & Essex railroad line. This gated community of commuters proved immensely successful, eventually attracting residents like Thomas Edison. Though designed to feel far removed from the city, its residents remained deeply dependent on it.

Urban critic James Howard Kunstler later pinpointed this contradiction, observing that "the streets were crooked and winding, gardens rambled, asymmetrical houses sprouted towers like fairy-tale castles to create a fanciful sense of timeless historicity—where, in reality, there would dwell just so many widget manufacturers who depended for their fortunes on the implacable routines of business conducted in the gridded streets of Manhattan."[65]

Even Manhattan would receive its own share of Downing's vision of rolling hills. Before his death, Downing had advocated for a grand public park. He had also recruited Vaux during his travels in England to work as his partner. After Downing's passing, Vaux teamed up with Olmsted and together they won the competition to design Central Park. Impressed with their design, the planners of Riverside commissioned Olmsted and Vaux to bring their talents to the Chicago suburb.

For Riverside, Olmsted and Vaux implemented strict regulations, unlike lesser versions of garden suburbs that simply subdivided land for sale without restrictions. Residents could not stray from the original plan: lot sizes had to be at least 100 by 200 feet, homes had to be set back 30 feet or more from the street, and fences were prohibited to maintain the parklike feel. What's more, the houses were required to cost a minimum of $3,000—a fortune at the time—effectively limiting the community to the wealthy.

However, technological advances were already beginning to democratize the suburban dream. The Industrial Revolution introduced cheap machine-made nails and standardized lumber like the two-by-four stud cut at sawmills. These innovations enabled lighter structures, initially derided as "balloon frames."[66] Unlike the labor-intensive process of carving mortises and tenons out of timber, these new homes could be assembled with simple nails.

The implications were staggering. This construction method required less expertise, less material, and less time—allowing unskilled workers to build homes without the help of joiners or master carpenters. It catalyzed the rapid rise of North America's western boomtowns. More significantly, it transformed the very nature of housing itself from a craft into an industry. The house, once a tailor-made product, increasingly became a commodity.

By 1856, Chicago emerged as the nation's wholesale lumber center. Capitalizing on balloon-frame construction, it played a major role in what became known as "Chicago Construction"—prefabricated frames shipped to the treeless western prairies for easy assembly. Its riverfront boasted an extensive lumber district, serving as a node for timber trains traveling all over the country. "They are now beginning to dispatch timber in the form of ready-made houses," marveled the *Atlantic Monthly* in 1867.[67]

In the mid-1800s, many forests around the Great Lakes, Appalachia, the Southeast, and West remained largely intact. When the railroad and steam power transformed lumber into an industrial commodity, timber production exploded from one billion board feet in 1840 to 46 billion in 1904.[68] Lumbering surpassed agriculture as the leading cause of deforestation, heavily impacting forests that had covered almost half of the United States.[69] By 1920, over two-thirds of American forests, particularly in the East, had been logged at least once. Timber companies would move through an area like a wave of destruction, often leaving behind ecological damage and struggling communities. Only when they reached the Pacific coast, with nowhere else to go, did a nascent awareness of sustainable forestry practices begin to emerge.

Meanwhile, by the late nineteenth century, a new era of accessibility had begun to tip the scale toward suburban living. Train travel became more affordable. Horse-drawn streetcars, or horsecars, emerged in several American cities. These were revolutionary in their simplicity—because they only carried passengers, not freight, the rails could be laid directly into ordinary streets between cobblestones. With an average speed of six miles per hour and affordable fares, they made suburban living accessible to a broader population. Around Chicago, streetcar suburbs flourished, featuring a dense mix of housing types, from detached single-family homes to small apartment buildings, all within walking distance of the streetcar lines.

By the turn of the century, however, the reign of the humble horsecar and steam locomotive was coming to an end. In 1879, Werner von Siemens, a German engineer, introduced the first electric train. It offered a quieter, cleaner mode of urban transport than coal-powered trains. A year later, he created the first electric elevator, enabling faster and safer vertical transportation compared to steam-powered elevators. These innovations would reshape cities. Electric trains and subways stretched them outward, while electric elevators propelled them skyward. Few architects embodied this dual transformation more clearly than William LeBaron Jenney, who designed one of the first steel-framed skyscrapers in Chicago in 1885—the Home Insurance Building—and also built his own Gothic Revival–style home in the garden suburb of Riverside.

Yet for all these technological leaps of the era, early suburban communities remained strikingly human in scale. The train station was not merely central—it was the organizing principle of the suburb itself. Around it, a walkable village center often emerged, with shops and services clustered in close proximity. Most homes, too, lay within

Schermerhorn residence, Riverside, Illinois,
William LeBaron Jenney, architect, 1869.

a comfortable stroll, creating a tight-knit, self-sufficient world tethered to transit. One suburban resident from that period described suburbia as "a railway state . . . a state of existence within a few minutes' walk of the railway station, a few minutes' walk of the shops, and a few minutes' walk of the fields."[70] That essential character—walkable, transit-oriented—still defines many railroad suburbs today.

Unfortunately, the very qualities that made places like Riverside so desirable—generous setbacks, low density, and an abundance of green space—have also made them exclusionary. Over time, these design prescriptions hardened into zoning policies and regulations that restrict density and thus hamper affordability, often pushing lower-income residents to the car-dependent fringes. What started as a hopeful experiment in blending nature with living has, in many places, calcified into a geography of privilege.

Nevertheless, these early railroad suburbs offer a compelling alternative to the car-centric development that would later sprawl across the American landscape. Their walkable cores, human-scaled streets, and proximity to rail lines embody many principles of what we now call transit-oriented development: a planning model that clusters housing, commerce, and services around public transit to reduce car dependence and encourage sustainable growth. Born from steam, these nineteenth-century experiments remain surprisingly relevant today.

As I board the Morris & Essex line in my own railroad suburb—on the same line as Llewellyn Park—I'm struck by how gracefully the town has aged. The curved streets still invite moments of discovery. The mature trees, now towering, transform each road into a natural arcade. Though cars have made the streets less pedestrian-friendly, much of the town retains its walkable spirit. The train station continues to shape the town's cadence of life.

Our home, now entering its second century, wears its history with grace. High ceilings and deep-set windows still flood the rooms with light and air. The sunken living room adds a kind of architectural drama that invites pause. The L-shaped plan—out of step with today's ideas about curb appeal—still captivates me with its sculptural silhouette. I've come to appreciate this house, time-polished floorboards and all. The past echoes in the modest closets, the enclosed kitchen that quietly resists the open-plan trend, the petite bathrooms that defy modern cravings for freestanding tubs. Domestic tastes may have changed, but its rooms remain functional, their windows still opening onto a canopy of trees. In its bones, Olmsted's dream continues to pulse—a railroad garden still thriving amid the rush of today.

FIVE

Machines for Living

Home as Machine

In 1920s Frankfurt, the newly developed suburb of Westhausen broke with convention: Eleven hundred dwellings in long, linear apartment buildings, each set apart by generous green expanses, made a stark contrast to the cramped, dimly lit rental barracks of the city. Designed by architect Ernst May and his team, Westhausen embodied a groundbreaking approach to urban housing known as *Zeilenbau*, or "row-building"—a scientific architecture calibrated to human needs, down to the angle of the sun. Each building faced south and was deliberately spaced from the others at a precisely calculated distance based on winter sun angles, ensuring that even in the depths of winter, sunlight would stream into every lower-level apartment. Westhausen would become a prototype influencing urban living worldwide: a rational form to promote health in an age of the machine.

May and his collaborators had become evangelists for what they called *Licht, Luft und Sonnenschein* (light, air, and sunshine) in their designs. These heliotropic design principles were thought to promote health and well-being.[1] However, they also helped to reduce depen-

Siedlung Westhausen, Frankfurt am Main, Ernst May, architect, 1931. (Later representation of the settlement with mature landscaping.)

dence on expensive heating amid Germany's postwar energy crisis, triggered by the Allied occupation of the coal-rich Ruhr region in 1923. When American housing advocate Catherine Bauer visited in the 1930s, she captured May's almost spiritual devotion to these principles in her 1934 book *Modern Housing*: "The great desiderata of the German planners were sunlight and order," she noted.[2] "A maximum of *light* for every room in a block of apartments means single open-ended rows, carefully spaced, and no more than two rooms deep in any part."

The green spaces between buildings were integral to the concept, a deliberate departure from the dark courtyards of old Frankfurt. On one side, laundry lines stood alongside children's sandboxes. On the other, as a response to recent food shortages, personal garden plots offered urban dwellers a chance to grow their own vegetables. The buildings sat within a large superblock that restricted vehicular traffic to the periphery. This cut infrastructure costs by 35 percent[3] while creating safe pedestrian spaces, all within a new network of walkways, bike paths, and sports fields.

This innovative approach emerged from *das Neue Frankfurt* (New Frankfurt), an ambitious modernization effort with May as its chief strategist. When he accepted the role of city architect in 1925, Frankfurt was in the grip of a housing crisis.[4] The city's population had more than doubled from 189,000 in 1890 to 454,000 by 1919, leaving shelters overflowing with returning soldiers and refugees after World War I. The situation had grown so desperate that even military barracks were opened to civilians.

This explosive growth coincided with a wave of technological breakthroughs. The Haber-Bosch process, introduced in 1913, enabled mass production of fertilizers, dramatically boosting food supply—today, it supports about half the global population.[5] Meanwhile, medical advances—from antibiotics to modern sanitation—meant cities were no longer the death traps they once were. For the first time, urban populations could grow without relying on a constant influx of migrants to offset mortality. Cities were swelling at unprecedented rates, demanding a radical rethinking of how people should live.

May realized that a new approach was needed. The overcrowded tenements, with their narrow, airless courtyards, were affordable but inhumane. Artist Heinrich Zille famously observed, "You can kill a man with an apartment as with an axe—it takes only a little longer."[6]

May's answer lay in the machine age. He set out to bring efficiency and standardization to housing. The so-called May system employed large precast concrete components, allowing entire housing units to be erected in just a few days.[7] "Dwellings are articles made in the mass," he argued. "To supply them in good quality and cheaply one must adopt the methods invariably followed by industry when producing goods for mass consumption."[8] This assembly-line approach so impressed a visiting member of the New York State Housing Board that he dubbed May's creations "machine-made houses."[9]

May's architectural vision was shaped in rural Silesia, where he had overseen the construction of more than four thousand housing units as head of the Rural Settlement Authority. There, across scattered villages in eastern Germany, he saw what industrialized housing could become. "We have experienced the triumphant accession of the standardized building," he proclaimed in 1925. "We will soon see the first steps toward mechanizing house construction."[10]

The zeitgeist of the Weimar Republic gave these ideas fertile ground. Through their building, May and his peers aspired to create a new way of life, a so-called *Wohnkultur*, or "dwelling culture." It also dovetailed with the rising Bauhaus movement, which abandoned ornament in favor of clean lines and rational function. Together, this new architectural avant-garde approached human dwelling with scientific precision. They diagrammed everything from sleeping patterns to car storage in what they dubbed, with typical German thoroughness, the "functional diagram."

Perhaps nowhere was this union of science and domestic life more evident than in the kitchen. Here, Margarete Schütte-Lihotzky—May's sole female team member and a protégé of modernist pioneer Adolf Loos (who famously declared "ornament is crime")—created her masterwork: the Frankfurt Kitchen. She drew on Frederick Taylor's principles of scientific management, which had revolutionized factory workflows, as well as on the compact efficiency of ship galleys and railroad dining cars. Applying industrial logic, she reinvented the kitchen, almost as a precise instrument.

She mapped out what later became known as the "golden triangle"—

an invisible line connecting the worktop, sink, and cooker, designed to minimize unnecessary movement. Measuring just six by eleven feet, the Frankfurt Kitchen featured continuous counter space, a day-lit window, labeled storage, and carefully selected materials. These included black linoleum counters and deep-blue enamel cabinets—chosen, in part, to deter the housefly.[11]

These kitchens were mass-produced, built in the factory, transported to the site, and lowered into place by crane. Eventually, they became available as consumer products beyond Frankfurt. Through films and publications, including May's own magazine, *Das Neue Frankfurt*, they inspired standardized kitchen designs across Europe.

Every facet of domestic life was modernized. Schütte-Lihotzky would also design schools, community buildings, student homes, and kindergartens that embraced Maria Montessori's educational philosophy. She even reimagined the ironing board as a Murphy bed–like device that could disappear into the wall. May's team tackled each element of the home as a problem to solve—from window openers to furniture—prioritizing clean lines for easy cleaning and eliminating dust-trapping ornamental nooks.

In Römerstadt, they built Germany's first fully electrified settlement, with major implications for residential living. "The main thing is electricity," a local newspaper proclaimed. "In the new home it is 'the servant girl who performs all tasks': it cooks the soup, grills the meat, bakes the cake, heats the bath and the cooking water—and, of course, lights the house."[12] These innovations promised domestic liberation. According to Schütte-Lihotzky's calculations, their arsenal of washers, dryers, and irons slashed laundry time from fifteen hours to five. Yet the promise carried a contradiction. Even as it aimed to free women from drudgery, it left them anchored to domestic roles.

The Frankfurt initiative's influence spread rapidly through architectural circles. In 1929, Frankfurt became the epicenter of modernist housing theory when it hosted the second Congrès Internationaux d'Architecture Moderne (CIAM-2). Architects and urban planners descended upon Westhausen to study its innovative approach to the minimum dwelling. Soon, *Zeilenbau* principles surfaced across Europe—from Britain's garden cities to Sweden's *folkhemmet* (the people's home) public housing and Dutch worker estates—all bearing the imprint of May's vision.[13]

By 1930, May had achieved the improbable: 12,000 apartments built. But dark clouds loomed on Germany's political horizon. As the Nazi Party rose to power, May and his team departed for the Soviet Union, carrying their modernist dreams eastward. Tasked with designing twenty new cities, they soon saw their vision collide with the realities of Stalinist bureaucracy and resource shortages—though fragments of their work would later shape the Soviet microdistrict system. Meanwhile, in Frankfurt, the Nazis dismantled social housing programs. Schütte-Lihotzky, who had joined the resistance, narrowly escaped execution and was sentenced to fifteen years of hard labor and imprisonment. The Frankfurt Kitchen's production lines halted in 1930. Yet it would continue to influence kitchen design for years.

The *Zeilenbau* concept and the Frankfurt Kitchen delivered real progress. Working-class families finally had their own kitchens, bathrooms, and sometimes even balconies. But as modernist ideas went global, they often shed their social core. Critics would later coin the term "tombstone urbanism" to describe the derivative housing blocks that mimicked May's parallel buildings but neglected the social infrastructure that made them work. The spaces between buildings often translated to windswept no-man's-lands. Even the celebrated Frankfurt kitchen later came under criticism—its efficient design, some argued, had inadvertently created a domestic "isolation chamber," too cramped for interacting with family or supervising children.

Perhaps the most seductive legacy of modernism emerged not in the worker housing of Frankfurt or the rational kitchens of Schütte-Lihotzky, but in the sleek curtain walls now synonymous with corporate towers. These shimmering nonstructural glass facades began modestly enough with the Bauhaus school's 1926 design, where the beauty of glass transparency collided head-on with the physics of heat loss. Architects responded with a simple fix: radiators installed directly against the windows—a patch that foreshadowed modern architecture's growing reliance on mechanical solutions to overcome environmental shortcomings.

The trouble became clear in Ludwig Mies van der Rohe's infamous Farnsworth House. Exposed and unshaded, this glass house became modernism's cautionary tale. Without air-conditioning, it transformed into a glass oven under the Illinois sun. In the winter, it racked up expensive heating bills. Its owner, Dr. Edith Farnsworth, who later sued Mies, captured the psychological toll of this radical transparency. "The house is transparent, like an X-ray," she noted, and living in it made her feel exposed: "like a prowling animal, always on the alert . . . always restless . . . like a sentinel on guard day and night."[14]

Then came Willis Carrier's air conditioner. Initially conceived to stabilize humidity in printing plants, it became modern architecture's enabler. By 1932, a Carrier publicist was already sketching out a brave new world freed from the tyranny of natural ventilation: buildings "unfettered by the erstwhile necessity of 'ventilating shafts,' 'light wells,' 'outside exposures,' and such considerations"[15]—features now recognized as essential to sustainable design. By 1952, a Carrier demonstration house boasted its divorce from nature: "This house

Edith Farnsworth House, Illinois, Ludwig Mies van der Rohe, architect, 1951.

started a revolution. It need not depend on natural ventilation. Ells [L-shaped extensions] and wings wouldn't be necessary.... Windows, doors, and even rooms themselves could be placed to suit the convenience of the owner, not to catch a breeze."[16]

The consequences reverberated worldwide. Modernist glass-curtainwall buildings could now appear even in desert climates—and they did. Glass-and-steel towers rose in climates where they made little environmental sense. What began as a quest for better working-class housing had morphed into a luxury aesthetic. The International Style, once grounded in egalitarian ideals, had drifted toward abstraction—bulldozing local and climatically adapted traditions in pursuit of universal form.

Climatic considerations often yielded to aesthetic dogma. Flat roofs in rainy weather leaked, glass walls in sunny environments turned buildings into greenhouses, and centuries-old building traditions that had evolved to address local conditions were dismissed as obsolete. This rejection of vernacular wisdom proved especially problematic in lower-income countries. Modernist buildings often required costly mechanical systems just to remain habitable. The modernist ideal of rational solutions had become a form of architectural imperialism, imposing energy-intensive designs regardless of local climate or resources. Despite improvements such as triple-glazed windows, most all-glass buildings still depend heavily on mechanical heating and cooling.

Yet modernism's original vision still holds profound lessons for contemporary architecture. As a student of modern architecture steeped in Bauhaus principles, I admire the audacious spirit of pioneers like May and Schütte-Lihotzky. I'll never forget visiting the Rietveld Schröder House in Utrecht, a building that looks like a modernist painting come to life—its primary colors standing out against the Dutch grey sky. Gerrit Rietveld's background as a furniture maker was beautifully evident in his architecture. He created a wraparound corner window that opens like a door, momentarily unifying inside and outside, dissolving the house's corner. It was one of those breakthrough moments that captured modernism's original promise—to radically rethink how buildings could connect humans to their environment.

But even architectural poetry must answer to gravity. On my graduation day, my mother's heel caught in the steel grating of our Brutalist architecture school's floor. Her offhand comment about the building's odd hostility to its occupants struck a deeper chord—especially in a structure meant to teach future architects. In retrospect, it seems a fitting metaphor for modernism's broader challenges: a movement born from the desire to improve human life through rational design had, in its pursuit of aesthetic purity, sometimes created spaces that worked better as manifestos than as shelter.

Driveway to Dreams

In 1932, the renowned American architect Frank Lloyd Wright conceived a radical vision for the future American landscape: an idealized community he called Broadacre City. He envisioned each family living on at least an acre of land to grow their own food, engage in small-scale manufacturing, and achieve self-sufficiency. Working with his students, Wright built a massive twelve-by-twelve-foot model to illustrate this dream. Within the four square miles it represented, he imagined "little farms, little homes for industry, little factories, little schools, and a little university." On two plywood panels, Wright declared in capital letters: "A NEW FREEDOM FOR LIVING IN AMERICA," followed by a list detailing the attributes of his design: "No traffic problem . . . No poles. No wires in sight. No glaring cement roads or walks . . . No roadside advertising."[17] Wright believed Broadacre City would replicate itself elegantly across the vast American landscape.

It never materialized. Postwar America took a different path. It was characterized less by careful planning or architectural vision, and more by uncoordinated suburban subdivisions. Meanwhile, commercial roadside strips featured crisscrossing webs of electrical wires and a cacophony of billboards. Wright lamented this fate. In 1958, just a year before his death, he remarked, "America needs no help to Broadacre City. It will haphazard[ly] build itself."[18]

In place of Broadacre City, postwar America built Levittown. Instead of integrated communities and refined architecture, what emerged were mass-produced homes designed to meet unprecedented housing demand. One man epitomized this transformation: William "Bill" Levitt, a former Navy lieutenant with experience in large-scale homebuilding. Levitt saw an opportunity on a vast potato field on Long Island, New York, just twenty-five miles east of Manhattan. Unlike the exclusive, wealthy garden suburbs of the late nineteenth century, Levitt intended to democratize the suburban ideal, making it affordable to returning war veterans and their young families.

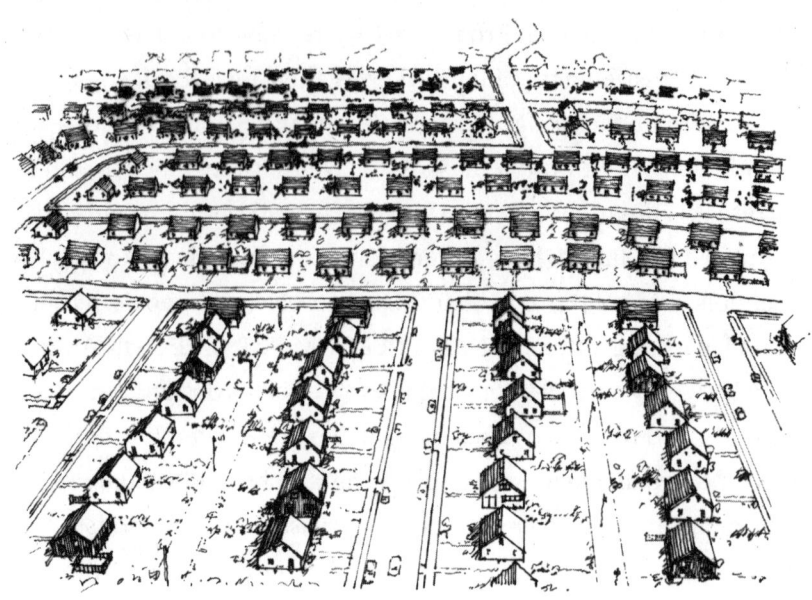

Levittown, New York, Levitt & Sons, developers, 1947.

The timing was perfect. After World War II, millions of veterans returned home flush with savings and aspirations to start families—the beginning of the Baby Boom. However, the Great Depression and wartime restrictions had severely limited residential construction, creating a housing shortage. Levitt's solution would transform not just the housing industry, but the fabric of American life.

"We are not builders," William Levitt proclaimed, "we are manufacturers." With his brother Alfred, he developed "the 26 steps,"[19] an assembly-line approach where specialized crews handled one task each—pouring foundations, installing tiles, painting interiors, even applying particular paint colors, like red and white.[20] Levitt described this as a "reversal of the Detroit assembly line,"[21] where instead of moving the product (the car) to stationary workers, the workers moved from house to house. This efficiency enabled them to build up to thirty homes a day.

Writer W. D. Wetherell vividly described this orchestration: "A truck comes along, stops in front of the house, half a dozen men pile out... in fifteen minutes they've put in a bathroom. Pop! Off they go to the next house, just in time, too, because here comes another truck with the kitchen. Pop! In goes the kitchen."[22] Levitt further reduced costs by employing nonunion workers and controlling a vertically integrated supply chain, producing his own nails, lumber, and other materials. This mastery of logistics made his homes faster and cheaper to build.

The result was staggering: By 1951, Levittown had become a community of 17,447 homes housing over 70,000 people. The first Levittown house, a Cape Cod–style dwelling, was compact and simple, bordering on caricature—a single-story rectangular structure with minimal decoration and a classic gabled roof, set on a sixty-by-hundred-foot lot. Though only a third the size of a typical prewar single-family house, it managed to include two bedrooms, a living room with a fireplace, a bathroom, and an "expansion" attic.[23] Homes were built on radiant-heated concrete slabs, to avoid having to excavate basements. Instead of traditional plaster, the walls were made of Sheetrock, with rooms sized in multiples of four feet, the width of a standard panel.[24]

Critics dismissed these homes as cookie-cutter, calling them "degraded in conception and impoverished in form,"[25] yet their impact was undeniable. As *Life* magazine noted in 1949, "He may not build the most attractive house in the world, but he has brought down the price of a well-equipped house."[26] Paul Goldberger, *The New York Times* architecture critic, later captured their significance, observing that "they turned the detached, single-family house from a distant dream to a real possibility for thousands of middle-class American families."[27]

Compared to earlier garden suburbs, Levittown represented significant aesthetic compromises. Its streets were neither quite curvilinear nor straight, and often too wide. The homes were sited with slight variations in their distance from the street, creating an illusion of diversity. Still, the uniformity was such that anecdotes emerged of residents mistakenly entering the wrong homes. "The houses might look quite attractive if there weren't so incredibly many of them,"[28] one critic observed.

Yet for many buyers, affordability trumped uniformity. Homes were later sold for $6,990, with mortgage and taxes costing at times half that of a small, two-bedroom rental in New York City.[29] The GI Bill of 1944 made them even more accessible. It offered veterans low-interest loans with no down payment and monthly payments of just $56.[30] To sweeten the deal, a washer and television were included in the purchase price as part of the mortgage.[31]

"SEVEN THOUSAND BUCKS! ONE HUNDRED DOLLARS DOWN! We were cowboys out there. We were the pioneers," reflects the narrator in Wetherell's story "The Man Who Loved Levittown." "Thanks to Big Bill Levitt we all had a chance. You talk about dreams. Hell, we had ours. We had ours like nobody before or since ever had theirs."[32]

Americans may have been culturally inclined toward single-family homes instead of apartments—the 1915 *Child Welfare Manual* criticized apartments as "diminutive pigeon-holes."[33] But as historian Gwendolyn Wright argues in *Building the Dream*, broader policy decisions further entrenched this pattern of life. The automobile, now affordable and widely available, extended the radius of viable housing into North America's vast tracts of inexpensive farmland. Federal investment in highway infrastructure created the arteries of suburban expansion. Corporations further promoted the lifestyle with aggressive advertising campaigns in newspapers, women's magazines, and radio broadcasts pushing suburban living as the pinnacle of modern life. This new American dream was captured in the words of a 1950s women's magazine heroine: "I'm thankful for my good health and faith in God, and such material possessions as two cars, two TVs, and two fireplaces."[34]

The suburban project became entangled with Cold War politics as well. Levitt aligned with a broader national agenda, promoting Levittown as the American way of life. He asserted, "No man who owns his own house and lot can be a Communist. He has too much to do."[35] He even posed with Senator McCarthy, who led anticommunist investigations, in front of Levittown washing machines. America was transforming into what one critic called a "Consumers' Republic." As *Brides* magazine declared: By purchasing "the dozens of things you never bought or even thought of before ... you are helping to build greater security for the industries of this country.... What you buy and how you buy it is very vital in your new life—and to our whole American way of living."[36]

Inside these suburban homes, a new American way of living was emerging: open-plan layouts and a flood of new products filling suburban garages and living rooms. Equipped with the era's cutting-edge built-in appliances, the 1949 Levittown homes boasted an electric range, washing machine, and refrigerator. By 1950, Levitt further enticed buyers with a twelve-inch television set integrated into the side of the staircase.

As demand soared, Levitt replicated his success with a second Levittown near Philadelphia. He introduced more refined models such as the Levittowner, which featured an open living room with a three-way fireplace. It was inspired by Frank Lloyd Wright. Yet Alfred Levitt, having briefly worked with Wright, managed to build these homes at a fraction of the cost of Wright's masterpieces. This positioned Alfred, according to architecture critic Witold Rybczynski, as "an unlikely conduit for disseminating Wright's ideas into the American mainstream."[37] When the Levittown model homes in Pennsylvania opened in 1951, more than 50,000 people toured them during the first weekend alone—an event hailed by national media as "the most spectacular buyers' stampede in American housebuilding history."[38]

Many of the homes merged the kitchen with the living area. This arrangement allowed women, then often responsible for domestic tasks, to cook while remaining close to domestic life. These new interiors felt less formal and more spacious. Contemporary studies now validate these choices, indicating that humans are naturally drawn to open spaces, which captivate us with their informational richness.[39]

Meanwhile, other large-scale developers were constructing mass-produced suburban subdivisions across the nation, from San Francisco to Baltimore and from Phoenix to Chicago. Architectural styles reflected regional preferences. On the East Coast, more traditional designs such as saltbox, colonial, and Cape Cod were common. On the West Coast, more experimental plans dominated, including modern ranch-style homes with open L-shaped floor plans.[40] There, builders like Joseph Eichler built midcentury modern homes, making California modernism more accessible to middle-class buyers.[41]

Yet this suburban ideal was not accessible to all. Through the discriminatory practice known as redlining, minority neighborhoods were labeled too "risky" for federally backed mortgages. Restrictive covenants embedded in deeds further barred nonwhite families from homeownership in many subdivisions. Levittown became an emblem of such exclusionary policies. Clause 25 of its lease agreement explicitly noted, in capital letters, that the homes could not "be used or occupied by any person other than members of the Caucasian race."

In 1957, when a Black family moved into Levittown, Pennsylvania, a violent backlash erupted—vandalism, rock-throwing, and even cross-burning. Tensions only eased after state intervention.[42] One white resident admitted to *Life* magazine, "He's probably a nice guy, but every time I look at him I see $2,000 drop off the value of my house."[43] As American historian Thomas Sugrue later noted, such reactions were not anomalies but part of a broader pattern of white resistance to integration. He cited the fear in Levittown that another sale to a black family "might touch off panic selling and even start the development of a 'Negro' section."[44]

This stark racialization of the suburban dream also reflected a broader pattern of "white flight," which rapidly hollowed out many American cities. As wealthier, predominantly white families relocated to the suburbs, urban centers were left with shrinking tax bases. As resources poured into new highways prioritizing suburban commuters, city neighborhoods were neglected. Urban residents had to contend with poorly maintained sidewalks, with schoolchildren walking single file along dangerous, traffic-filled streets.

At the core of this transformation was the rise of the automobile. Earlier in the century, streetcars and cars had competed for dominance. But government investment in highways reached its apex with the 1956 Federal-Aid Highway Act, which funded 41,000 miles of interstate highways, decisively favoring the automotive industry. This policy not only entrenched the car's supremacy but also shaped housing options, directing most new development into suburban sprawl.[45] By the 1950s, most new housing was suburban, and by the end of the decade, almost one-third of Americans lived in suburbs.

By 1970, the shift was complete: more Americans lived in suburbs than in central cities.

This new landscape came with new forms of organization. Zoning laws rigidly separated residential, commercial, and industrial uses, ensuring quiet "bedroom communities" devoid of local industry. Inside this commercial vacuum came malls, which soon arose as surrogate town centers. Victor Gruen, the Austrian-born architect who designed the first enclosed mall—Southdale Center in Minnesota (1956)—envisioned these spaces as all-in-one hubs with apartments, offices, parks, and schools. Instead, developers cherry-picked only the retail portion, building isolated shopping complexes surrounded by seas of parking. A dismayed Gruen later denounced them as "those bastard developments."[46]

As malls proliferated, they encouraged more driving and heightened consumerism. Suburban Americans no longer walked to local stores on a main street; they drove to climate-controlled malls. These shifts molded suburbia into a landscape routinely criticized for sterile monotony and the alienation of its inhabitants. Yet reality was more complex. Sociologist Herbert Gans, who in an experiment lived in a Levittown community in New Jersey, concluded in his 1967 book *The Levittowners* that it did not breed "depression, boredom, loneliness, and ultimately mental illness."[47] Residents, he found, were ordinary people who valued affordable homes, good schools, and stable neighborhoods.

Nevertheless, car-oriented suburban living exacted its own toll. Since work, shops, and entertainment were often miles away, residents who couldn't drive or lacked cars found themselves isolated. Suburban women, in particular, bore the brunt of this system, physically distanced from employment centers and socially tethered to domestic duties. The automobile, initially a symbol of freedom, increasingly became a source of stress as long commutes, traffic congestion, and solitary hours behind the wheel eroded that liberation. Meanwhile, sedentary lifestyles contributed to widening waistlines and shortening lifespans—leading some health advocates to declare, "Sitting is the new smoking."

The physical architecture of suburbia reflected these priorities. Homes retreated from their relationship to the street, abandoning the semi-public front porches of earlier suburbs. By the mid-twentieth century, garages dominated home fronts—creating what urban designers Michael Southworth and Peter Owens described as a "garage scape."[48] Lot sizes increased—from about sixteen homes per acre in earlier twentieth-century neighborhoods to around four per acre in postwar suburbs—even as family sizes shrank.[49] The result was a low-density environment incapable of effectively supporting public transport, further reinforcing the primacy of the car. Streets were wide but not pedestrian-friendly and few gathering places were accessible without driving. Cultural critics, such as James Howard Kunstler, aptly called it a "drive-in civilization."[50]

The expansion of this car-enabled suburbanism also relied on other less-visible technologies. As *The New York Times* noted in the 1960s, "The humble air-conditioner has been a powerful influence in circulating people as well as air in this country."[51] As people migrated to Sunbelt cities like Houston and Dallas, air-conditioning became "almost as common a device in the warmer sections of the United States as the automobile and the television set." With window units readily available at the local mall, Americans could replicate Minnesota's summer weather, even in Florida.

Outside, the suburban ideal demanded another machine: the sprinkler. What had once required an army of gardeners to sustain the grand estates of European aristocrats could now be achieved with sprinkler systems and mechanical lawnmowers. This democratization of the aristocratic lawn made the green grass a status symbol for millions, even in the driest regions. As a result, grass became the nation's third most widespread "crop." Frank Lloyd Wright had imagined farms; instead, as Kenneth T. Jackson alluded to in his book, suburban America became a *Crabgrass Frontier*. Today, lawns consume nearly one-third of residential water use in the US—approximately nine billion gallons daily, or two bathtubs per household.

The environmental costs mounted. The pesticides maintaining these green pastures became health hazards to children and pets. The relentless expansion of suburban areas required the bulldozing of forests and farmlands, necessitating environmental workarounds in less fertile lands such as water imports and synthetic fertilizers. By the 1960s, environmental repercussions were unmistakable. Acid rain, primarily caused by emissions from vehicles and coal-fired power plants, acidified hundreds of now fishless lakes in the state of New York alone.

Wright's Broadacre City had envisioned decentralized freedom. Instead, what emerged were "car suburbs." The result was an unintended experiment in mass suburbanization, one that would reshape the American landscape. Phoenix, Arizona, for instance, grew from about 107,000 residents in 1950 to nearly 1.7 million today—its metropolitan existence almost entirely dependent on imported water and air-conditioning.

Wright dreamed of a "new freedom for living," but the reality proved messier than that. I learned this the hard way one Las Vegas summer, moving between air-conditioned oases and scorching asphalt. Sidewalks were few and often in poor condition. Walking or waiting for a bus meant defying a world built for cars. Even the cool relief of air-conditioning came with a tradeoff, intensifying the dryness of indoor air.

One day, my car wouldn't start. I sat in its baking metal shell, surrounded by acres of shimmering asphalt. What had been sold as freedom suddenly revealed itself as a mirage—mobility and comfort vanished the moment the engine fell silent, the entire system indifferent to anyone it left behind.

Cities in the Sky

In 1925, the world glimpsed a radical new vision for urban living at the International Exhibition of Modern Decorative and Industrial Arts in Paris. There, modernist architect Le Corbusier unveiled his audacious urban renewal scheme, "Plan Voisin." He proposed demolishing a vast section of historic Paris. In place of the thousands of existing buildings, he envisioned eighteen cruciform sixty-story glass towers set amid vast green spaces. Although the office towers would occupy less than 10 percent of the land area, their dramatic height promised to increase density, while still allowing people to live among greenery in modern blocks nearby. These "cities in the sky," Le Corbusier declared, were the future. "Modern life demands, and is waiting for, a new kind of plan, both for the house and for the city," he proclaimed. "The house is a machine for living in."[52]

Almost a century later, I rented a small studio in a Paris walk-up on a street Le Corbusier had once slated for demolition. My apartment was modest, but the narrow, lively street filled with restaurants and shops more than made up for it. Le Corbusier's tabula rasa approach would have erased centuries of history and vitality, all in pursuit of theoretical efficiency. Paris was spared, but his ideas took root elsewhere after World War II when many countries faced acute housing shortages.

In 1952, in Marseille, Le Corbusier realized a version of that vision in the Unité d'Habitation. It housed 1,600 residents in 337 duplex apartments, with shops, clinics, a kindergarten, and even a rooftop hotel integrated into a single concrete structure. He aimed to "provide with silence and solitude before the sun, space and greenery, a dwelling which will be the perfect receptacle for the family" while crafting "a magisterial work of architecture, the product of rigour, grandeur, nobility, happiness and elegance."[53]

If Plan Voisin was "towers in the park," this was among the earliest *megastructures*—enormous self-contained complexes that combined housing, shopping, schools, and public facilities under one roof. Another innovation emerged from constraint: With postwar steel in short supply, the structure was built in exposed concrete, or *béton brut*—raw concrete. It helped give rise to what became known as Brutalism. Many residents appreciated the building's bold design and amenities. Yet, others found the concrete aesthetic and long windowless corridors unsettling. Regardless, megastructures, towers in the park, and Brutalism moved into the mainstream, shaping postwar high-density housing worldwide.

Across the English Channel, architects expanded on this megastructure model. Projects like Ernő Goldfinger's Trellick Tower (1972) and the Barbican Estate (1982) in London imagined "cities within cities." But megastructures had their flaws. Many replaced older, human-scale neighborhoods with stark, imposing geometries. Patrick Hodgkinson's Brunswick Centre (1972) in Bloomsbury was criticized for its unfinished concrete exterior. Others, like Sheffield's Park Hill Flats, came to represent Brutalism's failures. The exposed concrete, a hallmark of the style, weathered poorly in Sheffield's cold, wet climate—unlike in Marseille—and its "streets in the sky" felt uninviting.

By the 1980s, enthusiasm had faded. J. G. Ballard's 1975 novel *High-Rise* captured the growing unease, depicting a luxury apartment complex descending into violent chaos: "With its forty floors and thousand apartments, its supermarket and swimming-pools, bank and junior school—all in effect abandoned in the sky—the highrise offered more than enough opportunities for violence and confrontation."[54]

Meanwhile, in the United States, "towers in the park" met a similar fate. In 1947, New York City's Stuyvesant Town–Peter Cooper Village superblock replaced eighteen city blocks and 600 buildings with 110 cruciform towers set amid lawns and trees. But it drew criticism for its lack of public facilities and for displacing 11,000 residents. Most infamously, the Pruitt-Igoe towers in St. Louis were razed on national television. "Modern architecture died in St. Louis, Missouri, on July 15, 1972, at 3:32 p.m. (or thereabouts)," declared architectural historian Charles Jencks, "when the infamous Pruitt-Igoe scheme, or rather several of its slab blocks, were given the final coup de grace by dynamite."[55]

So you can imagine my surprise when I first visited Hong Kong and saw a city that had fully embraced towers in the park and megastructures—on a scale that might have even astonished Le Corbusier. The city has the world's highest concentration of skyscrapers. Looking at the Victoria Harbour skyline, a crest of concrete-and-steel towers rises between harbor and forested mountains. Each night, a synchronized laser show animates dozens of harbor-front buildings—a scene so cinematic it has inspired movies such as *Blade Runner*.

While many Western cities retreated from modernist ideals, Hong Kong became an unexpected laboratory for vertical living—not out of utopian ambition, but necessity. Constrained by mountainous terrain and explosive population growth, the city had little place to grow but upward. After World War II and the establishment of the People's

Republic of China, Hong Kong faced a refugee surge. Its population grew from 600,000 in 1945 to two million by 1950. Many residents lived in poorly built squatter settlements on hillsides and rooftops, often without sanitation. One observer remarked, "Can you imagine sharing a single bed with six other people? ... The home space for a tenement dweller was less than he would have in his coffin!"[56]

Tragedy struck on Christmas Day 1953, when a fire razed the Shek Kip Mei squatter town, leaving 60,000 homeless. In response, within fifty-three days, authorities erected Hong Kong's first public housing blocks at Shek Kip Mei. These austere "Mark I" buildings offered basic shelter and shared amenities, such as schools on the roofs. Built with barrack-like efficiency, they were nonetheless an improvement over the squalor of the settlements. Each H-shaped block housed units as small as 120 square feet—smaller than a modern parking space—yet designed to accommodate entire families.[57] Toilets were communal. Over the next six years, 115 such blocks were built, each accommodating hundreds of rooms and thousands of residents.

Over time, the housing authority built hundreds of high-rise blocks, relocating squatters into modest but more humane homes. Densities reached nearly two thousand people per acre—six times denser than Stuyvesant Town. Yet these concrete apartments offered dignity and stability. "New or old, the resettlement estates are alive, they throb and pulsate with energy and human activity,"[58] an architect observed at the time. It was the beginning of Hong Kong's massive public housing program.

By the late 1960s, Hong Kong's planners had begun to move beyond merely providing basic shelter toward more integrated forms of urbanism. Estates like Wah Fu combined tall towers with schools, shops, and other communal facilities. With densities reaching 2,400 people per acre, Wah Fu challenged prevailing assumptions about what constituted livable. One American planner was astounded by this extreme density, writing: "Most orthodox planners would expect [these] densities to precipitate serious health and social problems."[59]

During this period, researchers began to explore how urban form affects human psychology and behavior. Anthropologist Edward Hall coined the field "proxemics," to describe how people use and experience space. He observed, "If one sees man surrounded by a series of invisible bubbles which have measurable dimensions, architecture can be seen in a new light. It is then possible to conceive that people can be cramped by the spaces in which they have to live and work." Some skyscrapers, he warned, collapsed these spatial bubbles entirely. "The world's populations are crowding into cities," he wrote, "and builders and speculators are packing people into vertical filing boxes."[60]

Sociologists shared similar concerns, drawing on the infamous "rat utopia" experiments—where mice, placed in enclosures with unlimited food, experienced population explosions followed by overcrowding, deviance, social collapse, and mass die-offs. Yet strangely, those predictions didn't hold in Hong Kong. As one observer noted, the expected "upper limit" to human density "is utterly absent."[61]

One key reason was that Hong Kong had introduced an important innovation. Unlike the isolated Western "towers in the park," estates like Wah Fu followed a "township" model—self-contained vertical neighborhoods with direct links to public transit. By embedding social infrastructure—such as schools, shops, and gathering spaces—into a megastructure at the heart of the neighborhood, the model became more socially viable. It fostered a genuine sense of community, despite being a radical departure from the traditional rhythm of streets and blocks.

In 1975, this model became even more integrated when Hong Kong launched the Mass Transit Railway Corporation (MTRC), which was granted development rights around transit stations. This marked the beginning of what might be called "rail-residential" urbanism: a fusion of housing, subway infrastructure, and mixed-use development.

Perhaps no project captures this model better than Union Square, a dozen interconnected towers built above a high-speed rail hub, crowned by the city's tallest skyscraper. With more than 70,000 residents and workers flowing through its apartments, offices, shops, and transit, Union Square may be the most complete realization of a vertical neighborhood to date.

This was not Le Corbusier's idealized vision of towers amid parkland. It was something far more pragmatic: towers built directly atop subway stations. And it worked. This symbiotic system—high-rise housing plus mass transit—enhanced both livability and efficiency. By the 1990s, Hong Kong had developed seven new towns, which collectively housed about 2.5 million people. Today, Hong Kong's overall population has surpassed 7.5 million. And yet the city moves without traffic gridlock. You can reach most neighborhoods, beaches, and the airport faster by train than by car.

As the city kept building upward, erecting more and taller skyscrapers, observers began to wonder about the human experience within this vertical world. Photographer Michael Wolf captured this condition perfectly. His *Architecture of Density* series portrays Hong Kong's towers as endless grids of windows, with no visible horizon—a visual metaphor for life lived inside pure verticality. It often raises the question, as he once put it: "How do people live in there?"

The answer lies partly in what these towers take away. Tightly packed towers restrict natural light and views of open skies and greenery, elements that support mental well-being. Studies suggest that when tall buildings are spaced too closely, people report heightened feelings of oppressiveness, a kind of ambient stress. One study, using immersive virtual reality, found that residents exposed to closely spaced towers experienced significantly higher levels of oppressiveness—especially when separation distances fell below ninety feet.[62] This psychological stress amplifies perceived noise from traffic and surroundings.

Nevertheless, Hong Kong's dramatic topography offers unexpected relief. Like Manhattan's rivers, Hong Kong's coastline and mountains break the visual monotony. In some neighborhoods, density may be inescapable. But in many others, nature reasserts itself.

And while apartments are relatively small, constraint often turns into invention. Sliding walls transform living rooms into bedrooms. Desks fold out from closets. Built-in cabinets occupy every available

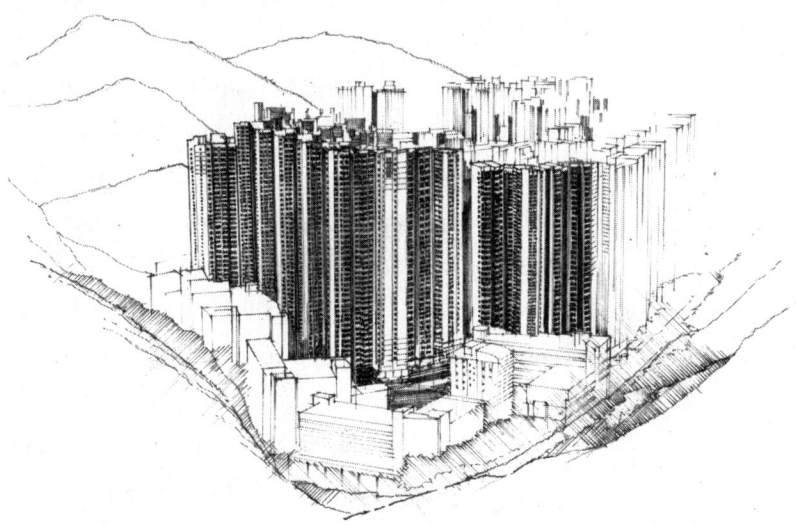

Kin Ming Estate, Hong Kong, Hong Kong Housing Authority, architects, 2003.

nook. Appliances and furniture are uniquely compact. With space at a premium, not a square inch is left to chance.

Still, the efficiencies of vertical life come with real tradeoffs: less privacy, less personal space, and less control over one's immediate environment. Having lived in Hong Kong for three years, I can attest to this. At times, I felt like a sardine in a can, just riding the elevator. Daily life often meant intrusions into what Hall defined as "intimate distance"—the eighteen-inch zone normally reserved for close friends or family. At that range, you can smell another person's body odor.

There are environmental tradeoffs, too. High-rises require vast quantities of steel and concrete, both carbon-intensive. They rely on elevators, pressurized plumbing, and mechanical ventilation. Yet even these resource-hungry towers can be sustainable when evaluated by how many people they house. Shared walls improve thermal performance, reducing energy use for heating and cooling. Economies of scale allow one team to maintain the building, while services like waste collection run more efficiently with more people per square meter. The towers' compact footprints reduce sprawl and preserve open land. Dense cities also require less road infrastructure per capita, lowering both maintenance costs and emissions.[63]

Thanks to its transit-oriented density, Hong Kong now has among the world's lowest per-capita transportation emissions.[64] Over 90 percent of all trips are made via public transit. The system works, not in spite of density—but because of it. That density supports a world-class transit system. It sustains local businesses. It powers efficient infrastructure. As transportation planner Robert Cervero wrote, "Hong Kong's [rail and property] model . . . is the best template available for achieving sustainable transit finance and sustainable urbanism."[65]

Other Asian cities have taken note. While Hong Kong represents an extreme of urban density, the principles of transit-oriented development have spread through many parts of China and Southeast Asia. In Singapore, for instance, 85 percent of the population lives in public high-rises, supported by a high-quality transit system. As incomes have risen, unit sizes have grown too, proving that vertical cities can evolve to offer both space and convenience.

The influence of this model of transit-integrated vertical urbanism continues to grow. From Bogotá to Melbourne, cities are adopting elements of this approach. Even in the United States, long skeptical of vertical living, residential towers are rising in high-demand areas. Without them, housing costs would skyrocket, and sprawl would consume more land. Especially in cities where land is expensive, apartment buildings, with shared infrastructure and economies of scale, offer a more efficient urban future.

A century after modernists dreamed of "cities in the sky," Hong Kong remains one of the few places where that vision has been realized. In a world facing rapid urbanization, it offers a functioning vertical model. It shows that vertical success requires more than stacking people in space. It demands orchestration of transit, amenities, and interior design.

Density, it seems, is destiny for many cities. But the story of vertical living is still being written. The towers of Hong Kong, imperfect as they are, preview an increasingly vertical urban future. In a city often branded as hyper-capitalist, Hong Kong has quietly extended the modernist housing legacy—using towering efficiencies to shelter millions.

Beyond the Modern Blueprint

At midnight on Christmas Eve, 1962, hundreds of families marched to the outskirts of Lima, Peru. Armed with wooden stakes and sheets of plastic, they would build a neighborhood by dawn. Their makeshift huts stood defiantly in the mud—a declaration of their right to exist in a city that had offered them no place. When police arrived to tear down the encampment, the families returned the following week to rebuild. What began as an "invasion" would become a permanent neighborhood.

Many of these settlers were indigenous migrants who had come to Lima in search of better lives. As one resident put it, "We are determined to invade any available land because we can't go on living as we are."[66] Faced with rising inequality and government inaction, they took housing into their own hands.

This act of desperation was part of a wider pattern. Two years earlier and 1,600 miles east, Brazil unveiled Brasília, meant to be its city of the future: orderly, egalitarian, and free from the slums plaguing other Brazilian cities. Designed by Lúcio Costa and with buildings by Oscar Niemeyer, this planned capital was laid out like an airplane: Government ministries ran along a monumental axis, while residential "wings" held superblocks complete with shops, churches, and schools. The plan followed the ideals of Le Corbusier's *Ville Radieuse*, with six-story blocks featuring white facades floating in green open space, neatly zoned.

But just outside the capital, another city was rising. In areas like Núcleo Bandeirante, wooden shacks sprang up along unpaved roads, housing the very laborers who had built the capital but were excluded from living in it. Brasília had no housing for workers. Planners assumed they would vanish after the job was done. Instead, they stayed—settling precariously on marginal lands, without sanitation or legal rights.

Anthropologist James Holston later noted that Brasília, conceived as the ultimate modernist city, had inadvertently produced the very kind of informal settlement its planners had sought to eliminate.[67] It revealed a central flaw in the modernist mindset: It imagined that cities could be designed top-down, with universal solutions, even when imposed on an unequal society. But affordability and access, it turned out, mattered just as much as aesthetics and order.

Today, over 1.8 billion people—nearly one in four globally—lack formal housing. They live in informal settlements, from the favelas of Rio to the slums of Lagos and Nairobi. They inhabit places like the "vertical slum" of Caracas, where squatters repurposed a forty-five-story office tower. These settlements are not anomalies. They are what happens when formal systems fail to keep up with rapid urbanization.

This is not to romanticize informal housing. Often built in floodplains or on dangerously sloping hillsides, homes frequently get inundated or collapse in mudslides. Without proper drainage, standing water invites mosquitoes and dengue. Without ventilation or insulation, rooms become ovens by day and fridges by night. Without garbage collection, waste piles up. In these places, the engineered comforts of modern life—clean water, sewage systems, basic safety—are often absent. But for billions, there is no alternative.

These types of settlements are not new. As historians Peter Kellett and Mark Napier noted, "Throughout history, the poor have constructed their dwellings around the urban centers of the rich and powerful."[68] Archaeologists have found evidence in Mesopotamian cities like Brak, classic Mayan cities like Copán, and pre-Incan cities like Chan Chan, where informal housing abutted the walled compounds.[69] As Plato once wrote, "For indeed any city, however small, is in fact divided into two, one the city of the poor, the other of the rich; these are at war with one another."[70]

What is new is the scale. After World War II, urban growth shifted from industrialized nations to poorer nations.[71] London added 93,000 people per year in the 1890s; a century later, Shenzhen added over half a million annually, and Delhi even more. Driven by migration, high birth rates, and modern transport, megacities have expanded at speeds unimaginable in earlier eras.[72]

By 2050, eight of the world's ten largest cities are projected to be in the Global South, with Mumbai expected to top 42 million.[73] The formal systems of housing production have not kept pace. For the urban poor, the options are limited: pay unaffordable rents, endure overcrowded tenements, or build informally. The result is that much of the world's housing has been produced without architects, without plans, without permission.

While governments such as Hong Kong's managed to integrate squatter populations into formal housing systems, many others ignored them—or bulldozed what people built. But in Lima, a different idea emerged. British architect John Turner, working in the *barriadas* in the 1960s, observed that residents were not passive squatters but resourceful builders. Turner argued that housing should not be a finished product delivered from above, but a process shaped from below. "The initiative, ingenuity, perseverance, and hope so evident in the housing action of such a large part of the population ... is, perhaps, the most important lesson an architect or urban planner can get."[74]

This was a radical notion, but not without precedent. Economist Jacob Crane, who led the international office of the US Housing and Home Finance Agency, had observed that the path to homeownership often ran through self-construction. By harnessing "the hard labor of many a homeseeker's own hands," he co-wrote, housing could be made cheaper and more responsive to local needs.[75] His idea—*aided self-help*—meant governments would provide land, sanitation, and materials, while families did the rest.

In the 1970s, Lima embraced this idea at scale with Villa El Salvador. Rather than resisting invasions, the government prepared for them—laying out a grid of streets and plazas and installing basic infrastructure on desert land. People were invited to participate in the planning. Over time, they built better homes, received municipal services, and turned the area into a thriving community. Villa El Salvador now has electricity, transit access, and literacy rates above the national average. It became a model of aided self-help.

Building on that idea, architects introduced the concept of "core housing"—small starter homes with essential services, designed to be expanded over time. Chilean architect Alejandro Aravena's "Half a House" follows this logic. In 2003, to house ninety-one low-income families in Iquique, he provided only a basic structure: foundations, plumbing, electricity, and a few rooms. Residents were left to build the rest. "Instead of producing a tiny house you build half of a good one,"[76] Aravena noted. "And by doing so you're not only making a more efficient use of the scarce resources, but also creating an open system that allows for families to keep on adding in the way they want." This approach stretched the budget further while giving residents the freedom to adapt their homes to their needs. For this innovative approach to informal housing, Aravena was awarded the Pritzker Prize.

A century after Le Corbusier's bold visions, we have come to see them differently. What modernists overlooked in their pursuit of order was that cities thrive on human adaptability. The formal city, with its elaborate building codes and zoning requirements, is

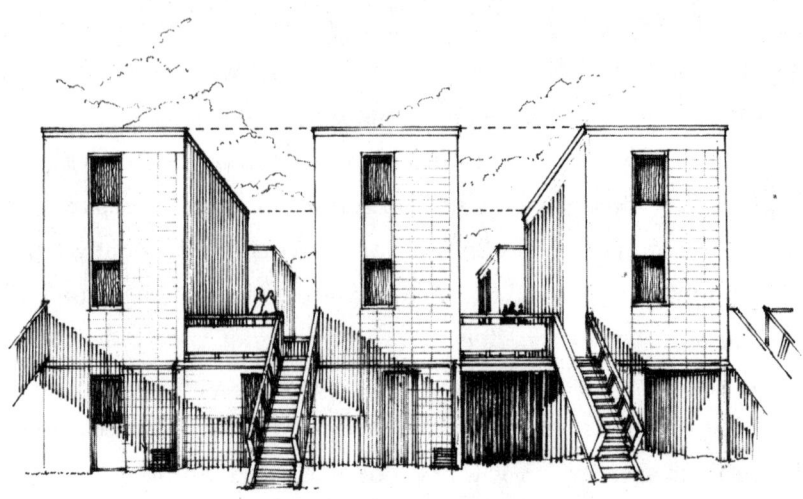

Quinta Monroy (Half a House), Iquique, Chile, Elemental, architects, 2004.

designed to make the built environment safer and more orderly. But it can also increase housing costs, slow down new housing starts, and often prohibit the very flexibility that allows communities to survive. In Lagos or Delhi, street vendors and home-based businesses support families in ways that would be zoned out of existence in New York or Paris.

The informal world challenges a core assumption of modernist planning: that cities must come from the top down. Often, they come from the bottom up. I saw this contrast in Shenzhen, China. I had grown accustomed to the city's skyscrapers, superblocks, and the sweeping geometry of master-planned megaprojects. But on one visit in 2010, what caught my eye were the urban villages. What had once been rural settlements were gradually being engulfed by Shenzhen's explosive growth. Built outside the bounds of zoning codes, these urban villages grew vertically and chaotically. Their "handshake houses"—sometimes just feet apart—were built so close together that neighbors could literally reach across and shake hands from their windows.

Wandering these villages, I often saw dilapidated buildings. But I also noticed everyday ingenuity: rooftop additions, shipping containers turned into workshops, old factories transformed into storefronts. Amid the apparent chaos there ran a clear logic: walkable streets, affordable rents, small stores, and human-scaled public life—elements often missing from the oversized modernist megablocks that characterized much of the city elsewhere. These informal villages offered what many planned communities could not: opportunity.

The urban village of Dafen, for instance, drew thousands of painters. They were even able to rent alleyway wall space to display work to passersby. One artist explained what brought him here: "In my spare time, I began painting, but my landlord complained about the strong smell of paint and quickly evicted me.... I quit the factory job and rented a small space in Dafen village... I picked up my paintbrush again—and now, I've become a painter."[77]

Unlike the perfectly drafted towers and luxury malls, these villages grew organically, offering not only affordable rents and walkable streets but also room to experiment. Though hundreds of urban villages have since been demolished, Shenzhen planners have recognized the value of some, including Dafen, which has become a cultural beacon with galleries.

These incremental housing solutions reflect a deeper history about dwelling. Long before blueprints or zoning codes, people built their own settlements and adapted them as needs changed. The modernist ideal of perfect cities, planned entirely from above, often proved inflexible or inaccessible. In contrast, informal cities continue to provide shelter and livelihoods for millions. As we anticipate billions more urban residents in the coming decades, most of them in lower-income countries, these issues grow more urgent. But, as Alejandro Aravena's "Half a House" demonstrates, we do not always need to choose between formal and informal approaches. The way forward may lie in finding ways to combine the best of both: the safety and infrastructure of formal planning with the adaptability and affordability of incremental growth.

SIX

The Intelligent Envelope

The Passive Haus

On a cold winter day in 1991, in the German city of Darmstadt, something remarkable was happening—or rather, not happening. In a newly built block of four houses, there was no rumble of furnaces, no hiss of radiators, yet the homes remained perfectly comfortable. This was no accident. Physicist Wolfgang Feist had created the first Passive House, a building that would maintain constant indoor temperatures with minimal energy input.

Through thick insulation, airtight construction, and careful orientation to the sun, Feist's home used only one-tenth of the energy of a typical German home.[1] The solution had an elegant simplicity to it. Rather than relying on complex mechanical systems, Feist's design worked with fundamental principles of thermodynamics and natural heat flow. Inside the walls, a thick layer of insulation—nearly a foot deep—wrapped the building like a thermos. Triple-pane windows welcomed sunlight while resisting heat loss. A heat exchanger recovered warmth from outgoing air, transferring it to fresh incoming air, to keep air ventilated without losing energy.

"We have optimal comfort conditions... healthy indoor air and... reduced overall costs because we save a lot of energy," Feist later said. "We have a solution to protect the Earth's atmosphere."[2]

In some ways, this breakthrough was a return to earlier ways of living, prior to mechanical climate solutions. For thousands of years, humans had crafted dwellings that worked with their local climate. But the Industrial Revolution disrupted that, allowing us to defy nature's limits with fossil fuels. We built everywhere, using mechanical systems to overcome any environmental challenge. And we built a lot more. It took nearly all of human history to reach a population of one billion by 1800 AD.[3] Two centuries later, we number more than eight billion. Meanwhile, fossil fuel use has increased by a factor of 1,400 since 1800.

Some have benefited from fossil fuels far more than others. Today, the average American consumes over twenty times more electricity than the average resident of Africa. But carbon pollution knows no borders. As early as 1938, English engineer Guy Callendar observed a relationship between fossil fuel use and global warming: "By fuel combustion, man has added about 150,000 million tons of carbon dioxide to the air during the past half-century... [and] world temperatures have actually increased."[4]

And emissions continue to rise, leading to more intense and frequent floods, fires, and storms. We are now breaching critical limits of our planetary boundaries that are essential to life's balance.[5] Our buildings bear much of the blame. They account for nearly 40 percent of global carbon emissions, mostly from heating and cooling.

Yet our ancestors never had air conditioners or mechanical heating. Instead, they developed remarkably ingenious strategies for staying comfortable, tailored to local climates. Persian architects built towering windcatchers that funneled cool air through entire buildings. The mudbrick towers of Shibam, Yemen—dubbed the Manhattan of the Desert—benefit from their compact urban layout that provides shade and the thermal mass of their walls to moderate temperatures. In ancient Greece, homes were positioned to capture the sun's warmth in winter. On Santorini, whitewashed facades still reflect heat while narrow lanes provide shade in summer.

Such designs emerged from necessity. Before fossil fuels, energy was scarce, and wood was often too precious to burn. So architecture became a form of environmental adaptation. Like wine shaped by the microclimatic conditions of its terroir, buildings reflected their climate.

Industrialization swept that wisdom aside. With mass-produced glass, modern air-conditioning, and cheap energy, buildings no longer had to respect the sun. Mechanical climate control allowed architects to design virtually everything, even when their designs made little climatic sense. An all-glass tower, for instance, makes for an excellent greenhouse, but not so much for human comfort—making air-conditioning a necessity, even in cold climates.

Where architects once holistically conceived of buildings and their climate, they increasingly delegated comfort to HVAC (heating, ventilation, and air-conditioning) consultants. These specialists established standard temperatures based on 1960s empirical models, which were calibrated to the metabolic rate of an average-sized middle-aged man wearing a suit. This has led to temperature settings that leave many women feeling cold[6]—a discrepancy dubbed by *The New York Times* as the "Great Arctic Office Conspiracy."[7]

The reliance on air-conditioning, particularly in densely populated or hot urban areas, created new problems. In Hong Kong, I noticed how my incessantly humming air conditioner moved heat from inside my apartment to the outside. However, with buildings so close to one another, this expelled hot air would find its way back inside. This paradox summarizes our modern predicament. We gained the ability to create our own climate, but at the cost of altering the Earth's climate itself. As global temperatures rise, we need to cool even more, and so the vicious cycle spirals out of control.

The path back toward more environmentally friendly homes began with a series of energy crises. In the 1940s, amid wartime fuel rationing and postwar energy anxieties, architects around the world experimented with solar-oriented design. They created "solar houses" with elongated, south-facing facades, outfitted with large glass panels to capture the low winter sun and roof overhangs precisely calculated to block summer heat. They also experimented with new forms of insulation and techniques for capturing and storing the sun's heat. Solar houses were so in vogue that a glass company sponsored a book, *Your Solar House* (1947), featuring designs by notable architects, such as Louis Kahn.[8]

Even Frank Lloyd Wright was intrigued by passive solar design. In 1948, he applied it masterfully in the Jacobs House—also known as the Solar Hemicycle. Shaped like an arc and shaded by deep southern overhangs, the house minimized solar gain in summer while maximizing winter warmth. To shield the building from chilling Wisconsin winter winds, Wright introduced a sunken garden. It helped form what he called "a ball of dead air." He quipped, "When it's finished, you can stand on the front terrace in a strong wind and light your pipe without any trouble."[9]

This early momentum faded as energy prices fell. But by the mid 1950s, concern over the limits of oil reserves revived interest in energy-conscious homes. Victor and Aladar Olgyay, twin architects and scholars, advanced the concept of "bioclimatic architecture"— building design optimized for environmental conditions. Their most significant contribution was a bioclimatic chart. Comfort,

Solar Hemicycle, Madison, Wisconsin, Frank Lloyd Wright, architect, 1948.

they found, was not a matter of controlling temperature alone. It could be achieved through natural means as well, such as through a breeze from cross ventilation. They offered an alternative to air-conditioning.

The 1970s oil embargo again propelled innovation. In Canada, researchers found that conventional homes leaked vast amounts of heat through poor insulation and air gaps. Their answer was the 1977 Saskatchewan Conservation House. This structure featured near-total airtightness, triple-glazed windows, and super-thick insulation—more than six times the required amount. Harold Orr, the home's lead engineer, later reflected, "We could make a strong argument that we should have put in even more insulation."[10] The project proved that a well-designed building envelope could reduce heating needs by up to 90 percent, even in Canada's harsh climate.

Yet the airtightness that made the home energy-efficient also posed a problem: Without proper ventilation, trapped moisture could lead to stale air, condensation, and mold. The solution: a heat-recovery ventilator. It allowed fresh air to circulate into the building without heat loss. By capturing the heat from outgoing air and transferring it to incoming air, it preserved energy. In doing so, it resolved one of the biggest dilemmas of early energy-efficient design.

Across the Atlantic, Europe had already begun exploring solar design decades earlier, though mostly because sunlight was valued for its health benefits, such as "heliotherapy." The 1933 Athens Charter, primarily written by modernist architect Le Corbusier, declared sunlight one of the "fundamental needs of men." It recommended that "builders must be required to submit a diagram showing that the sun will penetrate each dwelling for a minimum of two hours on the day of the winter solstice, failing which the building permit will be denied."[11]

Decades later, Feist expanded upon these legacies. He embedded hundreds of sensors throughout his Darmstadt home, turning it into a living lab. He covered it with a green roof, drawing inspiration from the sod-covered houses of rural Norway, which had long used vegetation as insulation. The outcome was impressive. The house stayed warm year-round while using less energy than a hair dryer. It remained mold-free, thanks to the heat-recovery ventilator.

This led to the founding of the Passivhaus Institut in 1996, which formalized this method into a rigorous building standard. To gain certification, a structure must pass a "blower door test," in which fans are installed in doors and windows to measure how airtight the building is. The less air is needed to create a pressure difference, the tighter the envelope—revealing how well the building holds its energy.

Today, tens of thousands of certified Passive Houses have been built across the globe—from suburban homes to urban high-rises. At first glance, they may look like any other building. But thermal imaging tells another story: Where typical buildings glow red with lost heat, Passive Houses appear cool blue, holding warmth like thermoses.

However, environmental tradeoffs persist. Some high-performance materials—such as insulation, membranes, and sealants—rely on oil-based foams and synthetic tapes. These may be highly effective at reducing operational carbon during a building's use, but they come with high embodied carbon due to the energy-intensive processes required for their production. Other "green" materials may be less durable or harder to recycle, meaning that addressing one environmental issue can inadvertently create another.

At the same time, cost remains a significant hurdle. In Germany, Passive House construction costs average 5 to 7 percent more than conventional methods.[12] But with enough time, these buildings more than pay for themselves. As energy prices rise, so too does the return on investment. And until recently, owners weren't held responsible for the carbon emissions of their buildings. This may be changing, with cities such as New York passing regulations to fine large buildings that do not meet carbon emission reduction targets.

Skeptics once questioned whether Passive House principles could work in high-rises. Thick insulation and modest window-to-wall ratios seemed incompatible with the demands of multistory commercial architecture. Yet today, Passive House skyscrapers stand in cities from New York to Vienna, proving that the principles can work at any scale.

But even these buildings must face a warming planet. In some areas, ultra-insulated structures may be prone to overheating in the future. These might still require active cooling systems within the next thirty to forty years.[13] This has led to a renewed interest in "adaptive comfort." Research suggests that varying temperatures can promote health and well-being. Prolonged periods outside the prescribed thermal comfort range can even result in higher perceived comfort ratings.[14] This may be due to the body and mind gradually acclimatizing and becoming more tolerant of a wider range of temperatures. Our narrow definition of thermal comfort may need to evolve.

The path forward may come from better building codes and standards. Germany's requirements for building insulation, airtightness, and HVAC systems show how regulatory frameworks can drive innovation. The amount of energy needed from sources like coal, gas, and renewables to power the country has decreased since 1990—even as its economy has grown—thanks in part to advancements in the building sector. "This is primarily the result of improved efficiency,"[15] Feist notes.

As a Dutch American architect practicing in the US, I've experienced different building landscapes. In the Netherlands, thick insulation is often the norm. In the US, however, I've sometimes pried open walls in older renovations to find surprisingly little insulation. Worse are what I call "obese buildings": structures so deep and wide they rely entirely on artificial lighting and cooling, cut off from natural light and air and almost impossible to adapt to new uses.

Climatic design isn't new knowledge. Millennia ago, Mesopotamian builders constructed their homes with open courtyards. These voids funneled breezes and soft light into their rooms, creating comfort without consuming a single watt. The basin of collected rainwater in the Roman atrium was a cooling strategy that also beautified the space. Long before mechanical systems, these builders understood that comfort begins with design.

Yet there is hope. From Passive House construction to simple upgrades in insulation, the solutions already exist. The path forward doesn't require radical reinvention—it requires raising the floor, tightening standards so that even the worst-performing buildings meet meaningful efficiency thresholds. We don't need to choose between good design and environmental performance. The future lies in buildings that embody both.

The Home as Powerplant

In 1883, inventor Charles Fritts covered a selenium plate with gold foil and installed it on a New York City rooftop, making the world's first solar array. His primitive selenium cells converted less than 1 percent of sunlight into electricity—hardly enough to power a light bulb. Yet Fritts was convinced this technology would be transformative. "The current is continuous, constant and of considerable force," he wrote, "and is not affected by heat and should be well suited to many purposes."[16] He boldly predicted, "We may ere long see the photoelectric plate competing, in high efficiency of conversion, with the dynamo electric machine itself," referring to coal-powered electricity plants, like Thomas Edison's Pearl Street Station, built the previous year.

Today, as solar cells approach 30 percent efficiency and the cost of panels has plunged 99 percent since Fritts's time, the vision of buildings as solar power plants is becoming reality. This would turn around architecture's relationship with energy. For millennia, homes consumed energy, first by burning wood, then coal, oil, and gas. Now, with ultraefficient design and solar technology, homes can generate more energy than they consume.

Yet Fritts wasn't the first to dream of solar energy. The earliest written reference to solar energy appears in *The Epic of Gilgamesh* (circa 2100 BC). It described "sacred glass" capturing sunlight to ignite fire on an altar. By 424 BC, Greek accounts mention "burning mirrors" that focused sunlight using crystal lenses. In Aristophanes's *Clouds*, a farmer imagines melting away a debt using a pharmacy-bought lens. "With this stone in the sun," the farmer noted, "I could make all the wax, upon which the words were written, melt."[17]

The Romans took it further, codifying solar access into the sixth-century Justinian Code, protecting the "right to the sun" for *heliocamini* (solar furnace rooms), built with transparent *lapis specularis* in southern walls. This ancient right to solar access persists today in various forms, from Japan's "Right to Sunshine" regulations to London's "Ancient Lights," still inscribed beneath the windows of London's older residential buildings to assert daylight protection.

Scientific understanding of solar power advanced in 1839, when French physicist Edmond Becquerel identified the photovoltaic effect—that light can produce electricity in an electrochemical cell. Fritts built upon this discovery with his rooftop installation, though it was silicon—abundant in Earth's crust as quartz and far more efficient—that eventually overtook his selenium.

In 1954, Bell Labs created the first practical silicon photovoltaic cell. It achieved 6 percent efficiency—up from Fritts's 1 percent. Originally intended to replace failing telephone batteries in humid climates,[18] the cells were hailed by *The New York Times* as "the beginning of a new era... to harness the almost limitless energy of the sun."[19] Yet, solar remained a niche technology for decades, used mostly in satellites and remote industrial sites.

The 1973 oil crisis revived interest in solar energy for everyday homes. At the University of Delaware, Dr. Karl Wolfgang Böer built Solar One, combining passive principles with the first building-integrated photovoltaics (BIPV). "It was built into the roof, not on top of it," he explained,[20] a concept similar to today's solar tiles. However, Böer chose copper sulfide solar cells, partially for their ease of production, topping out at 10 percent efficiency.

Meanwhile, solar *thermal* panels were developed to capture sunlight to heat water. In 1979, they were even installed on the White House. However, they required integration with a building's plumbing and storage tanks, and more frequent maintenance. And unlike photovoltaic systems, they produced only hot water, not electricity. Over time, many of these panels faded from use, outmatched by the broader utility and falling costs of solar photovoltaics. Several of the White House panels ended up as museum artifacts.[21]

Yet it was opposition to a proposed nuclear plant in the 1970s that helped transform Freiburg, Germany, into a hub for solar innovation. It initially galvanized a grassroots sustainability movement, eventually establishing the Fraunhofer Institute for Solar Energy Systems (ISE). By 1992, it built Freiburg's first fully solar-powered home. This experimental dwelling had a broad, semicircular south-facing facade clad in transparent insulation. Its roof, sloped at an ideal angle to capture the sun, was studded with photovoltaic panels, adding to its futuristic aesthetic. Hydrogen tanks stored excess energy, allowing the home to function completely off-grid. It supported a family of four without relying on external utilities.

Local architect Rolf Disch took this idea even further by creating a rotating, circular house, the Heliotrope. "We are entering a new era—an era without chimneys and exhaust pipes,"[22] Disch announced. "The house stands on a swivel base. It can rotate toward the sun. . . . The solar collectors, used as railings, generate heat and store it."

While rotating buildings remain a niche concept—a unique genre called "sunflower architecture"[23]—Disch brought the idea closer to the mainstream with the 2006 Solar Settlement (Solarsiedlung), which included several dozen row homes. Unlike the revolving Heliotrope, these buildings succeed through simple principles. Roofs angled at thirty degrees optimize solar collection, while the roof overhang blocks the southern sun from entering homes.

Initially, the project was controversial. "The real estate people said it wouldn't work,"[24] Disch noted. Germany's feed-in tariff for renewable energy, introduced in 2000, improved the economics, providing guaranteed payments for every kilowatt-hour of electricity fed back into the grid. The project proved that energy-positive buildings could work at neighborhood scale without complex moving parts. Residents were pleased with their up to 90 percent energy savings. Although, many valued the protected environment of the car-free neighborhood just as much as, if not more than, the solar technology itself.

Solar Settlement, Freiburg, Rolf Disch SolarArchitektur, 2006.

While large subsidies have declined, solar power is now cheaper than coal in many countries, with costs plummeting from $300 per watt in 1956 to between $0.20 and $0.50 per watt today—although this is for utility-scale installations, with residential being about $1.00 to $3.00 per watt.[25] Cities worldwide are revising their zoning codes to allow and encourage rooftop photovoltaics, and the use of smaller DIY solar panels is booming.

One emerging trend is the balcony solar system popular in Germany—plug-in panels about the size of a small door that are attached to balcony floors and railings. "I was absolutely thrilled to learn that such a thing even existed, that you can generate your own power and be more independent," one resident said. She had installed the panels herself. "You don't need to drill or hammer anything," she added. "You just hang them from the balcony like wet laundry in Italy."[26]

A single panel costs as little as 200 euros. Apps track energy output with scorecards that are often shared by proud owners, helping the idea of solar energy catch on among neighbors. "I am now completely hooked on how I can produce energy from the sun . . . it has become like taking a drug," said another resident. He is considering upgrading to an entire rooftop array—a common progression. "It's not like I'm saving the world, but I am doing my bit," he said. "It's a good feeling."

Today, solar panels and tiles cover millions of rooftops. Dropping battery costs make solar energy storage increasingly viable. This is particularly promising for underserved informal settlements, which could now leapfrog the fossil fuel infrastructure.

Still, there are many challenges, such as how to balance the mismatch between daytime solar output and evening demand. Some suggest electric vehicles could double as distributed batteries, storing excess solar energy during the day to power homes at night. And the supporting infrastructure must evolve as well. Traditional power grids still follow the same basic model as Thomas Edison's 1882 Pearl Street Station. They operate in a single direction: from plant to outlet. Smart grid technologies promise a two-way network, thanks to new sensors and smart meters. But power grid stability grows fragile as energy flows shift unpredictably, and cybersecurity risks multiply with each new connected device.

Another promising trend is solar glass. Perovskite solar cells are especially attractive for transparent applications. These cells can absorb specific wavelengths for energy purposes, while still allowing visible light to pass. Panasonic is developing inkjet-printed perovskite cells on glass, testing semitransparent panels. However, perovskite cells have shorter lifespans and rely on lead. If panels fail, this poisonous material could enter the environment. Once again, solving one problem risks creating another.

The electricity generated by integrated photovoltaics could even power smart glass itself. Electrochromic panes can shift from transparent to opaque when an electric current passes through them. This allows users to adjust the privacy level but also to save energy through better solar control. Occupants can manually change the glass tint via smartphones or let it automatically adapt to sunlight and glare. While these advancements can improve usability in otherwise over-illuminated spaces, they also add complexity to a previously simple building component. Fortunately, unlike the risk posed by smart doors, it's improbable that a hacker will target your window tint.

With all these technological advances, the tantalizing prospect of transforming buildings from energy consumers to producers is now within reach. Indeed, the International Energy Agency projects photovoltaics could become the largest global source of electricity by 2040. And the sun's immense power allows for a lot more. Capturing just ninety minutes of sunlight hitting Earth's surface could meet our planet's entire annual energy demand.

Yet the allure of seamlessly integrated technology within our built environment carries hidden risks. One such example is Tokyo's iconic 1972 Nakagin Capsule Tower, designed by Kisho Kurokawa of the avant-garde Metabolist architectural movement. Kurokawa envisioned a residential tower composed of individual self-contained capsules—each about a hundred square feet—equipped with the era's

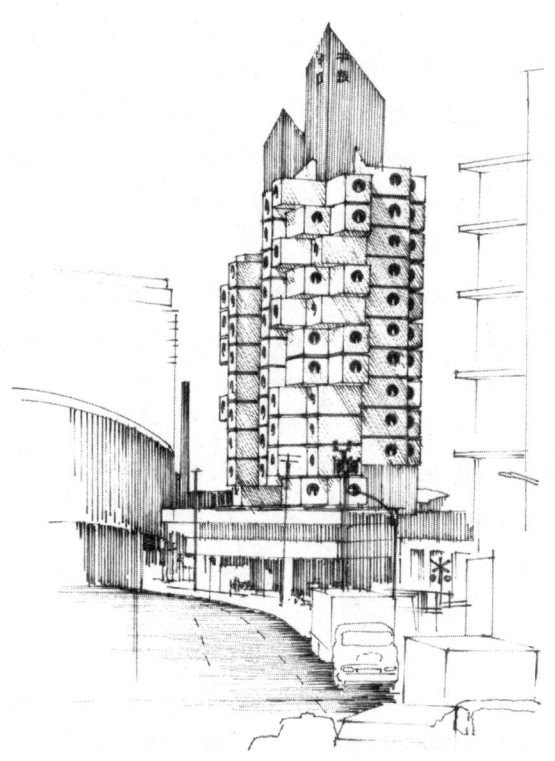

Nakagin Capsule Tower, Tokyo, Kisho Kurokawa, architect, 1972.

cutting-edge technology, such as built-in televisions, reel-to-reel tape players, and dial phones. While the capsules' amenities were designed for periodic replacement, these planned technological updates never happened. Over time, integrated systems became outdated and increasingly difficult to maintain. Hot water stopped working, mold spread, and the building was eventually covered with a protective net to shield passersby from falling debris. Technological obsolescence hastened its decline. It was demolished in 2022.

Solar homes face similar risks. The embodied carbon emissions from mining lithium for batteries and manufacturing solar panels and advanced materials can be significant—sometimes taking years of clean energy production to offset. If panels are not properly installed, they can become fire hazards. On university campuses, I've often seen the aftermath of solar house experiments: smart systems rusting in the rain, creating what amounts to high-tech ruins.

We have traveled far since Fritts's primitive solar array. We can now construct homes that produce more energy than they consume. But our goals should be twofold. We should build homes that conserve and generate energy while remaining structurally robust enough to outlast their technological components. We must ask not just what technology enables but also what it costs—in complexity, vulnerability, and environmental impact. The positive-energy home shows what's possible, but only if we remember that technology should support architecture, not dictate it.

The House That Prints Itself

In 2018, at the South by Southwest festival in Austin, Texas, a massive robotic arm extruded concrete through a nozzle, one layer at a time, and erected a remarkable structure in forty-eight hours. Built by construction technology company ICON, the project became the first permitted 3D-printed house in America. Despite an early setback when the printer collided with a partially constructed wall, the 350-square-foot home proved that automated construction could leap from science fiction into reality.

Within five years, ICON completed dozens of homes across Texas. In East Austin's East 17th Street development, the company's 3D-printed houses, recognizable by their distinctive curved and ribbed walls, sold at market rates, proving that robotic construction could appeal to mainstream buyers. More significantly, ICON proved that 3D printing could slash construction costs. It built America's first 3D-printed homes for the homeless: six 400-square-foot houses. When a *60 Minutes* reporter marveled that "the first person in North America to live in a 3D-printed home was homeless," the resident simply replied, "Yeah, isn't that something."[27]

In a curious case of life imitating art, 3D printing began as fiction in a 1974 issue of *New Scientist*. Chemist David Jones wrote of the amoral scientist Daedalus and his company, DREADCO, using UV light to polymerize liquid monomers into solid objects. "A laser beam aimed in the right direction zig-zags all around the tank to create an interlaced web of fibers," he imagined. "By proper settings of the mirrors anything from a Brillo-pad to a vest can be made ... silent, one-step, infinitely flexible mass production!"[28]

Actualizing these ideas took root in Japan with Hideo Kodama, who in the early 1980s pioneered a method for creating small plastic models by hardening photosensitive resin with UV light, a technique now known as photopolymerization, and "stacking the cross-sectional solidified layers."[29] This was the beginning of additive manufacturing, building objects layer by layer.

Scaling from small objects to entire buildings required fundamentally rethinking the printing process. Dr. Behrokh Khoshnevis at

USC in the 1990s first applied 3D printing to building construction, inspired by a crack in his wall after the 1994 Northridge earthquake.[30] "It occurred to me that a trowel, a very simple tool that has been used for ages, can actually create nice, smooth surfaces," he said. "Yet not a single automated manufacturing process used trowels."

Khoshnevis created a small machine that moved around three axes, similar to other 3D printers. But instead of moving around a beaming laser, it featured a nozzle that squeezed out cement-like material, like toothpaste. His invention of "contour crafting" demonstrated that 3D printing could work at architectural scale. This challenged assumptions about building form itself. Without the need for formwork for traditionally cast concrete, straight walls became optional. "They do not have to look like tract houses, because all you have to change is a computer program,"[31] Khoshnevis said. He was going to liberate the concrete building from the oppression of the rectangular mold.

Technical challenges, funding constraints, and liability concerns slowed progress. It wasn't until 2013 in China that a company claimed to have built ten houses in a single day.[32] In 2021, residents moved into the first 3D printed houses in Eindhoven, the Netherlands. "Project Milestone" includes five printed homes, their organic shapes somewhat reminiscent of the Flintstones' dwellings.

Back in Austin, a resident of one 400-square-foot printed home said: "There are no sharp corners in the house, and the roundness is embracing.... It feels warm, secure, and comforting inside—it's like I'm being hugged by my house."[33] Three-dimensional printing is uniquely suited to incorporate biophilic design principles, such as natural shapes and forms, which can improve psychological well-being and reduce stress. Indeed, organic shapes inherently offer more

3D-printed home, Project Milestone, Eindhoven, Netherlands, Houben & Van Mierlo Architects, 2021.

stability. This partially explains why ancient civilizations favored curvilinear structures before adopting rectangular forms.

Homes produced by 3D printing could offer potential economic advantages as well. ICON reduced 3D printing expenses from $315 per square foot in 2018 to $45 per square foot in 2023.[34] The process cuts many traditional construction steps, from wood-frame assembly to installing drywall. A large machine simply places a one-inch-tall, two-inch-wide layer of material at a time, which hardens in about thirty minutes—enough to hold the next layer. For interior walls, a single two-inch thickness is sufficient. For the building perimeter, two walls are spaced with insulation in between. The exterior wall is then coated with a waterproof paint—no siding is needed.

The precise material placement also has environmental benefits. According to the US Environmental Protection Agency (EPA), constructing a typical single-family home in the United States generates about three tons of waste—enough to fill multiple dumpsters. Three-dimensional printing has the potential to cut this waste by 30 to 60 percent.

On a deeper level, 3D printing signals a shift in the use of materials, one that paradoxically draws inspiration from ancient building practices. It enables a return to local materials, echoing the era before the Industrial Revolution introduced standardized components shipped from afar. Just as the ancient Mesopotamians used locally sourced clay, today's 3D printers can use site-specific materials, even earth itself. But instead of using many hands, they rely on a single robotic arm.

The technology is pushing innovation in sustainable building materials. Researchers and developers are working to reduce the cement content in building mixtures, a material responsible for roughly 5 to 8 percent of global carbon emissions. One solution is 3D printing with hempcrete, a mixture of the woody core of the hemp plant combined with lime and water. This material offers several benefits such as thermal insulation, moisture regulation, and carbon sequestration. However, it has slower curing times and limited structural strength, which make it better suited for non-load-bearing walls or insulation.

In 2018, Italian company WASP (World's Advanced Saving Project) 3D printed a pavilion with a mixture of earth, rice husks, and straw. These materials offer a path to carbon-negative construction by sequestering carbon within their walls. They can create more comfortable living spaces by naturally regulating humidity and temperature. And they could be healthier, avoiding volatile organic compounds and other chemicals that are common in conventional construction materials.

At Virginia Tech, my colleague Brook Kennedy and I experimented with clay as a 3D printing material for interior wall partitions. We suffered common setbacks, such as maintaining the right clay consistency—changes in humidity levels often disrupted print quality. Still, the technology unlocked exciting creative possibilities. Taking advantage of the printer's ability to produce curves without added cost, we began experimenting with patterned surfaces, like ripple effects. Research suggests that humans tend to prefer curved over rectilinear forms,[35] perhaps because they're so common in nature.[36] But beyond aesthetics, these designs offer functional benefits as well. Increased surface texture can improve acoustics and support passive cooling.

Nevertheless, the technology faces fundamental physical constraints. As Kodama, the Japanese inventor, already noted, "It is unable to fabricate a shape which is suspended and is not supported from below."[37] This is particularly true for contour crafting concrete, where each layer is heavy. Without support underneath the print, the layer would collapse. Thus, printing a complete house in one go remains impossible—human workers must still install structural supports for windows and doors during the printing process. Additionally, the layered structure of 3D printed concrete impacts structural performance. There could be voids or weaker adhesion between layers. This could reduce compressive strength by 10 to 25 percent compared to conventional concrete.[38]

There is also the challenge of reconciling old and new building methods. The ribbed surfaces created by layered extrusion often clash with standardized rectangular components—door frames, window fittings, and wall outlets—leaving gaps that are more than aesthetic concerns. They can compromise a building's thermal efficiency by allowing heat to escape.[39]

And even when erecting walls is automated, foundations, roofs, finishes, and utilities can still require months of manual installation. This raises the question whether construction can truly become fully autonomous. Residential construction remains fragmented into many small firms specializing in different segments, unlike car manufacturers for instance. This limits the coordination among design, supply, and construction, and can diminish innovation.[40]

Nevertheless, incremental automation is coming to other parts of the construction process. Companies like Caterpillar and Built Robotics are equipping traditional machinery with autonomous capabilities—excavators, bulldozers, and dump trucks now operate with GPS and lidar guidance. Even robots and humanoids are being developed to handle repetitive time-intensive tasks, from tying rebar to laying bricks.[41] These machines mirror human ways of doing things, which eases their integration into the existing construction industry. This may lead to somewhat bizarre situations of machines operating machines, as researcher Nathan Melenbrink told me, like a "humanoid robot sitting in a forklift pulling levers."

Automated construction could be particularly useful after disasters or in difficult-to-reach areas where conventional construction methods are too costly. We may soon see fully autonomous construction sites, with swarms of robots or even drones working together to erect structures. Just as self-driving vehicles promise safer roads, automated construction could significantly reduce accident risks in an industry notorious for its dangers to human workers.

Yet, automation's reach extends beyond construction sites. Gradually, domestic life itself is becoming automated, reshaping how we live. Digital twins, virtual replicas of buildings, are powered by real-time data from sensors tracking air quality and human activity. Arti-

THE INTELLIGENT ENVELOPE

ficial intelligence then runs simulations in these "mirror worlds" to optimize the real-world in return.

In Busan, South Korea, one experiment hints at the future. Fifty-four families live in free housing, equipped with state-of-the-art technology including cleaning robots. But there's a catch. Their every move is monitored. Residents wear smartwatches tracking everything from their movements to heart rates. "It's mandatory that everyone wears a watch,"[42] said a manager from a company affiliated with the project. "It monitors your body and constantly assesses you."

The residents seem to like the deal. "At 7 a.m. the light in my bedroom automatically comes on, and a speaker says, 'Hi, Song-Lee, good morning. Please stretch your body,'" one resident said. "A few weeks ago, we burned something in the kitchen, and the air filter system just removed it immediately. The system sensed that something was wrong and dealt with it. It's a thinking house."

A century ago, servants catered to households. Today, AI-powered smart homes adjust lighting and temperature, vacuum floors, monitor fridge contents, and may even prepare meals. Yet there is no such thing as a free lunch. These systems could transform the home from a private retreat into a surveillance hub. As homes become increasingly connected, personal data could fuel targeted advertising, with even your fridge panel potentially flashing ads.

Architects are not immune to automation either. As AI analyzes vast datasets of existing blueprints and designs, anyone may soon be able to generate AI-assisted home plans. One day, AI might create digital house models and send them directly to robotic arms to print, bypassing architects and traditional blueprints. The construction process might even get approved by autonomous flying drones, serving as automated building inspectors.

However, automation's true potential may lie beyond our planet. In 2022, ICON partnered with NASA to develop construction systems for the Moon. The lunar environment serves as an ideal testing ground for automated construction. Building permanent bases and launchpads would require transporting materials into space, which is prohibitively expensive. Instead of bringing mortar from Earth, ICON's printers would use lunar regolith—moon dust and rocks—to construct humanity's first off-world habitats. Using lasers, their 3D printer can transform lunar regolith into a hard ceramic-like material that is both durable and radiation resistant.

Just as photovoltaics first powered satellites and now energize humanity, ICON's lunar 3D printing technology has the potential to enhance terrestrial projects through improved automation and new material mixes. "We needed to achieve 100 per cent automation on the Moon," architect Bjarke Ingels said, whose firm was hired to design the project. "And when you reach those levels of automation with those levels of perfection and predictability they become incredibly advantageous on Earth."[43]

The path from a homeless shelter in Austin to a habitat on Mars might seem long, but it's linked by a common thread: the need to build efficiently, using local materials under challenging conditions. Whether addressing Earth's housing crisis or enabling human expansion into the solar system, automated construction technology offers innovative solutions to age-old challenges: building more, with less.

The Street as Living Room

In Tempe, Arizona, a new kind of neighborhood is rewriting the rules of local residential life. Culdesac, one of the first purpose-built car-free communities in the United States, replaces the typical car-oriented sprawl of garages, driveways, and wide roads with narrow paths and shaded plazas. Deliveries and ride shares go to a central drop-off. Residents walk or bike to shops, restaurants, and open spaces. "It's one of the best things we can do for climate, health, happiness, low cost of living, even low cost of government," said Ryan Johnson, a resident and co-founder.[44] One blind resident put it simply, "In order to have a good time or have fun, I do not have to cross the street."

The city granted Culdesac a rare exemption from parking requirements. "Not needing to accommodate spaces for car storage or circulation," said the architect, "opened up the opportunity to focus on creating people-oriented spaces."[45] The buildings, clusters of three-story apartment complexes, are deliberately arranged in an organic pattern to create a series of interconnected outdoor spaces that foster a sense of discovery.

"It reminds me of Mykonos," one resident said. "The walkways, which limit sun and heat exposure, wind between bright-white

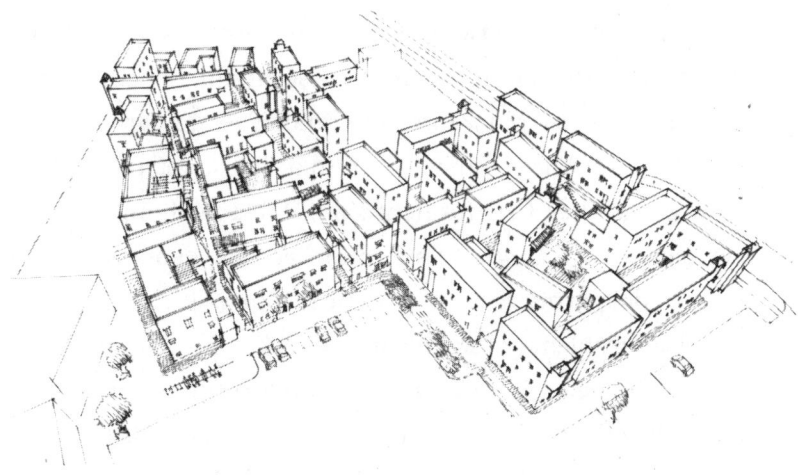

Culdesac, Tempe, Arizona, Opticos Design, 2023.

buildings while color accents make the whole thing feel bright and welcoming." Still, the transition away from car dependency is not absolute—while transit options are within walking distance, many residents still commute by car across the greater Phoenix metropolitan area.[46]

Culdesac is part of a broader shift in how we think about residential living. The most sustainable home is not just energy efficient. It is embedded in a walkable, well-connected community. As urban designer Peter Kindel told me, "People are doing these one-off interesting sustainable buildings, but they're not part of a larger idea. To me, the big moves are compact communities." Comfort is shaped not just by insulation and glazing, but by what lies just beyond the front door.

Normally, we don't think of streets as part of our home. But in many historic cities, streets were extensions of the domestic sphere. When doors open directly onto narrow streets, you are not just in public. You are in someone's lived world.

However, as automobiles flooded streets in the early twentieth century, the relationship between home and street was severed. This was the insight of Donald Appleyard, whose landmark book *Livable Streets* compared three blocks in San Francisco—similar in layout, but with differing traffic volumes. On the quietest street, most neighbors knew each other. One resident said, "I feel my home extends to the whole block."[47] On the most trafficked one, people saw only their building or apartment as their home territory. "It's not a friendly street," another resident noted, "no one offers help." Appleyard found that as traffic increased, residents retreated to the backs of their homes, avoiding the noise. Neighborliness and street pride declined.

The car transformed the home itself as well. Porches and front yards once served as social bridges between private life and the public street. But increasingly homes turned inward. Garage doors dominated front facades. Family life retreated to the backyard. The house became a machine for parking—garages often occupying over 30 percent of the ground floor.

One reason was how cities were being planned. Traffic engineers started to see streets as "pipelines" for cars, optimizing for "throughput"—using the same logic applied to sewer systems. If traffic was the problem, the answer was often to widen roads—even if that meant tearing through entire neighborhoods. Historian Peter Norton reveals how the car industry worked with its own handpicked consultants to reshape public opinion. So-called safety improvements often meant removing trees and reducing or eliminating sidewalks—encouraging faster speeds, not safer streets.[48] As Charles Marohn put it in his book *Confessions of a Recovering Engineer*, "The underlying values of the transportation system are not the American public's values. . . . They are not even human values."[49] He personally experienced the consequences of living on a residential road with "near-highway standards," calling it a "mini-highway."

And as driving enabled distance, zoning policies reinforced it. Shops, schools, and workplaces were zoned apart from homes, making car dependency inevitable. Meanwhile, social and civic life suffered. Political scientist Robert Putnam found that every extra ten minutes of commuting cuts civic engagement by 10 percent. He lamented, "Each generation that has reached adulthood since the 1950s has been less engaged in community affairs than its immediate predecessor."[50] Americans, as he famously argued in *Bowling Alone*, had shifted from team bowling to solitary play.

Our health and environment have paid the price. Cars disproportionately contribute to climate change, with passenger vehicles consuming about four times more energy per passenger-mile than public transit on average,[51] and accounting for roughly 10 percent of global carbon emissions. They also reshaped how we move. Our hunter-gatherer ancestors took roughly 16,000 to 17,000 steps per day.[52] Today, modern Americans average only 5,000. Every extra hour spent driving per day raises the risk of obesity by 6 percent.[53] Obesity brings higher chances of diabetes, stroke, and other illnesses.[54] And every year, road traffic accidents claim more than a million lives.

It took a tragedy to spark a reimagining of the street and its relationship to the home in the Netherlands. In 1982, in the village of Oudehaske, two children were killed by speeding cars. Locals turned to traffic engineer Hans Monderman; instead of installing speed bumps, he removed traffic lights, signs, and curbs.[55] He paved the street in red brick to make it more village-like. Without clear rules, drivers slowed down by over 40 percent[56] and made eye contact with pedestrians—and accidents dropped. Monderman rediscovered that when streets feel like places rather than traffic conduits, drivers behave differently.

Monderman benefited from earlier activism that had already begun challenging car-centric planning. These included 1970s grassroots movements such as the "*Stop de Kindermoord*" (Stop the Child Murder) campaign. Activist Maartje van Putten, a former Dutch politician, recalled, "The streets no longer belonged to the people who lived there, but to huge traffic flows. That made me very angry."[57] This movement gave rise to the *woonerf*, or "living street." First introduced in 1976, these residential streets were designed to prioritize pedestrians and cyclists ahead of cars. With trees, benches, and winding paths, the street becomes more like a shared space, almost an extension of the home itself. Studies found that *woonerfs* were not only safer but also encouraged greater social interaction and children's play.[58] Today, over two million Dutch people live on these streets.

This philosophy spread.[59] In 2009, two mothers in Bristol, England, asked a simple question about their children: "Why aren't they outside?"[60] Their solution—closing their street to traffic for two hours after school—revealed the latent social life buried under traffic. Children poured into the street. Parents began forming connections. With their kids now able to play outside with others, they even began questioning the need to chauffeur children to structured activities.

Today, walkable mixed-use neighborhoods are staging a comeback. Inspired by pre-car urbanism—from Paris's *quartiers* to Barcelona's *manzanas*—districts are being redesigned for people, not cars. In Barcelona, the "superblock" program reroutes cars around nine-block clusters. This opens interior streets for walking, biking, and public space. Since its implementation, pollution levels and traffic accidents have decreased while physical activity has increased. Businesses benefit from more foot traffic. Residents enjoy the new gathering spots and the improved street life. The changes have prevented hundreds of premature deaths annually, mostly due to decreased nitrogen dioxide levels.[61] Residents have reported better sleep, greater tranquility, and improved well-being due to less noise.[62]

In Paris, Mayor Anne Hidalgo promoted the idea of the "15-minute city," where everything residents need is just a short walk or bike ride away, including schools and shops. The concept, advanced by researcher Carlos Moreno, is not quite new[63]—but an older inevitability before the age of the car, a return to what cities once were. In the 1920s, Clarence Perry's "neighborhood unit" envisioned communities where children could walk to school without crossing major roads. But it took the COVID-19 pandemic to make this vision urgent again. As people worked from home and reevaluated their daily commutes, they began prioritizing access to essential services within their own neighborhood.

Under Paris's new plan, streets near schools become "children's streets," closed to traffic during school hours. The city expanded its cycling network, establishing over 600 miles of bike routes. Within a few years, bike trips overtook car trips in Paris, not just within neighborhoods but also linking the poorer outlying neighborhoods (banlieues) to the heart of the metropolis.[64]

Even in American suburbs, where the car-centered home reached its apex, change is underway. Many abandoned malls and underutilized suburban office parks are being retrofitted into walkable mixed-use districts.[65] One example is Santana Row in San Jose, California. Once the site of a strip mall, it is now a mixed-use district with apartments and restaurants centered around walkable tree-lined boulevards. Many of these areas can be transformed rapidly, thanks to large single-owner parcels and how easily asphalt can be removed.

One major reason behind these redevelopments is that developers have begun to embrace the market for walkable streets. Despite covering just about 1 percent of land in major US cities, walkable areas generate a disproportionate 19 percent of the country's GDP.[66] These neighborhoods tend to have higher property values and attract more investment.[67] The rise of tools like Walk Score, which measures how accessible daily needs are by foot, has even made walkability a feature in real estate listings.

One example is the Rosslyn-Ballston corridor in Arlington County, Virginia. It was once a car-dependent suburb with a declining commercial strip. Today, it has become a chain of urban villages centered around new Metro stations. These high-density mixed-use hubs host residential buildings, office spaces, and street-level retail, all linked by walkable sidewalks and bike paths. They attract a new generation of residents—from frustrated commuters escaping Washington traffic to empty nesters looking to downsize. Today, concentrated growth around transit in Arlington yields half the county's tax revenue from just 10 percent of its land.[68]

The health benefits of walkable neighborhoods are compelling as well. Perhaps the most vivid examples are the so-called blue zones, regions known for their residents' exceptional longevity. Walking is a daily habit among centenarians—thanks to built-in physical activity such as gardening and chores and, in some cases, steep terrain that naturally integrates exercise into daily routines. Walkable places also tend to foster innovation, fueled by serendipitous encounters—as seen even in the few walkable areas of Silicon Valley.[69]

Cycling, while riskier in traffic-heavy areas, can extend life expectancy by over a year due to the health benefits of regular exercise.[70] And in terms of efficiency, nothing compares. A study, once referenced by Steve Jobs, ranked the bicycle as the most efficient form of locomotion ever—more so than a condor in flight, when defined by energy used to move a unit of body weight.[71] On my Manhattan commute, weaving past stalled traffic on a shared bike, I like to imagine I am channeling that condor-like efficiency.

In our quest to create better homes, we tend to focus on the technology inside. Superinsulation, heat pumps, and solar panels matter. But many important decisions happen long before the first solar panel goes up—they happen when we design homes to connect with the street.

A century ago, the car promised freedom. But by reshaping our homes around driving, it often confined us instead—making us isolated, inactive, and dependent on fossil fuels. Now, a new kind of freedom is emerging. The freedom to access daily needs without a car, to move under one's own power, and to participate in the social life of the street.

Growing up in a Dutch town, I walked and biked to school freely, experiencing firsthand how *woonerfs* made residential streets into extensions of home life. Each time I visit Amsterdam, I am struck by its lively street culture—children playing, elders strolling, errands sparking conversations. The challenge today is to rekindle that link between home and street, inviting connection and community, one step or pedal stroke at a time.

SEVEN

Nature as Blueprint

From Forest to Frame

Rising 280 feet above the Norwegian countryside, Mjøstårnet might initially seem out of place. But on closer look, the tower, containing apartments, hotel rooms, and offices, connects quite seamlessly to the surrounding forests. Upon its completion in 2019, it became the world's tallest wooden building. Using timber from those very forests, Mjøstårnet offers a glimpse into the future of sustainable construction. It embodies a growing movement to reconnect buildings with bio-based materials such as timber.

For most of history, people built primarily with bio-based materials. Japan, for instance, is renowned for its timber architecture, with its intricate interlocking wooden joints that require no fasteners. In the United States, timber structures range from simple log cabins to lightweight balloon frames, standardized lumber pieces nailed together to quickly create homes. These traditional buildings often possessed qualities we are now coming to appreciate again: natural humidity control, excellent acoustic properties, and a textured aesthetic quality.

Mjøstårnet, Brumunddal, Norway, Voll Arkitekter, 2019.

Until the late twentieth century, engineers generally believed that wooden buildings could reach only six stories because of the inherent limitations of traditional lumber. While strong along the grain, traditional lumber is less reliable perpendicular to it. As a result, it is prone to failure under lateral forces such as wind, which is the dominant force on tall buildings. Compared to conventional materials like steel or concrete, wood lacked the necessary strength for taller structures.

The invention of cross-laminated timber (CLT) in the 1990s, drawing from glued laminated timber (glulam) developed a century earlier, changed this equation. These engineered wood products are made by gluing lumber lamellas—thin, planed boards cut from solid wood—together in precise orientations. CLT is a large panel created from alternating lamella layers set at ninety-degree angles—a similar principle to plywood but with thicker layers. It offers remarkable structural properties with compressive strengths not unlike a concrete slab. Glulam, with boards glued in the same direction, is used to form massive beams with high tensile strength. This makes it ideal for load-bearing columns or beams.

Modern engineered wood construction offers many practical advantages. At just one-fifth the weight of concrete by volume, it enables the use of smaller cranes, lighter foundations, and leaner construction crews. Unlike time-intensive concrete pours, engineered wood can be shaped using fast computer-controlled cutting machines and produced in several standard shapes and sizes. This precision manufacturing enables rapid assembly through prefabrication, where components arrive on site ready to slot together—like giant building blocks. Mjøstårnet's timber supplier and builder likened the process to "doing a Lego assembly with very large pieces. Everything is prefabricated."[1] The result is dramatically faster construction with significantly less material waste.

Perhaps engineered wood's potential to store carbon is its most compelling quality. Trees capture carbon dioxide as they grow, locking it into their wood. When those trees are harvested and turned into engineered wood products, that carbon remains sequestered for the life of the building. By planting new trees to replace those harvested, the carbon footprint of engineered wood can be effectively offset. The 18,000 trees required to construct Mjøstårnet will lock away roughly two thousand tons of carbon dioxide[2]—the equivalent of taking 435 cars off the road for a year. Through sustainable forestry practices, like the Norwegian legal requirement to replace felled trees, this becomes a renewable cycle.

While Mjøstårnet proudly displays a timber facade, many mass timber buildings conceal their wooden structure. This is to protect them from weathering and water damage. Inside, however, it's a different story. Because mass timber doesn't require additional finishes, it can become a defining feature of the interior. Exposed beams and columns create a warm atmosphere that invites inspection and even interaction. Mjøstårnet's builder noted, "People want to touch and smell the wood!"[3] Architect Øystein Elgsaas of Voll Arkitekter, who designed Mjøstårnet, described how the visible wood surfaces evoke "something growing up from the ground—rooted in the earth and reaching for the skies, like a tree."[4]

Wood even offers psychological and physiological benefits. Studies show that exposure to natural materials can lower stress and increase overall occupant satisfaction.[5] Wood's naturally varying grain patterns and color hues create a visual complexity that our brains find inherently engaging yet restful. It also softens harsh sounds and helps maintain speech clarity. Wood and other bio-based materials help regulate humidity and improve indoor air quality. Together, these elements create environments that are fundamentally different from spaces built with synthetic materials.

Understandably, fire safety remains a concern. Some locals called Mjøstårnet "the world's biggest torch." Yet mass timber performs remarkably well in fire. Heavy timber burns slowly, at about 1.5 inches per hour, since the charring that occurs on the surface acts as a protective seal, insulating the material below from oxygen and flame. This charred layer slows down the burn at a predictable rate, giving enough time to evacuate most buildings. In a surprising twist, steel structures face their own fire-related issues: steel becomes dangerously weak and malleable at intense temperatures. After a severe fire, steel-framed buildings often require complete demolition. Meanwhile, damaged mass timber panels can sometimes be replaced. Nevertheless, when left exposed without protective coverings, mass timber can add fuel to a fire, posing evacuation and firefighting risks particularly in high-rises—though this can be mitigated.[6]

Of course, mass timber is not without limitations. Mjøstårnet's architects used concrete in its upper floors to minimize swaying. Wooden columns and walls are often thicker than conventional materials, consuming valuable leasable floor space. However, these limitations primarily impact tall structures. The vast majority of buildings are much smaller and can fully capitalize on timber's advantages. Meanwhile, the adhesives used to bond wood layers have historically contained formaldehyde, a known carcinogen. Recently, however, stricter regulations and consumer demand have driven the adoption of formaldehyde-free adhesives in North America.

Cost is another hurdle. Mjøstårnet was about 11 percent more expensive than a comparable concrete-and-steel building.[7] However, in many cases, mass timber's premium can be partially attributed to production at a smaller scale. At the same time, faster construction times and smaller foundations can offset expenses. And as carbon emissions continue to face stricter regulations in some areas, mass timber can become increasingly economically viable.

Engineered wood's greatest promise lies in its potential to curb the environmental impact of construction. The building sector is a major carbon emitter: according to the World Green Building Council, buildings produce 39 percent of the world's energy-related carbon emissions—28 percent from daily operations and 11 percent from materials and construction. For decades, architects and engineers concentrated on reducing operational energy use, such as heating, cooling, and electricity. But as buildings become more energy efficient, attention has shifted to embodied carbon—the emissions embedded in materials and construction. This is quickly becoming the next frontier in sustainable design.

This has cast a new spotlight on concrete and steel. The production of cement, the key ingredient of concrete, alone accounts for 5 to 8 percent of global carbon dioxide emissions—more than the entire airline industry. If concrete were a country, it would be the third-largest emitter on Earth. Concrete is everywhere. Humanity uses around 30 billion tons annually,[8] the equivalent of more than eight bathtubs of concrete for every person on Earth.

But concrete has earned its place. This remarkable material enabled Roman aqueducts to carry water across valleys, created vast reservoirs through massive dams, and allowed for perfectly straight roads that enable fuel-efficient transportation. Yet, for small- and medium-sized buildings, mass timber offers a highly sustainable alternative, provided it is available locally. Shipping timber panels to the Middle East or North Africa, for instance, could negate the environmental benefits.

Unlike steel and concrete, which depend on energy-intensive extraction and processing—and require increasingly scarce resources like high-quality sand—engineered wood is renewable. With responsible forest management, harvested trees can be continually replenished, ensuring a sustainable supply. For a twenty-story building, timber architect Michael Green estimated, "We'll grow enough wood in North America every thirteen minutes."[9]

Nature offers even faster-growing alternatives. Bamboo, technically a grass, can shoot up to thirty-five inches in a single day. Iron Bamboo, denser and stronger than common bamboo, shows promise as a structural material, though its variability from stalk to stalk makes standardization challenging. Still, Green observes: "Wood is the only material, big material, that I can build with that's already grown by the power of the sun." And even when engineered for uniformity, no two pieces of engineered timber are exactly alike. "Just like snowflakes," Green notes, "no two pieces of wood can ever be the same anywhere on Earth."

Mass timber is just the beginning. As a structural material, it can be a major lever for emissions reduction, since the structure typically accounts for roughly half of a building's embodied carbon. But the potential of bio-based innovation reaches far beyond the frame. Straw bales, hempcrete, and mycelium (the root network of mushrooms) can serve as insulation and wall infill. These materials are often carbon-negative, sequestering more carbon dioxide during growth than they emit in processing.

They are already moving from the laboratory to the construction site. One example is The Phoenix, an affordable housing complex in Oakland, California, which uses mycelium-insulated composite panels with fiberglass cladding for weather protection. By replacing traditional polystyrene foam with mycelium-based insulation, the project addresses the roughly 20 percent of embodied carbon often found in building envelopes.[10]

Bio-based potential extends to finishes. Natural materials like wood, bamboo, cork, and linoleum have proven themselves as renewable, biodegradable alternatives to synthetic flooring. For walls, lime plasters and clay plasters tinted with natural pigments offer low-toxicity, breathable alternatives to conventional coatings.

The foundation of a single-family home can account for a substantial portion of its embodied carbon—sometimes nearly half. Yet even here, there are alternatives to concrete. Suspended timber floors can replace concrete slabs, and local stone can substitute for concrete in piers.

Nevertheless, concrete in buildings won't disappear entirely.

But there are several promising solutions to make it less harmful to the planet. Canadian company CarbonCure Technologies has developed a method to inject captured carbon dioxide into fresh concrete, where it mineralizes and becomes permanently stored, lowering emissions without compromising strength. Some innovators are going further, reimagining concrete entirely through biological processes. Biomason, founded by architect Ginger Krieg Dosier, grows cement. Drawing inspiration from the natural binders found in coral and seashells, the company uses biomineralizing bacteria to produce solid bio-cement tiles. By incubating these bacteria in a mix of urea, calcium, and recycled granite aggregate, engineers can guide the mineralization process—creating a biological building material that resembles stone, without the carbon footprint of conventional cement.[11]

The urgency of these innovations cannot be overstated. With global building volume expected to double by 2050, embodied carbon will continue to climb without intervention, and may even exceed the energy we use to operate our buildings. Without intervention, construction risks becoming one of the most significant unchecked sources of emissions.

Fortunately, policy is beginning to catch up. The International Building Code now allows mass timber structures up to eighteen stories, reversing centuries of restrictions on wood construction imposed after catastrophic fires. Since 2022, the builders of all new public, state-financed buildings in France—the birthplace of reinforced concrete—are encouraged to incorporate at least 50 percent bio-based materials, including timber. Amsterdam has followed suit, requiring that starting in 2025, at least 20 percent of all new housing be built with wood or other renewable materials, as a target. These policies will help accelerate research and development.

The potential for creating construction materials through biological systems is vast, with applications for biotechnology as diverse as nature itself. There are many possibilities to tap into, offered by numerous bacteria, fungi, and fast-growing plants. Janine Benyus, who coined the term biomimicry to describe nature-inspired design solutions, explains, "The organisms that we are surrounded by are trying to do exactly what we're trying to do: they're trying to build their homes, trying to make materials. And when you realize that, the false separation between us and the rest of the natural world starts to dissolve away."[12]

This return to natural materials, both ancient and futuristic, echoes my own journey with wood. In my grandfather's carpentry shop, he would hand me scraps of timber to play with. Wood's natural workability made it the perfect medium for young hands—light enough to lift, yet strong enough to build small tables and chairs. That early experience of building may well have inspired my path to architecture. But my formal architectural education immersed me in concrete and steel—the default materials of modernism. Today, as our profession rediscovers preindustrial material choices, we are beginning to realize that the future may have been growing all around us all along.

Tomorrow's Raw Material

Among Copenhagen's newest housing developments, Resource Rows—an apartment complex with integrated row houses—reveals an unexpected artistry in architectural salvage. Designed by Lendager Arkitekter, its walls form a mesmerizing patchwork of reclaimed three-by-three-foot brick panels. The brick surfaces, some salvaged from an old Carlsberg brewery, are arranged in geometric patterns that evoke haute couture textiles. Architect Anders Lendager noted, "We're recycling 12,000 square meters of building."[13]

Resource Rows, Copenhagen, Lendager Arkitekter, 2019.

These old bricks did not compromise the building's quality. In fact, the weathered bricks lent it gravitas in a neighborhood dominated by new construction. Wood salvaged from shipping crates serves as balcony decking. These strategies substantially reduce the building's environmental footprint. While only 10 percent of the project consists of reused materials, it achieves a 29 percent reduction in carbon emissions.[14]

This project upends the conventional approach to residential construction. It suggests that architecture's future lies not in novel materials, but in the creative reinterpretation of the existing. Any tailor can make a suit from fresh silk or cashmere—but the real challenge is to create beauty from what's already been worn. "It's the availability of the existing building that we have to respect and use no matter what," notes Lendager. He reframes the modernists' mantra—form follows function—into a new ethos: "Form follows availability."[15]

Resource Rows challenges our throwaway culture. In some ways, it is a return to the circular logic of human settlements from the past. Preindustrial buildings were typically made from biodegradable, locally sourced materials—wood, straw, clay—that could be reused or returned safely to the earth. The mud brick structures of Mesopotamia, for instance, as they crumbled, became the foundation for new buildings. They eventually formed earthen mounds—a closed-loop system that endured for thousands of years.

The Romans frequently salvaged and reused more permanent building materials, from marble columns to bronze fixtures. They repurposed material from abandoned structures or those in conquered territories into elements for other buildings, often as decorative elements. They coined a term for this practice, *spolia*, meaning "loot." Reuse extended beyond materials to entire structures. Along Rome's Via Teatro di Marcello, the upper floors of a 2,000-year-old amphitheater have been gradually transformed into apartment buildings—a layered adaptation that began in the Middle Ages and continues today.

The Industrial Revolution shattered this circular sensibility. In its place came an era of energy-intensive nonbiodegradable materials such as concrete, steel, and plastic. These materials promised permanence—and delivered. They were too durable to decompose naturally, yet too complex to reuse. Cement mortar, for example, binds bricks so tightly that disassembly becomes nearly impossible. Mass production made demolition cheaper than careful deconstruction. We began building as if resources were infinite and landfills limitless. Now, the consequences are clear.

Today, humanity extracts 100 billion tons of resources annually—equivalent to dismantling two-thirds of Mount Everest every year.[16] Construction consumes roughly half of that and produces about one-third of the world's total waste.[17] The challenge stems from how modern materials are designed: not for reuse, but for single-use assembly. Reinforced concrete, with its tangled mix of rebar, aggregate, and cement, is difficult to separate. As a result, concrete waste often ends up in landfills—especially in the Global South. In the United States, landfills like Puente Hills near Los Angeles sprawl across 1,300 acres and rise 500 feet—a monument to our failure to close the loop.

We are the only species that extracts from nature without reliably returning resources in usable form. As William McDonough and Michael Braungart note, the body mass of all the ants on the planet exceeds that of all humans. Yet their ecosystems flourish.[18] "Nature doesn't have a design problem. People do." In nature, one species' waste becomes another species' resource—a lesson modern architecture has largely ignored. To address this, they reframe the issue: "We have a materials-in-the-wrong-place problem."[19]

Biodegradable materials like straw and timber offer one path forward, but they aren't enough. Steel and plastic still have roles, particularly where structural strength and durability are paramount. What is needed is life-cycle thinking—from extraction and fabrication to disassembly and reuse. As critic Aaron Betsky argues in his book *Don't Build, Rebuild*, such projects not only promote sustainability but can generate new creative directions, too.

Rebuildable approaches already exist—especially in places where necessity drives innovation.[20] In many informal settlements, materials are reused by design—not glued or welded, but screwed or tied, ready for reassembly when homes need to move. Corrugated metal sheets might serve as walls today, roofs tomorrow. Though born of poverty, these practices reflect a pragmatic circularity that formal architecture is only beginning to discover.

That improvisational wisdom appears in unexpected places. In 1994, architect Shigeru Ban visited Rwandan refugee camps and saw how shelters made from local wood were worsening deforestation. His response—structural tubes made from recycled paper—offered a lightweight, low-cost alternative. Later, after the Kobe earthquake, he built a cathedral from cardboard and more than fifty shelters with cardboard tubes on beer-crate foundations. Intended as temporary, the cathedral stood for a decade. "I don't like waste,"[21] Ban said, pioneering a new genre: paper architecture.

Dutch firm Superuse advances this ethos through "urban mining," sourcing waste materials near project sites. In their Wikado playground, discarded wind turbine blades became sculptural play structures, large enough for children to crawl through. At Villa Wel-

Cardboard shelters, Kobe, Japan, Shigeru Ban Architects, 1995.

peloo, 60 percent of materials were locally salvaged—steel from textile machines, wood from discarded cable reels.

Yet scaling circular construction brings real challenges. Architects and builders face tight deadlines, but salvaged materials demand time to locate and adapt. Even seemingly straightforward types of reuse can be complicated. Shipping containers, for example. Retrofitting them for housing often requires costly modifications, from adding insulation to structural elements, which can make them less practical than building from scratch. And because they were designed for industrial freight, many carry traces of toxic materials, complicating their reuse.

The solution requires rethinking how we construct buildings. One promising strategy is design for deconstruction (DfD). This is a way of designing buildings whose parts can be easily disassembled and reused when the building is no longer needed. It avoids altering materials or using permanent adhesives like glues and mortars. Instead, it favors modular construction and components that can be taken apart and repurposed with minimal damage.

Timber architecture is particularly well-suited to DfD, since it often relies on bolted connections that can be disassembled. While such high-quality timber may cost more upfront, it can pay off in the end through eventual reuse. Steel, too, can be bolted instead of welded. Even facade panels can be built with interlocking joints for swift removal and reuse.

The CIRCL Pavilion in Amsterdam, designed by de Architekten Cie, puts these ideas into practice. It features a modular timber-frame, a facade made of recycled aluminum frames, and an interior with movable walls that can be reconfigured as needs change. Even lighting fixtures and elevators were leased rather than purchased—ensuring their return to the manufacturer for reuse. Every component is tracked with a "digital twin" and material passport, documenting origin, strength, and reuse potential. Just as passports enable people to travel, material passports allow components to "travel" into future buildings.

But challenges remain. There's no global standard for material passports, and the market for secondhand construction materials is still nascent. Supply chains will need new business models—such as leasing materials and implementing take-back schemes—to keep resources circulating through the economy.

It also requires rethinking the architect's role. As Hans Hammink, architect of the CIRCL, explains, it means shifting from designing buildings to stewarding materials. "You have to take care of the materials, not the building," he says. "A building is a collection of materials."[22]

This leads to a new aesthetic—less sleek, more improvised, more honest. In CIRCL, old jeans were upcycled as ceiling insulation. "Something arises that we could not have imagined beforehand," Hammink said. The result is a special type of architecture, with uniquely "unpolished" qualities.[23]

Circular construction is no longer confined to experimental architecture—it's becoming a broader movement. But to truly scale, it requires more than isolated ingenuity. Policy is starting to catch up. France's RE2020 policy requires whole life-cycle carbon calculations for new buildings, aiming for a 30 to 40 percent embodied carbon reduction by 2031. London now requires life-cycle assessments for major developments. California is developing a framework to lower the embodied carbon of construction materials for buildings, with plans to expand these standards to housing.

The logic of circular thinking has long been applied beyond individual buildings. Kalundborg, Denmark, is an eco-industrial park that began to take shape in the 1960s. Factories began to cluster around a power station to take advantage of its waste products—an example of "industrial ecology." Today, waste heat warms about 3,500 nearby homes and a fish farm. Fish sludge becomes fertilizer for local crops. A gypsum byproduct from the power plant feeds a wallboard factory. These symbiotic exchanges increase the efficiency of the entire system. Similar principles are being adapted in residential areas. In drought-prone regions of Australia, gray water from homes irrigates gardens.

All of this brings us back to a foundational idea: The best way to prevent waste is to avoid it through design. The most sustainable building is often the one that already exists. Yet modern architecture often prioritizes optimization over adaptability. Office buildings with expansive floor areas extending far from windows deny natural light to the interior; sprawling parking garages with continuously sloping decks and low clearances become "concrete tombs" as driving patterns change. The better approach is to design for change from the start—with higher ceilings, flexible layouts, and generous daylight—so that buildings can evolve rather than be demolished.

There are countless imaginative examples of adaptive reuse of historic buildings. In Vienna, four giant, century-old gasholders have been transformed into residential complexes, housing hundreds of apartments within their preserved brick cylinders. In the Netherlands, century-old water towers have become private apartments, their tall circular forms now offering residents panoramic views. Even a nineteenth-century military post, Fort Steurgat, has been repurposed into eleven dwellings, its ramparts now sheltering residents. These projects show that even highly specialized structures can find new purpose.

This lesson is especially clear in New York City. In the 1960s, powerful planner Robert Moses proposed razing hundreds of historic buildings in SoHo and the West Village to make way for the Lower Manhattan Expressway. Old buildings were seen as obstacles to progress. But locals, including urbanist Jane Jacobs, saw something different. Artists were already using SoHo's cast-iron warehouses as lofts and studios. These buildings, with their thick walls, high ceilings, and open spaces, were not obsolete. They were infinitely adaptable. The community managed to stop the expressway.

I once lived in an apartment a few blocks from where Jacobs lived in the West Village. The brownstones remain among New York's most beloved homes. In SoHo, the warehouses still thrive. These buildings endure not because of high-tech upgrades. They were well-built and generous in their design from the start.

They remind us that sustainability does not always mean starting fresh. It means building wisely—with care, with adaptability, and with the future in mind. As we face climate change and resource scarcity, we must relearn what our ancestors knew: Everything we construct today becomes the raw material of tomorrow's world.

Built to Endure

While filming a documentary about sustainable living, TV director Marjan de Blok visited a floating event venue and was inspired not just by the venue's environmental features—but by the possibility of creating an entire neighborhood that moved with the water. Despite being told that "building your own neighborhood, it's just impossible,"[24] de Blok rallied a group of like-minded visionaries. In a revitalized industrial canal they created Schoonschip, a community of thirty floating homes with roughly 150 residents. Some homes boast solar-paneled roofs. About half are semi-detached, shared by two households. A houseboat has been transformed into a floating community center, functioning as the heart of this waterborne village.

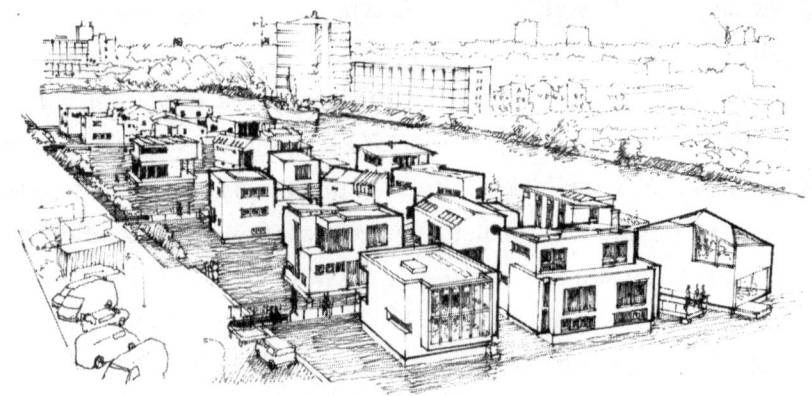

Schoonschip floating neighborhood, Amsterdam,
Space&Matter (master plan), 2019.

"It feels like living at the beach, with the water, the saltiness of the air and the seagulls," de Blok noted. "When it's dark and all the lights in the houses are on, it feels like a set from a film," she said.

Floating homes are not new to Amsterdam, where approximately three thousand registered houseboats dot the canals. Yet Schoonschip stands out, proving that communities can be both resilient and desirable—an increasingly important consideration in an era of climate change. The Netherlands already faces more frequent floods, and projects like Schoonschip show how adaptation can elevate, rather than compromise, quality of life.

These homes reimagine our relationship with water. Anchored to steel poles, they rise and fall with the tides. They require special infrastructure, such as waterproof cables for utilities and pumps for municipal services. But they also bypass a major construction hurdle: no need for extensive groundwork for foundations or sewage systems.

De Blok created a manifesto for Schoonschip, a Dutch maritime term meaning "getting the ship in order." The community committed to building their homes with environmentally friendly products, including bio-composites such as wood fiber for insulation. Informally, the community often cooks for each other or goes swimming together. In summer, children leap straight from bedroom windows into the water. "Living on water is normal for us, which is exactly the point," De Blok said.

Still, life on water has its quirks. Heavy furniture, like a piano, requires bricks as counterweights to balance the home. During storms, the motion is noticeable. Especially on the third floor. "You feel it in your stomach," said Siti Boelen, a Dutch TV producer and resident, who has grown accustomed to it.

Small adjustments aside, this lifestyle offers unique advantages. "Floating homes, you can turn them . . . [or] take them with you," said Sascha Glasl, a resident and the architect for several of the homes. "The flexibility on water is incomparable with the flexibility on land."

Schoonschip's innovation is timely as weather-related disasters surge. Our initial quest for dwelling was to escape from the elements. Yet today, the built environment contributes to roughly 40 percent of carbon emissions. In a cruel irony, our quest for shelter from the storm has led to more storms.

The climate challenge is unprecedented. The Little Ice Age, which drove the Norse from Greenland in the fifteenth century, caused a 0.6°C global temperature drop. Today, we face a projected 2.5°C rise by 2100, with some regions seeing 4°C to 5°C increases. By 2050, climate change could erase about 9 percent from the value of the global housing stock, a $25 trillion loss.[25] Extreme weather events, such as flooding and extended heatwaves, are recurring more frequently and with greater intensity. From forest fires to storms, climate change is increasingly coming to our homes.

Water, in particular, is the great displacer. Rising seas threaten to submerge coastal communities, potentially turning thriving metropolises into modern-day Atlantises. A three-foot rise in sea levels could submerge 17 percent of Bangladesh, displacing 20 million people. Coastal areas remain attractive—offering temperate weather and recreation—yet their continued urbanization compounds the risk. By 2100, rising seas could endanger hundreds of millions of homes.

Many cities have already felt the effects. In 2012, Superstorm Sandy left Lower Manhattan in darkness. Residents were trapped in their apartments without power, unable to use elevators or refrigerators, or even flush their toilets. Five years later, Hurricane Harvey flooded Houston. Today, in the low-lying areas surrounding Miami, king tides flood neighborhoods even on sunny days.

The best defense remains mitigation through cutting carbon emissions. But with the effects of climate change already being felt, some places have no choice but to adapt. The typical approach—evacuations, temporary shelters, insurance payouts—ultimately costs more than proactive measures would. For every dollar spent on disaster prevention, an estimated six dollars in future losses can be saved.[26]

While some cities are building levees and seawalls, others are rethinking how we live with water entirely. From the Mekong Delta to the Amazon Basin, cultures have long adapted by building on stilts or constructing floating homes. Today, these ancient techniques are being updated for the twenty-first century.

Waterstudio, a Dutch architecture firm specializing in floating structures, has designed a floating city project set in a lagoon near Malé, the capital of the Maldives. It will house five thousand homes and feature vertical farms and aquaponic systems, where fish and plants grow together symbiotically. These self-sustaining neighborhoods rest on large modular floating platforms, linked by walkways and anchored to the seabed.

"A floating city should look exactly the same [as] normal cities," said Koen Olthuis, founder of Waterstudio. Therefore, you would see "sandy roads, beautiful, colourful houses. But then if you look under the city, it's floating."[27]

The project is already under construction, with others planned worldwide. Still, questions remain about broader viability—from construction costs and hurricane resistance to concerns about isolating communities. Yet Olthuis is undeterred. He envisions a future on the sea: "We'll see large floating platforms that will move by themselves over the water, rotating with the sun, connecting and disconnecting with each other, like swarms of birds creating shapes in the sky."[28]

Back on land, adaptation takes many forms. Some are surprisingly small-scale but effective. In cities like Antwerp and The Hague, resilience means "rainproofing": replacing impermeable surfaces with community gardens that soak up rain, cool down summer streets, and strengthen neighborhood bonds. Those ties matter. Research shows that social cohesion helps communities bounce back faster, with neighbors pooling resources in times of crisis.[29] Resilience, in other words, is about upgrading individual homes as well as strengthening the community around them.

But while some regions face too much water, others are dealing with too much heat. In the US, extreme heat is the deadliest natural disaster.[30] The danger intensifies when storms knock out power and cooling systems. In the aftermath of Hurricane Ida, this deadly combination proved fatal—without air-conditioning, some New Orleans residents died from overheating in their homes.

That tragedy sparked new thinking. The concept of "passive survivability," developed by resilience advocate Alex Wilson, focuses on making homes livable even when the power grid goes down. Without relying on mechanical systems, it uses natural ventilation and insulation to keep temperatures safe.

Many of these solutions draw on wisdom from the past. Thick walls provide thermal mass. High ceilings and operable windows encourage natural ventilation. Courtyards with plants cool microclimates. But even these time-tested techniques need updating for our warming world. The atrium house—once an icon of Mediterranean passive cooling—is now overheating in places like Italy, prompting architects to add retractable shading and reintroduce evaporative cooling.

In wildfire-prone areas, the challenges shift again. Here, resilience hinges on sealable windows that protect against smoke along with proper ventilation and filtration. Homes could use fire-resistant concrete to withstand extreme heat. The most resilient homes use rainwater harvesting or solar power to become self-sufficient in case utilities go down for extended periods.

Yet sometimes the most resilient strategy is also the hardest—to move away from the risk. For some, this relocation is the only choice. After Hurricane Katrina, more than 300,000 residents—many low-income—left New Orleans, driven out by high rebuilding costs and unaffordable flood insurance. This serves as a stark reminder that climate change disproportionately affects the most vulnerable.

The challenge is to make these solutions accessible. While the wealthy may retreat to fortified off-grid bunkers, such measures are out of reach for most. Without affordability, low-income communities remain the most exposed.

Yet there is hope in human ingenuity. In Freetown, Sierra Leone, where urban heat is becoming intolerable, a low-cost initiative is bringing relief. By covering the roofs of informal homes with mirrored film, they reflect sunlight and lower indoor temperatures by as much as six degrees Celsius.[31] This helps residents stay safe as temperatures rise. "For those who are privileged to get it, there is some amount of relief," one resident said. "[Now] you can have rest in your home."[32]

For me, growing up in the Netherlands meant learning early that living with risk doesn't mean living in fear—it means learning to live with water. With a quarter of the country's land below sea level, Dutch children are taught to swim fully clothed to prepare for the possibility of falling into water. Water is ever-present, in a myriad of rivers and canals. I once worked in a floating office building. Every time I crossed the dock and felt the subtle sway, I was reminded of the water under my workspace.

A visit to Schoonschip left me hopeful. This is more than a stylish update of the houseboat. It is a compelling prototype for water-based living that does not sacrifice comfort. The dock almost feels like a typical residential street, complete with planters and benches and casually parked bikes—with the difference that a canoe is tied alongside the walkway.

Building resilient homes is not just a challenge. It's an opportunity: to create better neighborhoods and to redefine our relationship with the planet we call home.

Where Nature Lives

In many of today's densely populated cities, nature has become a scarce resource. Ho Chi Minh City, a metropolis of ten million, offers on average just four square feet of green space per resident—less than one-tenth the recommended area. Architect Vo Trong Nghia sees this as a design challenge. "We focus on connecting people to nature," he explains. "In Vietnam our cities have so few parks and so little nature."³³

Since founding VTN Architects, Nghia has crafted a signature style that fuses tropical modernism with vernacular wisdom. His 2014 House for Trees reimagines the typical Vietnamese shophouse. Located in a dense lane, the home features large rooms organized around a central courtyard—with the roof of each room doubling as a giant planter for native trees.

This approach challenges the assumption that buildings must be separate from nature. Instead, Nghia blurs the boundaries between inside and out, between the built environment and the living world. The trees he integrates into his designs are not just ornamental. They provide natural cooling, a lesson Nghia learned growing up in a vil-

House for Trees, Ho Chi Minh City, Vietnam, VTN Architects, 2014.

lage without electricity. "I very quickly learned the importance of trees in our environment," he said.

Nghia's work beautifully synthesizes tradition and innovation. It has modernist forms and clean lines. But it also draws from local techniques such as perforated bricks for cross ventilation. It shows that buildings do not necessarily need to rely on mechanical solutions. Natural ventilation and vegetation help keep the interiors cool. "We want to use vernacular and modern design together to help solve the problems of high-density cities like Ho Chi Minh City and Hanoi," Nghia explains. "Vernacular design really harmonizes with nature. It was already there before electricity. It knew how to deal with really hot weather."

His own workspace, dubbed the "urban farming office," serves as a working model of these ideas, with movable planter boxes cascading from the facade. "In our office we have air-conditioning," Nghia says, "but we don't use it. We have greenery all around us, irrigated through a rainwater harvesting system. A water system cools the air."

This integration of living systems into buildings—also known as biophilic design—is more than an environmental strategy. It's a vision of buildings as catalysts for health and well-being. "We want trees, and all-natural materials, to interact with the building," Nghia explains. "To limit water and flooding. To filter the sun. To filter sounds. To improve high-density living."

Research backs this up. In a landmark study, hospital patients recovering from gallbladder surgery healed more quickly and required fewer painkillers when their rooms had views of trees—compared to those whose windows faced a brick wall.[34] Another study found that office workers in spaces with natural elements reported a 15 percent higher well-being score compared to those in offices without natural features.[35] These findings suggest humans have an affinity with nature. As biologist E. O. Wilson argued in his biophilia hypothesis, this may come from millennia of evolution. "For more than 99 percent of human history people have lived in hunter-gatherer bands totally and intimately involved with other organisms," Wilson wrote.[36] "They depended on an exact learned knowledge of crucial aspects of natural history."

The environmental benefits extend beyond the building. Green walls can reduce surface temperatures by up to six degrees Celsius compared to bare concrete on sunny days.[37] They also invite urban biodiversity, attracting insects and birds. Nghia sees this as a feature, not a bug. "When you create a lot of greenery, of course, a lot of insects or birds are coming," he says. "And birds come to eat the insects, creating a really good ecosystem."[38]

Other examples of biophilic design are thriving worldwide. Singapore's Khoo Teck Puat Hospital, completed in 2010, was designed to feel more like a forest than a facility.[39] Gardens and green roofs cover over 40 percent of the site, creating habitats for more than a hundred species of birds, butterflies, and dragonflies. The absence of pesticides and the presence of native host plants even allowed locally endangered butterflies to return.[40] Inside, common spaces allow visitors views of greenery. Patients can garden in therapeutic rooftop plots or enjoy the restorative atmosphere of the central atrium, planted with green walls and a waterfall feature.

Singapore even brands itself as a "Biophilic City in the Garden." Through innovative policies such as Landscaping for Urban Spaces and High-Rises, it requires builders in select zones to incorporate greenery in their projects, whether via sky gardens, green roofs, or living walls. The policy provides bonuses for native plants with a higher leaf area index, which have more environmental benefits.[41] The result is developments like Marina One, whose residential and office towers are centered around a multilevel terraced garden with over 350 plant species and special drainage systems for tropical rainfall.

This movement is spreading globally. England now mandates that most new developments achieve a 10 percent net gain in biodiversity, meaning the site must end up more ecologically vibrant than before, even if that means creating or restoring habitat off-site. Paris is transforming schoolyards into green oases of trees, gardens, and natural water features. And in Utrecht, the Netherlands, the new Rijnvliet neighborhood blurs public and "edible" space—its streets and playgrounds are lined with bushes and trees bearing red currants, plums, and even kiwi berries and persimmons.

While such innovations are inspiring, some more ambitious projects reveal the complexities of urban greening. Bosco Verticale in Milan, designed by Stefano Boeri, has gotten global attention for its duo of forested towers, the tallest rising twenty-six stories. About 800 trees and 14,000 plants grow on cantilevered balconies. The towers reduce air pollution and create microclimates that support a surprising diversity of birds and pollinators. However, the buildings required extensive structural steel to support the weight of the planters, increasing their construction footprint. They also consume nearly four million gallons of water annually, for a relatively small number of luxury condo dwellers—though the buildings mitigate this impact by recycling on-site gray water. Maintenance is intensive. Teams of "flying gardeners" rappel down the facades for pruning and pest control. Critics argue it is more spectacle than solution. They question the livability challenges of so much vegetation, from potential pests to high humidity levels.

The solution to urban sustainability should go beyond simply adding greenery. As data scientist Hannah Ritchie notes, we tend to have a "natural fallacy": "Things that seem more grounded in 'natu-

Bosco Verticale, Milan, Stefano Boeri Architetti, 2014.

ral' properties must be better for us, where natural equals good, and unnatural equals bad."[42] In fact, dense urban living can be far more sustainable, leaving more land elsewhere for wilderness and biodiversity. The challenge lies in making dense cities more hospitable to other species while maintaining their efficiency advantages.

Yet this kind of hospitality is still rare. Most urban design continues to prioritize human convenience over the survival of wildlife. Glass skyscrapers are lethal to birds. Up to a billion perish annually in the US alone from collisions with reflective or transparent windows. In response, cities like New York have introduced bird-friendly building mandates that require patterned glass, UV coatings, or other visual cues to help birds detect and avoid these invisible barriers. At ground level, wildlife corridors and elevated parks are being built in many cities to help animals safely cross highways, reconnecting fragmented habitats into more functional urban ecosystems.

Traditional roofing is another problem. Asphalt shingles degrade from ultraviolet radiation and the thermal shocks from wild temperature swings. And since they absorb radiation, they also add to the buildings' cooling bills. Green roofs, by contrast, offer a living layer that insulates, filters stormwater, and provides habitat. More cities are adopting ordinances or offering incentives to encourage them.

Hard surfaces like asphalt roads and parking lots prevent water from soaking into the ground, causing runoff and pollution. They often have buried streams under them, which can lead to flooding. Cities are now responding with native landscaping and bioswales—vegetated trenches that capture and filter rainwater. One inspiring example of restoration comes from Seoul, which removed an elevated highway to restore the buried Cheonggyecheon Stream. Nearby residents once faced double the likelihood to suffer from respiratory illness compared to other people in Seoul. Today, they have access to a lush linear park that reduces flooding, cools temperatures up to six degrees Celsius, and absorbs air pollution.[43]

Together, these examples suggest a powerful idea. Cities do not need to always degrade nature. They can help regenerate it.

This requires rethinking the false dichotomy between nature and civilization. Nature is not the untouched Eden we often imagine. "I loathe that word 'pristine,'" says Indigenous ecologist Kawika Winter. "There have been no pristine systems on this planet for thousands of years. Humans and nature can co-exist, and both can thrive."[44] Research supports this perspective: Many of the world's most biodiverse "wild" landscapes were not preserved in isolation but actively shaped by centuries of human activity. This challenges the assumption that human presence always degrades ecosystems.

The implications are profound. Humans have been altering at least three-quarters of the planet's land for the past 12,000 years.[45] Today, humans and our domesticated species such as livestock account for 96 percent of Earth's mammal biomass. The question then becomes: How can we steward and regenerate the novel, human-influenced ecosystems that now dominate our planet?

The answer lies in a combination of active and passive approaches. One approach is to allow nature to regenerate through the process of "rewilding." In the Netherlands, the Oostvaardersplassen demonstrates this potential. What began as abandoned industrial land evolved into a thriving wetland ecosystem supporting wild horses, deer, and hundreds of bird species—with minimal human management. This philosophy is beginning to catch on in cities as well. In Paris, meticulously pruned street trees give way to wilder, more ecologically valuable species. These projects show that we do not always need to choose between human settlement and "wildness." In this worldview, we are part of nature, rather than removed from it.

We already possess the tools to build new types of living systems that unite human ingenuity with nature's regenerative power. For millennia, we have shaped ecosystems—from terracing hillsides for agriculture to domesticating plants and animals. Now we must consciously harness this capability to restore rather than degrade the living systems we depend on. Reimagining our dwellings in partnership with nature is a part of this challenge.

This shift is as much philosophical as it is technical. It demands respect for the natural world often absent from modernist design thinking. It also invites creativity. Nghia's work shows that every balcony can be a garden, every rooftop an opportunity for biodiversity.

At its heart, this approach reconceives the purpose of a home, from a fortress against nature to a thoughtfully designed part of it. We have a remarkable and sometimes terrifying power to shape our surroundings. The challenge is to channel this ability not solely toward a narrow definition of human comfort—often achieved at the expense of everything else—but toward the flourishing of our world.

ACKNOWLEDGMENTS

Writing this book, like building a house, has been a collaborative effort, shaped by many skilled hands. I'm deeply grateful to Matt Weiland at W. W. Norton for believing in this project, his enthusiastic support, and keen editorial eye, and to Yumiko Gonzalez Rios for guiding it to completion. Ira Brodsky provided meticulous copyediting. I thank my literary agent, Jud Laghi, for helping shape the book's framework. Pietro Calogero and Boris Tefsen deserve special recognition for their many readings and constructive comments. The graceful pen drawings are by architect and colleague Dave Dugas, whose archaeological interests brought additional depth to every illustration.

This book is built upon the work of countless researchers who have excavated ancient sites and combed through archives, and I am deeply grateful to them all. Several of these scholars were generous enough to correspond with me directly, sharing their expertise. Matt Pope illuminated the complexities of prehistoric settlements, while William Hafford offered many insights on Mesopotamian architecture and building practices. Margarete van Ess, Sebastian Hageneuer, and Sarah Graff further enriched my understanding of the Near East's early construction.

From the world of architectural scholarship, Gwendolyn Wright and Greig Crysler offered invaluable perspectives. I thank Tom

Vanderbilt for his example in writing with public resonance. Technical insights came from Andrew McCoy, Bill Braham, Ali Malkawi, Peter Kindel, Nathan Melenbrink, Paul Clemens Bart, and Jason Carlow.

This work benefited from a supportive academic ecosystem—my Hunter College colleagues Nicholas Dagen Bloom, Joseph Viteritti, Victoria Johnson, John Chin, Laura Wolf-Powers, Mehdi Heris, Jill Simone Gross, and Lily Baum Pollans, as well as Jim Bassett and Brook Kennedy at Virginia Tech.

My understanding of architecture was shaped early by my classics teachers, particularly Rob Tuizenga, who revealed connections between ancient texts and buildings. This foundation deepened at UC Berkeley through exposure to the intellectual legacy of Spiro Kostof, which taught me to look past grand monuments to the entire built landscape.

The idea for this book first took shape years ago during a transatlantic flight with my wife, Rebecca. It evolved over time, especially during the COVID years, when our extended time at home prompted deeper reflection on the spaces we inhabit and how they shape our lives. Above all, I'm deeply grateful to Rebecca and to our daughters, Maxine and Natalie, who remind me daily why home matters.

Finally, I thank you—the reader—for picking up this book. I hope these pages deepen your curiosity about the built environment and inspire you to look anew at the houses around you. May the homes you create bring beauty to this world.

NOTES

INTRODUCTION: Dwelling on Earth

1. Phillippa Carnemolla and Vivienne Skinner, "Outcomes Associated with Providing Secure, Stable, and Permanent Housing for People Who Have Been Homeless: An International Scoping Review," *Journal of Planning Literature* 36, no. 4 (2021): 508–25.
2. Lawrence D. Frank et al., "Obesity Relationships with Community Design, Physical Activity, and Time Spent in Cars," *American Journal of Preventive Medicine* 27, no. 2 (2004): 87–96; Margaret C. Weiss et al., "Transportation-related Environmental Mixtures and Diabetes Prevalence and Control in Urban/Metropolitan Counties in the United States," *Journal of the Endocrine Society* 7, no. 6 (2023).
3. Prospective Studies Collaboration, "Body-Mass Index and Cause-Specific Mortality in 900,000 Adults: Collaborative Analyses of 57 Prospective Studies," *Lancet* 373, no. 9669 (2009): 1083–96.
4. Rohan Nagare et al., "Access to Daylight at Home Improves Circadian Alignment, Sleep, and Mental Health in Healthy Adults: A Crossover Study," *International Journal of Environmental Research and Public Health* 18, no. 19 (2021): 9980.
5. Edward Glaeser and Bruce Sacerdote, "The Social Consequences of Housing," *Journal of Housing Economics* 9, nos. 1–2 (2000): 1–23.
6. Sophie Paddock et al., "Evaluating the Cardiovascular Benefits of Stair Climbing: A Systematic Review and Meta-Analysis," *European Journal of Preventive Cardiology* 31 (2024).
7. Mei Chen et al., "Residential Exposure to Pesticide During Childhood and Childhood Cancers: A Meta-Analysis," *Pediatrics* 136, no. 4 (2015): 719–29; Marcia Nishioka et al., "Distribution of 2,4-D in Air and on Surfaces Inside Residences after Lawn Applications: Comparing Exposure Estimates from Various Media for Young Children," *Environmental Health Perspectives* 109, no. 11 (2001): 1185–91.

8. Rohan Nagare et al., "Access to Daylight at Home," 9980.
9. Jeanne Arnold et al., *Life at Home in the Twenty-First Century: Thirty-Two Families Open Their Doors* (Cotsen Institute of Archaeology Press, 2012).
10. Kirsten Weir, "Nurtured by Nature," *Monitor on Psychology* 51, no. 3 (2020): 50–56.
11. Gaston Bachelard, *The Poetics of Space* (Penguin, 2014).
12. Mike Hansell, *Built by Animals: The Natural History of Animal Architecture* (Oxford University Press, 2007), 93.
13. Kamaljit Singh et al., "The Architectural Design of Smart Ventilation and Drainage Systems in Termite Nests," *Science Advances* 5, no. 3 (2019).
14. Priyadarshi Shukla et al., "Climate Change 2022: Mitigation of Climate Change," *Contribution of Working Group III to the Sixth Assessment Report of the Intergovernmental Panel on Climate Change* (2022).
15. Thibaut Abergel et al., *Global Status Report 2017* (International Energy Agency for the Global Alliance for Buildings and Construction, 2017).
16. Maria Moura et al., "120 Years of US Residential Housing Stock and Floor Space," *PLOS One* 10, no. 8 (2015): e0134135.
17. Noel Boaz and Russell Ciochon, *Dragon Bone Hill: An Ice-Age Saga of Homo erectus* (Oxford University Press, 2004).
18. Marc-Antoine Laugier, *An Essay on Architecture*, trans. Wolfgang Herrmann (Hennessey & Ingalls, 1977).
19. Paola Villa, *Terra Amata and the Middle Pleistocene Archaeological Record of Southern France*, University of California Publications in Anthropology 13 (University of California Press, 1983).
20. Richard B. Lee, *The !Kung Bushmen of Botswana* (Holt, Rinehart and Winston, 1972).
21. Herodotus, *The History of Herodotus*, ed. and ann. George Rawlinson (John Murray, 1858).
22. Spiro Kostof et al., *A History of Architecture: Settings and Rituals* (Oxford University Press, 1995).
23. Luís Bettencourt et al., "Growth, Innovation, Scaling, and the Pace of Life in Cities," *Proceedings of the National Academy of Sciences* 104, no. 17 (2007): 7301–6.
24. Luís Bettencourt et al., "Growth, Innovation, Scaling," 7301–6.
25. Enrico Berkes and Ruben Gaetani, "The Geography of Unconventional Innovation," *Economic Journal* 131, no. 636 (2021): 1466–1514.
26. Amos Rapoport, *House Form and Culture* (Prentice-Hall, 1969).

ONE: A Permanent Place

1. Marc-Antoine Laugier, *An Essay on Architecture*, trans. Wolfgang Herrmann (Hennessey & Ingalls, 1977).
2. Colin Groves and J. Sabater Pi, "From Ape's Nest to Human Fix-Point," *Man* (1985): 22–47.

NOTES

3. Joseph Stromberg, "Learn the Secrets of Ape's Sleeping Habits," *Smithsonian*, 15 April 2015.
4. Amy Clark et al., "Domestic Spaces as Crucibles of Paleolithic Culture: An Archaeological Perspective," *Journal of Human Evolution* 172 (2022): 103266.
5. Steven Kuhn and Mary Stiner, "Hearth and Home in the Middle Pleistocene," *Journal of Anthropological Research* 75, no. 3 (2019): 305–27.
6. Clark et al., "Domestic Spaces as Crucibles of Paleolithic Culture," 103266.
7. Kuhn and Stiner, "Hearth and Home in the Middle Pleistocene," 305–27.
8. Tim Fox et al., "Engineering the Anthropocene: Scalable Social Networks and Resilience Building in Human Evolutionary Timescales," *Anthropocene Review* 4, no. 3 (2017): 199–215.
9. Lawrence Barham et al., "Evidence for the Earliest Structural Use of Wood at Least 476,000 Years Ago," *Nature* 622, no. 7981 (2023): 107–11.
10. Clark et al., "Domestic Spaces as Crucibles of Paleolithic Culture," 103266.
11. Desmond Clark and John Harris, "Fire and Its Roles in Early Hominid Lifeways," *African Archaeological Review* 3, no. 1 (1985): 3–27.
12. Based on Y. González and E. Baquedano, illustration re-creating the Abrigo de Navalmaíllo where Neanderthals had their campsite, in Enrique Baquedano, "Neanderthals: More Sapiens Than We Ever Thought!," Springer Nature: Research Communities, 26 February 2023.
13. Kuhn and Stiner, "Hearth and Home in the Middle Pleistocene," 305–27; subsequent information and quotation from "Hearth and Home in the Middle Pleistocene," 305–27.
14. Rebecca Chisholm et al., "Controlled Fire Use in Early Humans Might Have Triggered the Evolutionary Emergence of Tuberculosis," *Proceedings of the National Academy of Sciences* 113, no. 32 (2016): 9051–56.
15. Jesse Roth, "Evolutionary Speculation About Tuberculosis and the Metabolic and Inflammatory Processes of Obesity," *JAMA* 301, no. 24 (2009): 2586–88.
16. Yafit Kedar et al., "The Influence of Smoke Density on Hearth Location and Activity Areas at Lower Paleolithic Lazaret Cave, France," *Scientific Reports* 12, no. 1 (2022): 1469.
17. Jessica Thompson et al., "Early Humans Used Fire to Permanently Change the Landscape," *PBS NewsHour*, 7 May 2021.
18. James Scott, *Against the Grain: A Deep History of the Earliest States* (Yale University Press, 2017).
19. Lyn Wadley et al., "Fire and Grass-Bedding Construction 200 Thousand Years Ago at Border Cave, South Africa," *Science* 369, no. 6505 (2020): 863–66.
20. Polly Wiessner, "Embers of Society: Firelight Talk Among the Ju/'hoansi Bushmen," *Proceedings of the National Academy of Sciences* 111, no. 39 (2014): 14027–35.
21. J. Jaubert et al., "Early Neanderthal Constructions Deep in Bruniquel Cave in Southwestern France," *Nature* 534 (2016): 111–14.

22. Julien Riel-Salvatore et al., "A Spatial Analysis of the Late Mousterian Levels of Riparo Bombrini (Balzi Rossi, Italy)," *Canadian Journal of Archaeology* 37, no. 1 (2013): 70–92.
23. Based on Pascale Galibert, *restitution hypothétique de La Folie*, 2009, in "*Le quotidien des chasseurs-cueilleurs nomades néandertaliens*" [The everyday life of nomadic Neanderthal hunter-gatherers], Muséum National d'Histoire Naturelle, 5 April 2019.
24. Amy Clark, "Time and Space in the Middle Paleolithic: Spatial Structure and Occupation Dynamics of Seven Open-Air Sites," *Evolutionary Anthropology: Issues, News, and Reviews* 25, no. 3 (2016): 153–63.
25. Randall White et al., "Context and Dating of Aurignacian Vulvar Representations from Abri Castanet, France," *Proceedings of the National Academy of Sciences* 109, no. 22 (2012): 8450–55.
26. Mikhail Gladkih et al., "Mammoth-Bone Dwellings on the Russian Plain," *Scientific American* 251, no. 5 (1984): 164–75.
27. Steven Mithen, *After the Ice: A Global Human History, 20,000–5000 BC* (Harvard University Press, 2006).
28. John Yellen, "Behavioural and Taphonomic Patterning at Katanda 9: A Middle Stone Age Site, Kivu Province, Zaire," *Journal of Archaeological Science* 23, no. 6 (1996): 915–32.
29. Dani Nadel et al., "Stone Age Hut in Israel Yields World's Oldest Evidence of Bedding," *Proceedings of the National Academy of Sciences* 101, no. 17 (2004): 6821–26.
30. John Yellen, "Settlement Patterns of the !Kung: An Archaeological Perspective," in *Kalahari Hunter-Gatherers: Studies of the !Kung San and Their Neighbors*, ed. Richard B. Lee and Irven DeVore (Harvard University Press, 1976), 47–72.
31. Based on Sharon Bar-Yehuda, reconstructed 19,000-year-old hut from Ohalo II [Locus I], based on identified botanical remains and comparisons to ethnographic examples, in Dani Nadel and Ella Werker, "The Oldest Ever Brush Hut Plant Remains from Ohalo II, Jordan Valley, Israel (19,000 BP)," *Antiquity* 73, no. 282 (1999): 755–64.
32. Based on figure in Gil Haklay and Avi Gopher, "A New Look at Shelter 131/51 in the Natufian Site of Eynan (Ain-Mallaha), Israel," *PLOS One* 10, no. 7 (2015): e0130121.
33. Ian Tattersall, "In Search of the First Human Home," *Nautilus*, 2 December 2013.
34. Nicolas Samuelian et al., "Final Natufian Architecture at 'Eynan ('Ain Mallaha): Approaching the Diversity Behind Uniformity," in *Domesticating Space: Construction, Community, and Cosmology in the Late Prehistoric Near East*, ed. E. B. Banning and Michael Chazan (Berlin Ex Oriente, 2006), 35–42.
35. Olivier Aurenche et al., "Theoretical Archaeology and Rhetorical Archaeology: Toward a 'History' of Architecture in the Ancient Near East," in *Representations*

in Archaeology, ed. Jean-Claude Gardin and Christopher S. Peeples (Indiana University Press 1992), 196–204.
36. Gil Haklay and Avi Gopher, "A New Look at Shelter 131/51 in the Natufian Site of Eynan (Ain-Mallaha), Israel," *PLOS One* 10, no. 7 (2015): e0130121.
37. Aurenche et al., "Theoretical Archaeology and Rhetorical Archaeology," 196–204.
38. Michael Balter, "The Tangled Roots of Agriculture," *Science* 327, no. 5964 (2010): 404–6.
39. Thomas Rocek and Ofer Bar-Yosef, eds., *Seasonality and Sedentism: Archaeological Perspectives from Old and New World Sites* (Peabody Museum Press, 1998).
40. Lior Weissbrod et al., "Origins of House Mice in Ecological Niches Created by Settled Hunter-Gatherers in the Levant 15,000 Years Ago," *Proceedings of the National Academy of Sciences* 114, no. 16 (2017): 4099–104.
41. Mithen, *After the Ice*.
42. Ian Kuijt and Bill Finlayson, "Evidence for Food Storage and Predomestication Granaries 11,000 Years Ago in the Jordan Valley," *Proceedings of the National Academy of Sciences* 106, no. 27 (2009): 10966–70.
43. Erle Ellis et al., "People Have Shaped Most of Terrestrial Nature for at Least 12,000 Years," *Proceedings of the National Academy of Sciences* 118, no. 17 (2021): e2023483118.
44. Patricia Gilman et al., "Substantial Structures, Few People, and the Question of Early Villages in the Mimbres Region of the North American Southwest," in *Becoming Villagers: Comparing Early Village Societies*, ed. Matthew Bandy and Jake Fox (University of Arizona Press, 2010), 67.
45. Carol Cope, "Gazelle Hunting Strategies in the Southern Levant," in *The Natufian Culture in the Levant*, ed. Ofer Bar-Yosef and François Raymond Valla (International Monographs in Prehistory, 1991), 341–57.
46. Spiro Kostof et al., *The History of Architecture: Settings and Rituals* (Oxford University Press, 1995).
47. Edward Banning, "Housing Neolithic Farmers," *Near Eastern Archaeology* 66, nos. 1–2 (2003): 4–21.
48. Howard Michael Hecker, "The Faunal Analysis of the Primary Food Animals from Pre-Pottery Neolithic Beidha (Jordan)" (PhD thesis, Columbia University, 1975).
49. Brian Byrd and Diana Kirkbride-Helbæk, "Early Village Life at Beidha, Jordan: Neolithic Spatial Organization and Vernacular Architecture, the Excavations of Mrs Diana Kirkbride-Helbæk," in *British Academy Monographs in Archaeology; Beidha Excavations* (Oxford University Press, 2005).
50. Ofer Bar-Yosef, "The Walls of Jericho: An Alternative Interpretation," *Current Anthropology* 27, no. 2 (1986): 157–62.
51. Arieh O'Sullivan, "World's First Skyscraper Sought to Intimidate Masses," *Jerusalem Post*, 14 February 2011.

52. Marcin Białowarczuk, "Early Neolithic Wall Construction Techniques in the Light of Ethnographical Observations on the Architecture of the Modern Syrian Village of Qaramel," *Polish Archaeology in the Mediterranean* 19 (2010): 586–600.
53. Aurenche et al., "Theoretical Archaeology and Rhetorical Archaeology," 196–204.
54. Kent Flannery, "The Origins of the Village Revisited: From Nuclear to Extended Households," *American Antiquity* 67, no. 3 (2002): 417–33.
55. Elizabeth Cashdan, "Egalitarianism Among Hunters and Gatherers," *American Anthropologist* 82, no. 1 (1980): 116–20.
56. Polly Wiessner, "Beyond Willow Smoke and Dogs' Tails: A Comment on Binford's Analysis of Hunter-Gatherer Settlement Systems," *American Antiquity* 47, no. 1 (1982): 173.
57. Peter Wilson, *The Domestication of the Human Species* (Yale University Press, 1991).
58. V. Gordon Childe, "The Urban Revolution," *Town Planning Review* 21, no. 1 (1950): 3.
59. Greger Larson et al., "Current Perspectives and the Future of Domestication Studies," *Proceedings of the National Academy of Sciences* 111, no. 17 (2014): 6139–46.
60. Jacques Blondel, "The 'Design' of Mediterranean Landscapes: A Millennial Story of Humans and Ecological Systems During the Historic Period," *Human Ecology* 34 (2006): 713–29.
61. Brian Hayden, "Nimrods, Piscators, Pluckers, and Planters: The Emergence of Food Production," *Journal of Anthropological Archaeology* 9, no. 1 (1990): 31–69.
62. Douglas Comer, "Environmental History at an Early Prehistoric Village: An Application of Cultural Site Analysis at Beidha, in Southern Jordan," *Journal of GIS in Archaeology* 1 (2003): 103–15.
63. Pierre Deffontaines, "Géographie et religions," *Géographie humaine* 21 (1948): 77.
64. Jeremiah 35:6–7 (New International Version).
65. James Mellaart, *Çatal Hüyük: A Neolithic Town in Anatolia* (Thames and Hudson, 1967), 27; subsequent quotations from *Çatal Hüyük*, 27.
66. Ian Kuijt and Arkadiusz Marciniak, "How Many People Lived in the World's Earliest Villages? Reconsidering Community Size and Population Pressure at Neolithic Çatalhöyük," *Journal of Anthropological Archaeology* 74 (2024): 101573.
67. Based on *The City of Catal Huyuk*, De Agostini Picture Library, Scala Archives.
68. Theya Molleson, "Times of Stress at Catalhoyuk," *BAR International Series* 1603 (2007): 140.
69. Kamilla Pawłowska, "The Smells of Neolithic Çatalhöyük, Turkey: Time and Space of Human Activity," *Journal of Anthropological Archaeology* 36 (2014): 1–11.
70. Clark Spencer Larsen et al., "Bioarchaeology of Neolithic Çatalhöyük Reveals Fundamental Transitions in Health, Mobility, and Lifestyle in Early Farmers," *Proceedings of the National Academy of Sciences* 116, no. 26 (2019): 12615–23.

71. Pawłowska, "The Smells of Neolithic Çatalhöyük," 1-11.
72. Wendy Matthews, "Defining Households: Micro-Contextual Analysis of Early Neolithic Households in the Zagros, Iran," in *New Perspectives on Household Archaeology*, ed. Bradley J. Parker and Catherine P. Foster (Eisenbrauns, 2012),183.
73. Ian Hodder, "Çatalhöyük in the Context of the Middle Eastern Neolithic," *Annual Review of Anthropology* 36, no. 1 (2007): 105-20.
74. Mithen, *After the Ice*.
75. Ian Kuijt, "Keeping the Peace: Ritual, Skull Caching, and Community Integration in the Levantine Neolithic," in *Life in Neolithic Farming Communities: Social Organization, Identity, and Differentiation*, ed. Ian Kuijt (Springer, 2000), 137-64.
76. Ian Hodder and Peter Pels, "History Houses: A New Interpretation of Architectural Elaboration at Çatalhöyük," in *Religion in the Emergence of Civilization: Çatalhöyük as a Case Study*, ed. Ian Hodder (Cambridge University Press, 2010): 163-86.
77. Theya Molleson, "The Eloquent Bones of Abu Hureyra," *Scientific American* 271, no. 2 (1994): 70-75.
78. Ian Hodder, "More on History Houses at Çatalhöyük: A Response to Carleton et al.," *Journal of Archaeological Science* 67 (2016): 1-6.
79. Hodder, "Çatalhöyük in the Context of the Middle Eastern Neolithic," 105-20; subsequent quotation from "Çatalhöyük in the Context."
80. Larsen et al., "Bioarchaeology of Neolithic Çatalhöyük," 12615-23.
81. Nigel Goring-Morris and Anna Belfer-Cohen, "Great Expectations, or, the Inevitable Collapse of the Early Neolithic in the Near East," in *Becoming Villagers: Comparing Early Village Societies*, ed. Matthew S. Bandy and Jake R. Fox (University of Arizona Press, 2010): 62-77.
82. Gary Rollefson and Ilse Köhler-Rollefson, "Early Neolithic Exploitation Patterns in the Levant: Cultural Impact on the Environment," *Population and Environment* 13, no. 4 (1992): 243-54.
83. Rollefson and Köhler-Rollefson, "Early Neolithic Exploitation Patterns," 243-54; Anna Belfer-Cohen and Nigel Goring-Morris, "Becoming Farmers: The Inside Story," *Current Anthropology* 52, no. S4 (2011): S209-20.
84. Goring-Morris and Belfer-Cohen, "Great Expectations," 62-77.
85. "Neolithic Site of Çatalhöyük," UNESCO.org.
86. Anne Whiston Spirn, *The Granite Garden: Urban Nature and Human Design* (Basic Books, 1984), 5.

TWO: Cities of Mud

1. J. A. Black et al., *The Debate Between Bird and Fish: Translation*, Electronic Text Corpus of Sumerian Literature. Oxford, 1998.

2. Seton Lloyd et al., "Tell Hassuna Excavations by the Iraq Government Directorate General of Antiquities in 1943 and 1944," *Journal of Near Eastern Studies* 4, no. 4 (1945): 255–89.
3. Based on P. Veale, model of a mud brick house at Tell Hassuna, Mesopotamia, Science Museum Group.
4. Kent Flannery, "The Origins of the Village Revisited: From Nuclear to Extended Households," *American Antiquity* 67, no. 3 (2002): 417–33.
5. Lloyd et al., "Tell Hassuna Excavations," 255–89.
6. Flannery, "The Origins of the Village Revisited," 417–33.
7. Olivier Aurenche et al., "Theoretical Archaeology and Rhetorical Archaeology," 196–204.
8. Flannery, "The Origins of the Village Revisited," 417–33.
9. Hans Helbaek, "Early Hassunan Vegetable Food at Tell es-Sawwan Near Samarra," *Sumer* 20, nos. 1 and 2 (1964): 45–48.
10. Kadim Hasson Hnaihen, "The Appearance of Bricks in Ancient Mesopotamia," *Athens Journal of History* 6, no. 1 (2020): 73–96.
11. David Oates, "Innovations in Mud-Brick: Decorative and Structural Techniques in Ancient Mesopotamia," *World Archaeology* 21, no. 3 (1990): 388–406.
12. Flannery, "The Origins of the Village Revisited," 417–33.
13. Leonard Woolley, *Ur Excavations, Vol. 4: The Early Periods* (British Museum, 1955).
14. Stephen Bertman, *Handbook to Life in Ancient Mesopotamia* (Infobase Publishing, 2003), 188; Jason Ur, "Households and the Emergence of Cities in Ancient Mesopotamia," *Cambridge Archaeological Journal* 24, no. 2 (2014): 262.
15. Michael Roaf, *Cultural Atlas of Mesopotamia and the Ancient Near East* (Facts on File, 1990), 51.
16. Gertrude Lowthian Bell, *The Letters of Gertrude Bell*, vol. 1 (Ernest Benn, 1927).
17. Uwe Sievertsen, "Private Space, Public Space and Connected Architectural Developments Throughout the Early Periods of Mesopotamian History," *Altorientalische Forschungen* 29, no. 2 (2002): 307–29.
18. Based on John Brennan, "Site Plan of Tell Madhur" in *Cultural Atlas of Mesopotamia and the Ancient Near East* by Michael Roaf (Facts on File, 1990).
19. Pascal Butterlin, "The Great Houses of Mesopotamia: Tripartite Houses and the Formation of the City-State," in *From House Societies to States: Early Political Organisation, From Antiquity to the Middle Ages*, ed. Juan Carlos Moreno García (Oxbow Books, 2022): 28–55.
20. Kenneth Hirth, "From Households to Palaces," in *The Organization of Ancient Economies: A Global Perspective* (Cambridge University Press, 2020).
21. Butterlin, "The Great Houses of Mesopotamia," 39.
22. Shamil Kubba, "The Ubaid Period: Evidence of Architectural Planning and the Use of a Standard Unit of Measurement—the 'Ubaid cubit' in Mesopotamia," *Paléorient* 16, no. 1 (1990): 45–55.

23. Butterlin, "The Great Houses of Mesopotamia," 39.
24. Agatha Christie, *Come, Tell Me How You Live* (William Collins, 1946; repr. Harper-Collins, 2006).
25. Jason Ur et al., "Proto-Urbanism in the Late 5th Millennium BC: Survey and Excavations at Khirbat al-Fakhar (Hamoukar), Northeast Syria," *Paléorient* 37, no. 2 (2011): 151–75.
26. Jason Ur, "The Birth of Cities in Ancient West Asia," in *Ancient West Asian Civilization: Geoenvironment and Society in the Pre-Islamic Middle East*, ed. Akira Tsuneki et al. (Springer, 2017): 133–47.
27. Bisserka Gaydarska, "The City Is Dead! Long Live the City!," *Norwegian Archaeological Review* 49, no. 1 (2016): 40–57.
28. Augusta McMahon, "Early Urbanism in Northern Mesopotamia," *Journal of Archaeological Research* 28 (2020): 289–337.
29. Andrew Lawler, "North Versus South, Mesopotamian Style," *Science* 312 (2006): 1458–63.
30. Ur, "Households and the Emergence of Cities," 249–68.
31. Amy Lavoie, "New Research Challenges Previous Knowledge About the Origins of Urbanization," *Harvard Gazette*, 30 August 2007.
32. Jason Ur, "Urban Form at Tell Brak Across Three Millennia," in *Preludes to Urbanism: Studies in the Late Chalcolithic of Mesopotamia in Honour of Joan Oates* (Archaeopress, 2014).
33. Lawler, "North Versus South, Mesopotamian Style," 1458–63.
34. Augusta McMahon and Adam Stone, "The Edge of the City: Urban Growth and Burial Space in 4th Millennium BC Mesopotamia," *Origini: Preistoria e protostoria delle civiltà antiche* 35 (2013): 83–110.
35. Tony Wilkinson et al., "The Geoarchaeology of Route Systems in Northern Syria," *Geoarchaeology* 25, no. 6 (2010): 745–71.
36. Tony Wilkinson et al., "The Structure and Dynamics of Dry-Farming States in Upper Mesopotamia [and Comments and Reply]," *Current Anthropology* 35, no. 5 (1994): 483–520.
37. Augusta McMahon, "Urbanism and the Prehistory of Violent Conflict: Tell Brak, Northeast Syria," ArchéOrient - Le Blog, 2 May 2014.
38. Augusta McMahon et al., "Late Chalcolithic Mass Graves at Tell Brak, Syria, and Violent Conflict During the Growth of Early City-States," *Journal of Field Archaeology* 36, no. 3 (2011): 201–20.
39. Ur, "The Birth of Cities in Ancient West Asia," 144.
40. Augusta McMahon, "Urban Heterogeneity in the Early Cities of Northern Mesopotamia," *Journal of Urban Archaeology* 8 (2023): 47–63.
41. *The Oriental Institute 2008–2009 Annual Report*, University of Chicago (Oriental Institute, 2009); Clemens Reichel, "Beyond the Garden of Eden—Competition and Early Warfare in Northern Syria (4500–3000 BC)," in *Schlachfeldarchäologie—Battlefield Archaeology*, ed. H. Meller (Landesdenkmalamt, 2009): 17–30.

42. "Inana and Enki," Electronic Text Corpus of Sumerian Literature, t.1.3.1, Oxford, 1998.
43. Robert Adams, "Critique of Guillermo Algaze's 'The Sumerian Takeoff,'" *Structure and Dynamics* 1, no. 1 (2005).
44. Andrew Robinson, "Excavating Uruk," *Science* 366, no. 6468 (2019): 959.
45. W. Ludwig, "Mass, Sitte und Technik des Bauens in Habuba Kabira-Süd" [Measurements, customs and building techniques in Habuba Kabira South], in *Le Moyen Euphrate* (Brill, 1980), 63–74; Sievertsen, "Private Space, Public Space and Connected Architectural Developments," 307–29.
46. Roaf, *Cultural Atlas of Mesopotamia and the Ancient Near East*, 80.
47. Jacques W. Delleur, "The Evolution of Urban Hydrology: Past, Present, and Future," *Journal of Hydraulic Engineering* 129, no. 8 (2003): 563–73.
48. Andrew Wilson, "Drainage and Sanitation," in *Handbook of Ancient Water Technology* (Brill, 2000), 151–79.
49. Augusta McMahon, "Waste Management in Early Urban Southern Mesopotamia," in *Sanitation, Latrines and Intestinal Parasites in Past Populations* (Routledge, 2016), 19–40.
50. Nicola Crüsemann et al., eds., *Uruk: First City of the Ancient World* (Getty Publications, 2019).
51. "MS 1717—Beer Production at the Inanna Temple in Uruk," The Schøyen Collection.
52. Lewis L. Mumford, *The City in History: Its Origins, Its Transformations, and Its Prospects* (Houghton Mifflin Harcourt, 1961), 34.
53. Spiro Kostof, *The City Shaped: Urban Patterns and Meanings Through History* (Little, Brown, 1991).
54. Gwendolyn Leick, *Mesopotamia: The Invention of the City* (Penguin UK, 2002).
55. Karen Radner et al., eds., *The Oxford History of the Ancient Near East*, vol. 1 (Oxford University Press, 2020), 220.
56. Mary Shepperson, "Planning for the Sun: Urban Forms as a Mesopotamian Response to the Sun," *World Archaeology* 41, no. 3 (2009): 363–78.
57. Martin Sauvage, *La brique et sa mise en oeuvre en Mésopotamie, des origines à l'époque achéménide* [Brick and its implementation in Mesopotamia, from its origins to the Achaemenid Period] (Research Editions on Civilizations, 1998), 22.
58. Nicolò Marchetti et al., "The Rise of Urbanized Landscapes in Mesopotamia: The QADIS Integrated Survey Results and the Interpretation of Multi-Layered Historical Landscapes," *Zeitschrift für Assyriologie und Vorderasiatische Archäologie* 109, no. 2 (2019): 214–37; Robert McCormick Adams, *Heartland of Cities: Surveys of Ancient Settlement and Land Use on the Central Floodplain of the Euphrates* (University of Chicago Press, 1981), 138.
59. Martha Roth, *Law Collections from Mesopotamia and Asia Minor*, vol. 6 (SBL Press, 1997).

NOTES

60. Karen Nemet-Nejat, *Daily Life in Ancient Mesopotamia* (Hendrickson, 2002), 121.
61. Genesis 11:3 (New International Version).
62. Hnaihen, "The Appearance of Bricks in Ancient Mesopotamia," 73–96; subsequent information from "The Appearance of Bricks in Ancient Mesopotamia."
63. "Foundation Figure of Ur-Namma Holding a Basket," Metropolitan Museum of Art.
64. Leonard Woolley, *The Sumerians* (AMS Press, 1929).
65. Leonard Woolley, "The Excavations at Ur, 1926–7," *Antiquaries Journal* 7, no. 4 (1927): 392.
66. Andrew George, *The Epic of Gilgamesh: A New Translation* (Penguin Press, 1999), VII 120.
67. Stefano Anastasio, *Building Between the Two Rivers: An Introduction to the Building Archaeology of Ancient Mesopotamia* (Archaeopress, 2020).
68. William Hafford, personal correspondence.
69. Sievertsen, "Private Space, Public Space and Connected Architectural Developments," 307–29.
70. Shiyanthi Thavapalan, "Mesopotamian Megacity Re-Imagined in Berlin," *Curator: The Museum Journal* 57, no. 1 (2014): 137–45.
71. George, *The Epic of Gilgamesh*, I 20.
72. Marvin Powell, "Metrological Notes on the Esagila Tablet and Related Matters," *Zeitschrift für Assyriologie und Vorderasiatische Archäologie* 72, no. 1 (1982): 106–23.
73. Eleanor Robson, *Mesopotamian Mathematics, 2100–1600 BC: Technical Constants in Bureaucracy and Education* (Oxford University Press, 1999), 233.
74. Peter Miglus, "Babylonian Domestic Architecture," in *Uruk: First City of the Ancient World*, ed. Crüsemann et al. (Getty Publications, 2019).
75. "Ur Digitization Project: January 2013," University of Pennsylvania Museum of Archaeology and Anthropology.
76. John Perlin, *A Forest Journey: The Story of Wood and Civilization* (Countryman Press, 2005).
77. Yoshinori Yasuda et al., "The Earliest Record of Major Anthropogenic Deforestation in the Ghab Valley, Northwest Syria: A Palynological Study," *Quaternary International* 73 (2000): 127–36.
78. Richard N. Frye, review of *The Uruk Countryside: The Natural Setting of Urban Societies* by Hans J. Nissen and Robert McC. Adams, *American Historical Review* 79, no. 5 (December 1974): 1523–24.
79. Oates, "Innovations in Mud-Brick," 388–406.
80. McMahon, "Waste Management in Early Urban Southern Mesopotamia," 19–40.
81. Edward Chiera, *Sumerian Epics and Myths*, Cuneiform Series, vol. 3 (University of Chicago Press, 1934).
82. Augusta McMahon, "Urban Heterogeneity in the Early Cities of Northern Mesopotamia," *Journal of Urban Archaeology* 8 (2023): 47–63.

83. Emily Hammer and Angelo Di Michele, "The Suburbs of the Early Mesopotamian City of Ur (Tell al-Muqayyar, Iraq)," *American Journal of Archaeology* 127, no. 4 (2023): 449–79.
84. "The Lament for Urim," Electronic Text Corpus of Sumerian Literature t.2.2.2, Oxford, 1998.

THREE: Order and Ornament

1. Robin Waterfield, ed., *Conversations of Socrates* (Penguin, 1990), 159–60.
2. Aristotle, *Metaphysics: Books X-XIV, Oeconomica and Magna Morali*a, trans. Hugh Tredennick and G. Cyril Armstrong (William Heinemann, 1947), 343.
3. Aeschylus, *Suppliant Maidens; Persians; Prometheus; Seven Against Thebes*, trans. Herbert Weir Smyth (William Heinemann, 1922), 255, 257.
4. Thucydides, *History of the Peloponnesian War*, trans. Charles Forster Smith (Harvard University Press, 1919), 1.58.2.
5. Bradley Ault, "Greek Domestic Architecture," in *A Companion to Science, Technology, and Medicine in Ancient Greece and Rome* (Wiley-Blackwell, 2016): 656–71.
6. Aristotle, *Politics*, 1253b.
7. Xenophon, "Oeconomicus," in *Not in God's Image: Women in History from the Greeks to the Victorians*, ed. Julia O'Faolain and Lauro Martines (Temple Smith, 1973).
8. Aristophanes, *Thesmophoriazusae*, in Nicholas Cahill, *Household and City Organization at Olynthus* (Yale University Press, 2002), 151.
9. Eubulus, in Athenaeus, *The Deipnosophists*, trans. Charles Burton Gulick (William Heinemann, 1927), frag. 93.
10. Carla Antonaccio, "Architecture and Behavior: Building Gender into Greek Houses," *Classical World* 93, no. 5 (2000): 517–33.
11. Lysias, *On the Murder of Eratosthenes*, 1.9.
12. Aeschines, *Against Timarchus*, in *The Speeches of Aeschines*, trans. Charles Darwin Adams (William Heinemann, 1919), 101.
13. Plutarch, *Plutarch's Morals*, vol. 4, ed. William Goodwin (Little, Brown, 1871), 428–29.
14. "Terracotta oinochoe: chous (jug)," Metropolitan Museum of Art, object no. 37.11.19.
15. Aristotle, *Athenian Constitution*, in *Aristotle in 23 Volumes*, vol. 20, trans. H. Rackham (Harvard University Press, 1952), 50.
16. George Kubler, "Mexican Urbanism in the Sixteenth Century," *Art Bulletin* 24, no. 2 (1942): 160–71.
17. Roger Paden, "The Two Professions of Hippodamus of Miletus," *Philosophy & Geography* 4, no. 1 (2001): 25–48.
18. Harold Schmeck, "Research Finds Greeks Used Solar Energy," *New York Times*, 24 April 1979.

19. Seneca, *Moral Letters to Lucilius*, trans. Richard Mott Gummere (William Heinemann, 1918), letter 90.
20. Francis Lazenby, "Greek and Roman Household Pets," *Classical Journal* 44, no. 5 (1949): 299–307.
21. Marcello Mogetta and Jeffrey A. Becker, "Archaeological Research at Gabii, Italy: The Gabii Project Excavations, 2009–2011," *American Journal of Archaeology* 118, no. 1 (2014): 171–88.
22. Andrew Wallace-Hadrill, *Houses and Society in Pompeii and Herculaneum* (Princeton University Press, 1994), 83.
23. Based on Francis Ching, elements of a typical Roman house, in *A Global History of Architecture* by Francis Ching et al. (John Wiley, 2010).
24. Steven Tuck, "Roman Housing," Metropolitan Museum of Art, October 2009.
25. Vitruvius Pollio, *The Ten Books on Architecture*, trans. Morris Hicky Morgan (Harvard University Press, 1914), bk. 3, chap. 1; subsequent quotations from *Ten Books on Architecture*, bk. 6, chap. 3; bk. 6, chap. 4; bk. 6, chap. 1; bk. 1, chap. 1.
26. Frontinus, *The Stratagems and the Aqueducts of Rome*, trans. Charles Bennett (William Heinemann, 1925), 357, 359.
27. Christer Bruun, "The Water Supply of Ancient Rome: A Study of Roman Imperial Administration," *Commentationes Humanarum Litterarum* 93 (Societas Scientarum Fennica, 1991).
28. Ann Olga Koloski-Ostrow, *The Archaeology of Sanitation in Roman Italy: Toilets, Sewers, and Water Systems* (UNC Press Books, 2015).
29. Aelian, *On the Characteristics of Animals, Books 12–17*, trans. A. F. Scholfield (Harvard University Press, 1959), 85.
30. Luigi Spina, *Inside Pompeii* (Thames & Hudson, 2023), 367.
31. Janet DeLaine, "Some Observations on the Transition from Greek to Roman Baths in Hellenistic Italy," *Mediterranean Archaeology* 2 (1989): 111–25.
32. Marcus Tullius Cicero, *Epistulae ad familiares*, bk. 9, letter 4.
33. Clelia Cirillo et al., "Pompeii—Nature and Architecture," *Proceedings of the 19th IPSAPA/ISPALEM International Scientific Conference, Naples, Italy*, 2015.
34. Marcus Tullius Cicero, *On the Nature of the Gods* 2.61, translation adapted from H. Rackham.
35. Lynley McAlpine, "Marble, Memory, and Meaning in the Four Pompeian Styles of Wall Painting" (PhD thesis, University of Michigan, 2014).
36. "The House of the Vettii in Historic Context," MIT OpenCourseWare, Massachusetts Institute of Technology.
37. Pliny the Younger, *The Letters of the Younger Pliny*, trans. Betty Radice (Penguin, 1963).
38. John Coulston and Hazel Dodge, eds., *Ancient Rome: The Archaeology of the Eternal City* (Oxford University School of Archaeology, 2000), *Corpus inscriptionum Latinarum* 6.7193a, 281.
39. Titus Livius (Livy), *The History of Rome*, bk. 21, chap. 62.

40. Based on Italo Gismondi, "Ostia: Casa Di Diana Vista Dalla Piazzetta Dei Lari," in Guido Calza, *Le origini latine dell'abitazione moderna* (Bestetti & Tumminelli, 1923).
41. Roger Ulrich, "Courtyard Architecture in the Insulae of Ostia Antica," in *A Companion to Roman Architecture* (Blackwell, 2014): 324–41.
42. Plutarch, *Plutarch's Lives*, trans. Bernadotte Perrin (William Heinemann, 1916), 317.
43. Vitruvius, *Ten Books on Architecture*, bk. 2, chap. 8.
44. Juvenal, *Satires*, in *Citizens of Rome: A Fascinating Insight into Everyday Life 2,000 Years Ago*, by Simon Goodenough (Crown Publishers, 1979), 62.
45. Vitruvius, *Ten Books on Architecture*, bk. 2, chap. 8.
46. John Clarke, *Physical Science in the Time of Nero, Being a Translation of the* Quaestiones Naturales *of Seneca* (Macmillan, 1910).
47. Ulrich, "Courtyard Architecture in the Insulae of Ostia Antica," 324–41; subsequent information from "Courtyard Architecture in the Insulae of Ostia Antica."
48. Gregory Aldrete, *Daily Life in the Roman City: Rome, Pompeii and Ostia* (Bloomsbury USA, 2004), 78.
49. Anthony Barrett, *Rome Is Burning: Nero and the Fire That Ended a Dynasty* (Princeton University Press, 2020), 177.
50. Marcus Tullius Cicero, *The Letters of Cicero,* trans. Evelyn Shuckburgh (George Bell and Sons, 1908), bk. 14, letter 8.
51. Aldrete, *Daily Life in the Roman City*, 79.
52. Juvenal, *Satires*, trans. Jerome Mazzaro (University of Michigan Press, 1965), 45.
53. Ann Olga Koloski-Ostrow, "Talking Heads: What Toilets and Sewers Tell Us About Ancient Roman Sanitation," The Conversation, 19 November 2015.
54. Martial, *Epigrams* (Bohn's Classical Library, 1897), bk. 7.
55. Petronius, *The Satyricon*, 74.14.
56. Alexander McKay, *Houses, Villas, and Palaces in the Roman World* (Johns Hopkins University Press, 1975), 99.
57. Aldrete, *Daily Life in the Roman City*.
58. Barrett, *Rome Is Burning*, 178.
59. James Packer, "The Insulae of Imperial Ostia," *Memoirs of the American Academy in Rome* 31 (1971): 18.
60. Nicholas Purcell, "Ostia," *Oxford Research Encyclopedia of Classics* (Oxford University Press, 2016).
61. H. H. J. Brouwer, *Bona Dea: The Sources and a Description of the Cult* (E. J. Brill, 1989), 26–27.
62. Packer, "The Insulae of Imperial Ostia."
63. Robert Sallares, "Role of Environmental Changes in the Spread of Malaria in Europe During the Holocene," *Quaternary International* 150, no. 1 (2006): 21–27.
64. Purcell, "Ostia."
65. Walter Scheidel et al., eds., *The Cambridge Economic History of the Greco-Roman World*, vol. 1 (Cambridge University Press, 2007), 47.

NOTES

66. Claudian, "On Stilicho's Consulship," in *Claudian*, vol. 2, trans. M. Platnauer (Harvard University Press, 1922), bk. 3, p. 53.
67. Kyle Harper, *The Fate of Rome: Climate, Disease, and the End of an Empire* (Princeton University Press, 2018), 1.
68. Publius Vergilius Maro, *Aeneid*, bk. 1, lines 278–79.
69. Marcus Tullius Cicero, *Nature of the Gods*, in *The Treatises of M. T. Cicero*, trans. Charles Duke Yonge (Henry Bohn, 1853), 101.
70. William Vernon Harris, "Defining and Detecting Mediterranean Deforestation, 800 BCE to 700 CE," in *The Ancient Mediterranean Environment Between Science and History* (Brill, 2013), 173–94.
71. John Perlin, *A Forest Journey: The Story of Wood and Civilization* (Countryman Press, 2005).
72. Harper, "The Fate of Rome," 51.
73. Harris, "Defining and Detecting Mediterranean Deforestation," 173–94.
74. Donald Hughes and Jack Thirgood, "Deforestation, Erosion, and Forest Management in Ancient Greece and Rome," *Journal of Forest History* 26, no. 2 (1982): 60–75.
75. Russell Meiggs et al., *Roman Ostia* (Clarendon Press, 1973).
76. Robert Sallares, *Malaria and Rome: A History of Malaria in Ancient Italy* (Oxford University Press, 2002).
77. D. F. Cheeseman, "Varro and the Small Beasts," *Nature* 203 (1964): 911–12.
78. Michelle Ziegler, "Malarial Landscapes in Late Antique Rome and the Tiber Valley," *Landscapes* 17, no. 2 (2016): 150.
79. Lara O'Sullivan et al., "Deforestation, Mosquitoes, and Ancient Rome: Lessons for Today," *BioScience* 58, no. 8 (2008): 756–60.
80. Ziegler, "Malarial Landscapes in Late Antique Rome," 139–55.
81. Scheidel et al., *The Cambridge Economic History of the Greco-Roman World*, 39.
82. Tim Dyson, "The Role of the Demographic Transition in the Process of Urbanization," *Population and Development Review* 37 (2011): 34–54.
83. Guillermo Algaze, "Entropic Cities: The Paradox of Urbanism in Ancient Mesopotamia," *Current Anthropology* 59, no. 1 (2018): 23–54; William McNeill, *Plagues and Peoples* (Anchor, 2010).
84. Roland Fletcher, "Angkor, Food Production, Water Management and Climate Change: The Trajectory of Urbanism in SE Asia to the Mid-Second Millennium CE," in *Water and Society from Ancient Times to the Present* (Routledge, 2018), 238–58.
85. Amy Styring et al., "Isotope Evidence for Agricultural Extensification Reveals How the World's First Cities Were Fed," *Nature Plants* 3, no. 6 (2017): 1–11; Vernon Scarborough et al., "Low Density Urbanism, Sustainability, and IHOPE-Maya: Can the Past Provide More Than History?," *UGEC Viewpoints* 8 (2012): 20.
86. Arlen Chase et al., "Airborne LiDAR, Archaeology, and the Ancient Maya Land-

scape at Caracol, Belize," *Journal of Archaeological Science* 38, no. 2 (2011): 387–98.
87. Lisa Lucero et al., "From 'Collapse' to Urban Diaspora: The Transformation of Low-Density, Dispersed Agrarian Urbanism," *Antiquity* 89, no. 347 (2015): 1139–54.
88. Based on Thomas Chandler et al., digital reconstruction of Angkor Wat complex in the twelfth century, based upon data from airborne lidar surveys, Monash University, media, 2022.
89. Fletcher, "Angkor, Food Production, Water Management and Climate Change," 238–58.
90. Roland Fletcher, "Sprawl at Risk: Lessons from Angkor, Tikal and Anuradhapura," in *Disrupted Balance: Society at Risk*, ed. Jan Wouter Vasbinder (World Scientific, 2018), 89–95.
91. Fletcher, "Angkor, Food Production, Water Management and Climate Change," 238–58.
92. Damian Evans et al., "Uncovering Archaeological Landscapes at Angkor Using Lidar," *Proceedings of the National Academy of Sciences* 110, no. 31 (2013): 12595–600.
93. Fletcher, "Sprawl at Risk," 89–95.
94. Roland Fletcher, "Low-Density, Agrarian-Based Urbanism: A Comparative View," *Insights* 2, no. 4 (2009): 1–19.
95. Rubina Raja and Søren M. Sindbæk, "A Not-So-Dense Idea," *Current World Archaeology* 120 (2023), 58–59.
96. Fletcher, "Sprawl at Risk," 89–95.

FOUR: The Industrial Home

1. Jona Lendering, "The Edges of the Earth (3)," Livius.org.
2. Pliny the Elder, *Natural History: A Selection,* trans. John Healy (Penguin, 1999) 16.2–3 (206).
3. Russell Shorto, *Amsterdam: A History of the World's Most Liberal City* (Vintage, 2014), 29.
4. Jan Bieleman, *Five Centuries of Farming: A Short History of Dutch Agriculture 1500–2000,* vol. 8 (Brill, 2023); Willem Jacob Diepeveen, *De vervening in Delfland en Schieland tot het einde der zestiende eeuw* [Peat extraction in Delfland and Schieland until the end of the sixteenth century] (E. IJdo, 1950).
5. Robin Evans, "Figures, Doors and Passages," *Architectural Design* 48 (1978): 267–78.
6. Witold Rybczynski, *Home: A Short History of an Idea* (Penguin, 1987).
7. Helmer Helmers and Geert Janssen, eds., *The Cambridge Companion to the Dutch Golden Age* (Cambridge University Press, 2018).

8. Jan de Vries and Ad van der Woude, *The First Modern Economy: Success, Failure, and Perseverance of the Dutch Economy, 1500–1815* (Cambridge University Press, 1997).
9. Emile Wennekes and Louis Peter Grijp, *De hele dag maar op en neer: Over heien, heiliedjes en hoofdstedelijke muziekgebouwen* [Up and down all day long: on pile driving, pile-driving songs and the capital's music buildings] (Meertens Instituut with Het Muziekgebouw, 2002).
10. Hentie Louw, "The Origin of the Sash-Window," *Architectural History* 26 (1983): 49–72.
11. Mary Mapes Dodge, *Hans Brinker, or, The Silver Skates: A Story of Life in Holland* (James O'Kane, 1867).
12. Owen Felltham and Graeme Watson, "A Brief Character of the Low-Countries Under the States (1652)," *Dutch Crossing* 27, no. 1 (2003): 89–141.
13. Margaret Horsfield, *Biting the Dust: The Joys of Housework* (St. Martin's Press, 1998), 203.
14. Philip Tabor, "Striking Home: The Telematic Assault on Identity," in *Occupying Architecture* (Routledge, 1998).
15. Simon Schama, *The Embarrassment of Riches: An Interpretation of Dutch Culture in the Golden Age* (University of California Press, 1988); subsequent quotations from *Embarrassment of Riches*.
16. Conrad Busken Huet, *Het land van Rembrand: Studien over de Noordnederlandsche beschaving in de zeventiende eeuw* [The land of Rembrandt, studies on the North-Netherlands civilization in the seventeenth century] (Tjeenk Willink, 1886).
17. Jaap Evert Abrahamse and Reinout Rutte, "Building Regulations and Urban Development in Late Medieval Elburg and Early Modern Amsterdam," in *Building Regulations and Urban Form, 1200–1900* (Routledge, 2017), 139–56; subsequent information and quotation from "Building Regulations and Urban Development."
18. John Evelyn, *Diary*, ed. E. S. de Beer (Oxford University Press, 1959), 27–28.
19. "Decision 34 COM 8B.30: Seventeenth-Century Canal Ring Area of Amsterdam Inside the Singelgracht, Netherlands," UNESCO World Heritage Convention, UNESCO World Heritage Centre.
20. De Vries and Van der Woude, *The First Modern Economy*, 304.
21. S. P. W. Chave, "The DUNCAN Memorial Lecture: 'Duncan of Liverpool—and Some Lessons for Today,'" *Journal of Public Health* 6, no. 1 (1984): 61–71.
22. W. H. Duncan, "Report on the Sanitary State of the Labouring Classes in the Town of Liverpool," in Poor Law Commissioners, *Local Reports on the Sanitary Condition of the Labouring Population in England: In Consequence of an Inquiry Directed to be Made by the Poor Law Commissioners* (HM Stationery Office, 1842): 287.

23. Stefan Muthesius, *The English Terraced House* (Yale University Press, 1984), 3.
24. Duncan, "Report on the Sanitary State of the Labouring Classes in the town of Liverpool," 288.
25. Frederick Engels, *The Condition of the Working Class in England*, trans. Florence Kelley Wischnewetzky (Swan Sonnenschein, 1892), 27.
26. Margaret Jacob, *Scientific Culture and the Making of the Industrial West* (Oxford University Press, 1997).
27. Chave, "The Duncan Memorial Lecture," 61–71.
28. Muthesius, *The English Terraced House*, 14.
29. Nicholas Crafts, "Forging Ahead and Falling Behind: The Rise and Relative Decline of the First Industrial Nation," *Journal of Economic Perspectives* 12, no. 2 (1998): 193–210.
30. Joanne Harrison, "The Origin, Development and Decline of Back-to-Back Houses in Leeds, 1787–1937," *Industrial Archaeology Review* 39, no. 2 (2017): 101–16.
31. Muthesius, *The English Terraced House*, 19.
32. Gareth Carr, "Victorian Workers' Housing: The Development of the Bye-Law Terraced House," transcript of public lecture, March 2023.
33. Elizabeth Barrett Browning, *Aurora Leigh, and Other Poems* (J. Miller, 1872).
34. Peter Ackroyd, *London: The Biography* (Random House, 2001).
35. Ellen Ross, "'Not the Sort That Would Sit on the Doorstep': Respectability in Pre-World War I London Neighborhoods," *International Labor and Working-Class History* 27 (1985): 39–59.
36. Charles Dickens, *Our Mutual Friend* (TB Peterson, 1865).
37. *New York Tribune*, 11 November 1869.
38. Junius Henri Browne, *The Great Metropolis: A Mirror of New York* (American Publishing, 1869), 398.
39. Elizabeth Cromley, *Alone Together: A History of New York's Early Apartments* (Cornell University Press, 1990), 22.
40. Andrew Sandoval-Strausz, *Hotel: An American History* (Yale University Press, 2007).
41. Elizabeth Blackmar, *Manhattan for Rent, 1785–1850* (Cornell University Press, 1989).
42. Joseph Camp Griffith Kennedy, *Preliminary Report on the Eighth Census, 1860, of the United States* (Government Printing Office, 1862).
43. "European Social Reforms: Liverpool, Its Sanitary Condition, Over-Crowding, Cellar Dwellings, Courts, &c," *New York Times*, 2 September 1865.
44. Cromley, *Alone Together*, 12; subsequent quotations from *Alone Together*, 18, 2.
45. J. R. Hamilton, "Houses for the Hard Times," *New York Times*, 23 March 1862.
46. Cromley, *Alone Together*, 72.
47. Christopher Gray, "Apartment Buildings, the Latest in French Ideas," *New York Times*, 11 July 2013.

NOTES

48. Spiro Kostof, *America by Design* (Oxford University Press, 1987), 49.
49. Gray, "Apartment Buildings, the Latest in French Ideas."
50. Cromley, *Alone Together*, 2.
51. Cromley, *Alone Together*, 159.
52. Gwendolyn Wright, *Building the Dream: A Social History of Housing in America* (MIT Press, 1983), 142.
53. "Apartment Houses - II," *American Architect and Building News*, 15 November 1890, 97.
54. David Katzman, *Seven Days a Week: Women and Domestic Service in Industrializing America* (University of Illinois Press, 1981), 286.
55. Cromley, *Alone Together*, 4.
56. Blackmar, *Manhattan for Rent*, xiii.
57. Moses King, ed., *King's Handbook of New York City: An Outline History and Description of the American Metropolis* (Moses King, 1892), 242–43.
58. J. E. Ives, "Studies in Illumination. III. A Study of the Loss of Light due to Smoke on Manhattan Island, New York City, During the Year 1927, Especially in its Relation to the Nature of the Weather, the Relative Humidity of the Air, and the Velocity and Direction of the Wind," *Public Health Bulletin* (1930).
59. Olmsted, Vaux and Co., *Preliminary Report Upon the Proposed Suburban Village at Riverside, near Chicago* (Sutton, Bowne, 1868), 275; subsequent quotations from *Preliminary Report upon the Proposed Suburban Village*, 280, 286.
60. Staten Island Improvement Commission, *A Letter Introductory from Messrs. Olmsted, Harris, Trowbridge, and Richardson* (New York, 1871), 9.
61. Andrew Downing, *The Architecture of Country Houses* (Courier Corporation, 2013).
62. Kostof, *America by Design*, 26.
63. Andrew Jackson Downing, *Essential Texts*, ed. Robert Twombly (W. W. Norton, 2012), 156.
64. *History of Cincinnati and Hamilton County, Ohio: Their Past and Present*, Glendale Ohio Archive (S. B. Nelson, 1894).
65. Kunstler, James Howard, *The Geography of Nowhere: The Rise and Decline of America's Man-Made Landscape* (Simon and Schuster, 1994), 47.
66. Kostof, *America by Design*, 24.
67. Michael Williams, *Americans and Their Forests: A Historical Geography* (Cambridge University Press, 1992), 186.
68. Whit Bronaugh, "North American Forests in the Age of Man," *American Forests* (22 June 2012).
69. Williams, *Americans and Their Forests*.
70. Peter Hall, *Cities of Tomorrow: An Intellectual History of Urban Planning and Design Since 1880* (Wiley-Blackwell, 2014), 326.

FIVE: Machines for Living

1. Anthony Denzer, "Modern Architecture and Theories of Solar Orientation," *2014 Proceedings of the American Solar Energy Society National Solar Conference* (2014).
2. Catherine Bauer, *Modern Housing* (University of Minnesota Press, 2020).
3. Susan Henderson, "Rationalization Takes Command: Zeilenbau and the Politics of CIAM," in *Building Culture: Ernst May and the New Frankfurt Initiative, 1926–1931* (Peter Lang, 2013), 410.
4. John Robert Mullin, "City Planning in Frankfurt, Germany, 1925–1932: A Study in Practical Utopianism," *Journal of Urban History* 4, no. 1 (1977): 3–28.
5. Vaclav Smil, *Enriching the Earth: Fritz Haber, Carl Bosch, and the Transformation of World Food Production* (MIT Press, 2004).
6. Joseph Wechsberg, "Letter from Berlin," *New Yorker*, 5 December 1958.
7. Mullin, "City Planning in Frankfurt, Germany," 3–28.
8. Ernst May, "*Die Frankfurter Wohnungspolitik*" [Frankfurt's housing policy], *Proceedings of the International Housing Association* (1929), 21.
9. Louis Heaton Pink, *The New Day in Housing* (John Day, 1928), 50.
10. Susan Henderson, "Ernst May and the Campaign to Resettle the Countryside: Rural Housing in Silesia, 1919–1925," *Journal of the Society of Architectural Historians* 61, no. 2 (2002): 188–211.
11. Henderson, "Rationalization Takes Command."
12. Susan Henderson, "A Revolution in the Woman's Sphere: Grete Lihotzky and the Frankfurt Kitchen," in *Architecture and Feminism*, ed. Debra Coleman et al. (Princeton Architectural Press, 1996), 240; subsequent information from "Revolution in the Woman's Sphere," 240.
13. Mullin, "City Planning in Frankfurt, Germany," 22.
14. Alice Friedman, *Women and the Making of the Modern House: A Social and Architectural History* (Yale University Press, 2006).
15. Stan Cox, *Losing Our Cool: Uncomfortable Truths About Our Air-Conditioned World (and Finding New Ways to Get Through the Summer)* (New Press, 2010), 9.
16. Marsha Ackermann, *Cool Comfort: America's Romance with Air-Conditioning* (Smithsonian Institution Press, 2010), 121.
17. Jennifer Gray, "Reading Broadacre," Frank Lloyd Wright Foundation, 1 October 2018.
18. James Dougherty, "Broadacre City: Frank Lloyd Wright's Utopia," *Centennial Review* (1981), 241.
19. Joseph Koenenn, "The Man Who Created Suburbia," *Chicago Tribune*, 3 February 1985.
20. Kenneth T. Jackson, *Crabgrass Frontier* (Oxford University Press, 1985), 234.
21. Bruce Lambert, "William J. Levitt, 86, Pioneer of Suburbs, Dies," *New York Times*, 29 January 1994.

22. W. D. Wetherell, *The Man Who Loved Levittown* (University of Pittsburgh Press, 1985).
23. Robert Gordon, *The Rise and Fall of American Growth: The US Standard of Living Since the Civil War* (Princeton University Press, 2017), 365.
24. "The Six Thousand Houses That Levitt Built, *Harper's* 197, no. 1180 (1948): 79–83.
25. Vincent Scully, *American Architecture and Urbanism* (Praeger, 1969), 165.
26. "Building Costs: Be Big Enough to Fight," *Life*, 31 January 1949, 74.
27. Jackson, *Crabgrass Frontier*, 236.
28. "The Six Thousand Houses That Levitt Built," 79–83.
29. Jackson, *Crabgrass Frontier*, 206.
30. Barry Checkoway, "Large Builders, Federal Housing Programmes, and Postwar Suburbanization," *The City: Critical Concepts in the Social Sciences* 4, no. 1 (2002).
31. Jackson, *Crabgrass Frontier*, 236.
32. Wetherell, *The Man Who Loved Levittown*.
33. Gwendolyn Wright, *Building the Dream: A Social History of Housing in America* (MIT Press, 1983), 148.
34. Peter N. Carroll and David W. Noble, *The Free and the Unfree: A Progressive History of the United States* (Penguin, 2001), 377.
35. Dolores Hayden, *Redesigning the American Dream: Gender, Housing, and Family Life*, rev. and expanded ed. (W. W. Norton, 2002), 25.
36. Lizabeth Cohen, *A Consumers' Republic: The Politics of Mass Consumption in Postwar America* (Vintage, 2003), 119.
37. Witold Rybczynski, "The Pioneering 'Levittowner,'" Working Paper 556, Zell/Lurie Real Estate Center, Wharton School, University of Pennsylvania.
38. Checkoway, "Large Builders, Federal Housing Programmes," 38.
39. Alexander Coburn et al., "Psychological and Neural Responses to Architectural Interiors," *Cortex* 126 (2020): 217–41.
40. Kostof, *America by Design*, 60.
41. Ryan Smith, *Prefab Architecture: A Guide to Modular Design and Construction* (John Wiley, 2010).
42. David Kushner, *Levittown: Two Families, One Tycoon, and the Fight for Civil Rights in America's Legendary Suburb* (Bloomsbury USA, 2009).
43. "Integration Troubles Beset Northern Town," *Life*, September 2, 1957: 43.
44. Thomas J. Sugrue, *Sweet Land of Liberty: The Forgotten Struggle for Civil Rights in the North* (Random House, 2009), 228.
45. Kostof, *America by Design*, 39.
46. Jeffrey Hardwick, *Mall Maker: Victor Gruen, Architect of an American Dream* (University of Pennsylvania Press, 2010), 216.
47. Herbert Gans, *The Levittowners: Ways of Life and Politics in a New Suburban Community* (Columbia University Press, 2017).

48. Michael Southworth and Peter Owens, "The Evolving Metropolis: Studies of Community, Neighborhood, and Street Form at the Urban Edge," *Journal of the American Planning Association* 59, no. 3 (1993): 271–87.
49. Robert Bruegmann, *Sprawl: A Compact History* (University of Chicago Press, 2019), 44.
50. James Howard Kunstler, *The City in Mind: Notes on the Urban Condition* (Simon and Schuster, 2003), 74.
51. "The Air-Conditioned Census," *New York Times*, 6 September 1970.
52. Le Corbusier, *Towards a New Architecture* (Courier Corporation, 2013).
53. James Ronald Firth, "The Work of the Hong Kong Housing Authority," *Journal of the Royal Society of Arts* 113, no. 5103 (1965): 175–95.
54. J. G. Ballard, *High-Rise: A Novel* (Liveright, 2012), 13.
55. Charles Jencks, *The Language of Post-Modern Architecture* (Rizzoli, 1977).
56. Firth, "The Work of the Hong Kong Housing Authority," 175–95.
57. Charlie Q. L. Xue, *Hong Kong Architecture 1945–2015: From Colonial to Global* (Springer, 2016); subsequent information from *Hong Kong Architecture*, 13.
58. Firth, "The Work of the Hong Kong Housing Authority," 175–95.
59. Robert C. Schmitt, "Implications of Density in Hong Kong," *Journal of the American Institute of Planners* 29, no. 3 (1963): 210–17.
60. Edward T. Hall, *The Hidden Dimension* (Anchor, 1969), 129.
61. Eugene Anderson, "Some Chinese Methods of Dealing with Crowding," *Urban Anthropology* 1, no. 2 (1972): 141–50.
62. Wai Kit Chung et al., "Modelling Perceived Oppressiveness and Noise Annoyance Responses to Window Views of Densely Packed Residential High-Rise Environments," *Building and Environment* 157 (2019): 127–38.
63. Paavo Monkkonen et al., "A Global Analysis of Land Use Regulation, Urban Form, and Greenhouse Gas Emissions," *Cities* 147 (2024): 104801.
64. Peter Newman and Jeffrey Kenworthy, "Transport and Urban Form in Thirty-Two of the World's Principal Cities," *Transport Reviews* 11, no. 3 (1991): 249–72.
65. Robert Cervero and Jin Murakami, "Rail + Property Development: A Model of Sustainable Transit Finance and Urbanism," UC Berkeley: Center for Future Urban Transit, 2008.
66. John Turner, *A Roof of My Own*, United Nations Centre for Building and Planning, 1964.
67. James Holston, *The Modernist City: An Anthropological Critique of Brasilia* (University of Chicago Press, 1989).
68. Peter Kellett and Mark Napier, "Squatter Architecture? A Critical Examination of Vernacular Theory and Spontaneous Settlement with Reference to South America and South Africa," *Traditional Dwellings and Settlements Review* 6, no. 2 (1995): 8.
69. Michael Smith, "Sprawl, Squatters and Sustainable Cities: Can Archaeological Data Shed Light on Modern Urban Issues?," *Cambridge Archaeological Journal* 20, no. 2 (2010): 229–53.

NOTES 281

70. Plato, *Republic*, trans. G. M. A. Grube, rev. C. D. C. Reeve, in *Complete Works*, ed. John M. Cooper and D. S. Hutchinson (Hackett, 1997), 423a–b.
71. Remi Jedwab and Dietrich Vollrath, "Urbanization Without Growth in Historical Perspective," *Explorations in Economic History* 58 (2015): 1–21.
72. "Urbanization," *Encyclopedia of Urban Studies*, vol. 1, ed. Ray Hutchison (Sage, 2010), 889.
73. "2018 Revision of World Urbanization Prospects," Population Division, United Nations, 2018.
74. John Turner and Robert Fichter, *Freedom to Build: Dweller Control of the Housing Process* (Macmillan, 1972), 145.
75. Jacob Crane and Edward Paxton, "The World-Wide Housing Problem," *Town Planning Review* 22, no. 1 (1951): 16.
76. Justin McGuirk, *Radical Cities: Across Latin America in Search of a New Architecture* (Verso Books, 2014), 96.
77. Stefan Al et al., eds., *Villages in the City: A Guide to South China's Informal Settlements* (Hong Kong University Press, 2014), 89.

SIX: The Intelligent Envelope

1. Wolfgang Feist et al., "Durability of Building Fabric Components and Ventilation Systems in Passive Houses," *Energy Efficiency* 13, no. 8 (2020): 1543–59.
2. Wolfgang Feist, "30 Years: the First Passive House," YouTube, International Passive House Association, posted 25 June 2021.
3. William Rees, "The Human Ecology of Overshoot: Why a Major 'Population Correction' Is Inevitable," *World* 4, no. 3 (2023): 509–27.
4. Guy Callendar, "The Artificial Production of Carbon Dioxide and Its Influence on Temperature," *Quarterly Journal of the Royal Meteorological Society* 64, no. 275 (1938): 223–40.
5. Katherine Richardson et al., "Earth Beyond Six of Nine Planetary Boundaries," *Science Advances* 9, no. 37 (2023): eadh2458.
6. Boris Kingma and Wouter van Marken Lichtenbelt, "Energy Consumption in Buildings and Female Thermal Demand," *Nature Climate Change* 5, no. 12 (2015): 1054–56.
7. Pam Belluck, "Chilly at Work? Office Formula Was Devised for Men," *New York Times*, 4 August 2015.
8. Daniel Barber, "Overview: Solar Architecture and Solar Design, 1930s–1950s," Energy History Online, Yale University, 2023.
9. Maron J. Simon, ed., *Your Solar House* (Simon and Schuster, 1947).
10. Martin Holladay, "Forgotten Pioneers of Energy Efficiency," Green Building Advisor, 24 April 2009.
11. Le Corbusier and Anthony Eardley, *The Athens Charter* (Grossman, 1973).
12. Elisabeth Rosenthal, "No Furnaces but Heat Aplenty in 'Passive Houses,'" *New York Times*, 26 December 2008.

13. Robert McLeod et al., "An Investigation into Future Performance and Overheating Risks in Passivhaus Dwellings," *Building and Environment* 70 (2013): 189–209.
14. Wouter van Marken Lichtenbelt et al., "Healthy Excursions Outside the Thermal Comfort Zone," *Building Research and Information* 45, no. 7 (2017): 819–27.
15. "Prof. Wolfgang Feist: 'We Can Still Do It!'," Passive House Accelerator, 8 June 2020.
16. John Perlin, *Let It Shine: The 6,000-Year Story of Solar Energy* (New World Library, 2022), 305.
17. Aristophanes, *The Clouds*, MIT Internet Classics Archive.
18. John Perlin, *Silicon Solar Cell Turns 50* (No. NREL/BR-520-33947), National Renewable Energy Lab, 2005.
19. John Perlin, *From Space to Earth: The Story of Solar Electricity* (Earthscan, 1999), viii.
20. Karl Wolfgang Böer and Esther Riehl, *The Life of the Solar Pioneer Karl Wolfgang Böer* (iUniverse, 2010), xi.
21. David Biello, "Where Did Carter's White House's Solar Panels Go?," *Scientific American*, 6 August 2010.
22. Rolf Disch, "Ohne Schornstein und Auspuff" [Without chimney and exhaust], YouTube, posted by TEDx Talks, 25 January 2017.
23. Rosenthal, "No Furnaces but Heat Aplenty."
24. "Rolf Disch wird siebzig" [Rolf Disch turns seventy], YouTube, posted by Solarsiedlung, 12 March 2014.
25. Steven Chu and Hartmut Michel, "Energy: Fuelling the Future," *Nature* 502, no. 7471 (2013): S60–61.
26. Melissa Eddy, "Germans Combat Climate Change from Their Balconies," *New York Times*, 29 July 2024; subsequent quotation from "Germans Combat Climate Change."
27. "3D Printing a 100-home Community in Texas, and Someday on the Moon," *60 Minutes*, posted to YouTube, 22 January 2023.
28. "Ariadne," *New Scientist*, 3 October 1974.
29. Hideo Kodama, "Automatic Method for Fabricating a Three-Dimensional Plastic Model with Photo-Hardening Polymer," *Review of Scientific Instruments* 52, no. 11 (1981): 1770–73.
30. Brad Lemley, "The Whole-House Machine," *Discover*, 28 April 2005.
31. Behrokh Khoshnevis, "Contour Crafting: Automated Construction." YouTube, posted by TEDx Talks, 15 May 2012.
32. Jack Nicas, "3-D Printed Gun Debate Unlikely to Be Put to Rest," *Wall Street Journal*, 7 May 2013.
33. Lauren Gallow, "What It's Really Like to Live in a 3D-Printed Home," *Dwell*, 23 May 2022.
34. "ICON's SXSW 2024 Showcase: DOMUS EX MACHINA," YouTube, posted by ICON, 12 March 2024.

35. Moshe Bar and Maital Neta, "Humans Prefer Curved Visual Objects," *Psychological Science* 17, no. 8 (2006): 645–48; Helmut Leder and Claus-Christian Carbon, "Dimensions in Appreciation of Car Interior Design," *Applied Cognitive Psychology* 19, no. 5 (2005): 603–18; Sibel Seda Dazkir and Marilyn A. Read, "Furniture Forms and Their Influence on Our Emotional Responses Toward Interior Environments," *Environment and Behavior* 44, no. 5 (2012): 722–32.
36. Alexander Coburn et al., "Psychological Responses to Natural Patterns in Architecture," *Journal of Environmental Psychology* 62 (2019): 133–45.
37. Kodama, "Automatic Method for Fabricating a Three-Dimensional Plastic Model," 1770–73.
38. Maximilian Meurer and Martin Classen, "Mechanical Properties of Hardened 3D Printed Concretes and Mortars—Development of a Consistent Experimental Characterization Strategy," *Materials* 14, no. 4 (2021): 752.
39. Rob Wolfs et al., "Lessons Learned of Project Milestone: The First 3D Printed Concrete House in the Netherlands," *Materials Today: Proceedings* (2023).
40. Ayodeji Emmanuel Oke et al., "Robotics and Automation for Sustainable Construction: Microscoping the Barriers to Implementation," *Smart and Sustainable Built Environment* 13, no. 3 (2024): 625–43.
41. Nathan Melenbrink et al., "On-site Autonomous Construction Robots: Towards Unsupervised Building," *Automation in Construction* 119 (2020): 103312.
42. David Belcher, "A New City, Built upon Data, Takes Shape in South Korea," *New York Times*, 28 March 2022; subsequent quotations from "A New City, Built upon Data."
43. Jackie Daly, "How to Solve the Housing Crisis," *Financial Times*, 7 December 2022.
44. Cara Buckley, "Living Car-Free in Arizona, on Purpose and Happily," *New York Times*, 25 March 2025.
45. Ben Ikenson, "America's 'First Car-Free Neighborhood' Is Going Pretty Good, Actually?," *Dwell*, 4 February 2025; subsequent quotation from "America's 'First Car-Free Neighborhood.'"
46. Joseph W. Kane, "Banning Cars Won't Solve America's Bigger Transportation Problem: Long Trips," *Brookings*, 6 January 2020.
47. Donald Appleyard, *Livable Streets* (University of California Press, 1981), 23; subsequent quotation from *Livable Streets*, 21.
48. Peter Norton, *Fighting Traffic: The Dawn of the Motor Age in the American City* (MIT Press, 2011).
49. Charles L. Marohn Jr., *Confessions of a Recovering Engineer: Transportation for a Strong Town* (John Wiley, 2021).
50. Robert Putnam, "The Strange Disappearance of Civic America," *The American Prospect*, 19 December 2001.
51. Peter Newman and Jeff Kenworthy, "Peak Car Use: Understanding the Demise of

Automobile Dependence," *World Transport Policy and Practice* 17, no. 2 (2011): 35–36; *Planning and Design for Sustainable Urban Mobility: Global Report on Human Settlements 2013* (UN Habitat, 2013).

52. Evan L. O'Keefe and Carl J. Lavie, "A Hunter-Gatherer Exercise Prescription to Optimize Health and Well-Being in the Modern World," *Journal of Science in Sport and Exercise* 3 (2021): 147–57.
53. Lawrence D. Frank et al., "Obesity Relationships with Community Design, Physical Activity, and Time Spent in Cars," *American Journal of Preventive Medicine* 27, no. 2 (2004): 87–96.
54. "Global Status Report on Road Safety," World Health Organization, 2009.
55. Stephen Johnson, "Want Fewer Car Accidents? Remove Traffic Signals and Road Signs," *Big Think*, 31 August 2017.
56. Jonathan Coppage, "Put a Stop to Stoplights," *American Conservative*, 31 March 2015.
57. Renate van der Zee, "How Amsterdam Became the Bicycle Capital of the World," *Guardian*, 5 May 2015.
58. "Neighbourhoods as Childhood Habitats," *Children's Environments Quarterly* 1, no. 4 (winter 1984/1985).
59. Ben Hamilton-Baillie, "Shared Space: Reconciling People, Places and Traffic," *Built Environment* 34, no. 2 (2008): 161–81.
60. Stephanie H. Murray, "What Adults Lost When Kids Stopped Playing in the Street," *Atlantic*, 29 July 2024.
61. Natalie Mueller et al., "Changing the Urban Design of Cities for Health: The Superblock Model," *Environment International* 134 (2020): 105132.
62. "Barcelona: Using Urban Design to Improve Urban Health," World Health Organization, 26 October 2021.
63. Carlos Moreno et al., "Introducing the '15-Minute City': Sustainability, Resilience and Place Identity in Future Post-Pandemic Cities," *Smart Cities* 4, no. 1 (2021): 93–111.
64. Sara González, "The Cycling Revolution in Paris Continues: Bicycle Use Now Exceeds Car Use," *El País*, 24 April 2024.
65. June Williamson and Ellen Dunham-Jones, *Case Studies in Retrofitting Suburbia: Urban Design Strategies for Urgent Challenges* (John Wiley, 2021).
66. Michael A. Rodriguez and Christopher B. Leinberger, "Foot Traffic Ahead: Ranking Walkable Urbanism in America's Largest Metros 2023," Smart Growth America, 24 January 2023.
67. John I. Gilderbloom et al., "Does Walkability Matter? An Examination of Walkability's Impact on Housing Values, Foreclosures and Crime," *Cities* 42 (2015): 13–24.
68. Rodriguez and Leinberger, "Foot Traffic Ahead."
69. Richard Florida and Charlotta Mellander, "Rise of the Startup City: The Chang-

NOTES 285

ing Geography of the Venture Capital Financed Innovation," *California Management Review* 59, no. 1 (2016): 14–38.
70. Jeroen Johan de Hartog et al., "Do the Health Benefits of Cycling Outweigh the Risks?," *Environmental Health Perspectives* 118, no. 8 (2010): 1109–16.
71. "Bicycle Technology," *Scientific American* 228, no. 3 (March 1973).

SEVEN: Nature as Blueprint

1. "Case Study: Mjøstårnet, Bergen—85.4m Tall Timber Tower," YouTube, posted by WoodSolutions, July 15, 2020.
2. Rebecca Mead, "Transforming Trees into Skyscrapers," *New Yorker*, 18 April 2022.
3. WoodSolutions, "Case Study: Mjøstårnet, Bergen."
4. Mead, "Transforming Trees."
5. Bianca C. Dreyer et al., "Beyond Exposure to Outdoor Nature: Exploration of the Benefits of a Green Building's Indoor Environment on Wellbeing," *Frontiers in Psychology* 9 (2018): 1583.
6. Thomas Gernay and Shuna Ni, *Timber High Rise Buildings and Fire Safety*, World Steel Association (2020).
7. Mead, "Transforming Trees."
8. "Concrete Needs to Lose Its Colossal Carbon Footprint," *Nature* 597, no. 7878 (2021): 593–94.
9. Michael Green, "Why We Should Build Wooden Skyscrapers," TED Talks, posted to YouTube 26 February 2013.
10. Miranda Lipton, "This Oakland Housing Complex Is Being Built with Mushroom Roots," *Fast Company*, 17 November 2023.
11. Lisa Melton, "How to Grow Cement," *Nature Biotechnology* 40 (2022): 286.
12. "Biocement: Growing Concrete with Bacteria," YouTube, posted by RE:TV, 8 December 2023.
13. "Resource Rows Part 1: New Construction Method with Reclaimed Materials | Eco Conscious Architecture," YouTube, posted by Reconstructing the World, 11 April 2024.
14. "The Resource Rows," EU Mies Award, Fundació Mies van der Rohe.
15. "'Anders Lendager: 'The Resourceful Architect,'" YouTube, posted by Architects Not Architecture, 14 October 2024.
16. "Circularity Gap Report 2021," Circularity Gap Reporting Initiative, 2021.
17. Norman Miller, The Industry Creating a Third of the World's Waste, BBC.com, 15 December 2021.
18. William McDonough and Michael Braungart, *Cradle to Cradle: Remaking the Way We Make Things* (North Point Press, 2010).
19. William McDonough and Michael Braungart, *The Upcycle: Beyond Sustainability—Designing for Abundance* (Macmillan, 2013).

20. Aaron Betsky, *Don't Build, Rebuild: The Case for Imaginative Reuse in Architecture* (Beacon Press, 2024).
21. Austin Williams, "Shigeru Ban (1957–)," *Architectural Review*, 16 March 2015.
22. "How to Design a Circular Building? Hans Hammink," YouTube, posted by Architektura Powinna, 18 October 2023.
23. "Circl: Clubhouse of Circularity," Archello.com.
24. Shira Rubin, "In Amsterdam, a Community of Floating Homes Shows the World How to Live Alongside Nature," *Washington Post*, 17 December 2021; subsequent quotation from "In Amsterdam."
25. "The Next Housing Disaster," *Economist*, 13 April 2024.
26. K. Porter et al., *Natural Hazard Mitigation Saves 2017 Interim Report: An Independent Study*, National Institute of Building Sciences, Multihazard Mitigation Council, December 2017.
27. "The Maldives Are Building a Floating City to Address Rising Sea Levels and Population," CBC Radio, 23 June 2022.
28. Emanuele Midolo, "Why I'm Building a Floating City in the Maldives," *Times* (UK), 4 June 2024.
29. Judith Rodin, *The Resilience Dividend: Being Strong in a World Where Things Go Wrong* (Public Affairs, 2014).
30. Terri Adams-Fuller, "Extreme Heat Is Deadlier Than Hurricanes, Floods and Tornadoes Combined," *Scientific American*, 1 July 2023.
31. Saidu Bah, "How Africa's First Heat Officer Is Protecting Women in Sierra Leone," BBC.com, 9 November 2023.
32. Eromo Egbejule, "'Now You Can Have Rest In Your Home': The Mirror Roofs Cooling Homes in Freetown," *Guardian*, 16 August 2024.
33. Sam Lubell, "Designed for Serenity, with Nature in Mind," *New York Times*, 10 October 2019; subsequent quotations from "Designed for Serenity."
34. Roger S. Ulrich, "View Through a Window May Influence Recovery from Surgery," Science 224, no. 4647 (1984): 420–21.
35. Cary Cooper and B. Browning, "Human Spaces: The Global Impact of Biophilic Design in the Workplace," Interface.com, 2015.
36. Edward O. Wilson, "Biophilia and the Conservation Ethic," in *Evolutionary Perspectives on Environmental Problems* (Routledge, 2017), 250–58.
37. Erdem Cuce, "Thermal Regulation Impact of Green Walls: An Experimental and Numerical Investigation," *Applied Energy* 194 (2017): 247–54.
38. "Spring 2022 UTSOA Lecture Series: Vo Trong Nghia," YouTube, posted by Texas Architecture, 21 February 2022.
39. "Khoo Teck Puat Hospital: Healing Through Nature," International Living Future Institute.
40. Tan Shao Yen, "The Practice of Integrated Design: The Case Study of Khoo Teck Puat Hospital, Singapore" (master's diss., University of Nottingham, 2012).

41. Urban Redevelopment Authority (Singapore), "Circular Package: LUSH Programme - Landscaping for Urban Spaces and High Rises," 29 April 2009.
42. Hannah Ritchie, *Not the End of the World: How We Can Be the First Generation to Build a Sustainable Planet* (Random House, 2024).
43. Alexander Robinson and Myvonwynn Hopton, "Cheonggyecheon Stream Restoration Project," Landscape Performance Series, Landscape Architecture Foundation, 2011.
44. Claudia Geib, "How 'Wilderness' Was Invented Without Indigenous Peoples," Sapiens.org, 3 February 2022.
45. Erle C. Ellis et al., "People Have Shaped Most of Terrestrial Nature for at Least 12,000 Years," *Proceedings of the National Academy of Sciences* 118, no. 17 (2021): e2023483118.

INDEX

Page numbers in italics refer to illustrations.

Abrigo de Navalmaíllo, Spain, *22*
Abu Hureyra, Syria, *38*
acid rain, 176
acoustics/soundproofing, 144, 145, 148, 213
adaptability of humans, 1, 3, 5–6, 24
    "adaptive comfort," 199–200
    in house design, 31, 33–34, 88, 134, 195, 200, 240–41, 244–45
    incremental growth and, 8, 191–92
adhesives, 229, 238
Aeschylus, 88
aesthetics, 57, 103, 134, 137, 165–66, 170, 178, 203, 213, 239
Africa, 1, 20, 24, 194
"agrarian urbanism," 116, 119
Agricultural Revolution, 10–11, 41–42. *See also* farming
"aided self-help," 189
'Ain Ghazal, Jordan, 49
'Ain Mallaha, *31*, 33
air conditioning, 16, 164–66, 174–77, 194–96, 198, 245, 249
airtightness, 4, 193, 197–200
Amsterdam, 121–24
    bio-based materials in, 232
    canal houses of, 121–31, *126*, 133
    designed for deconstruction (DfD) in, 238–39
    Fourth Extension of, 124–25, 129
    Schoonschip, 241–43, *242*, 247
andron, 91–93
Angkor, Cambodia, 117–20, *117*
animals
    dogs and cats, 33, 91, 97, 104
    domestication of, 10–12, 41–42, 47, 49, 54, 116, 254
    as material resource, 1, 10–12, 30, 34
    interpreting animal remains, 1, 64, 66
    niche construction by, 5–6, 7
    pollution from, 45–46, 49, 132
    swarm intelligence, 8, 64–65, 88, 214, 245
    for transport, 112
Antwerp, 122–23, 245
Anuradhapura, Sri Lanka, 119
apartment buildings, 138–48, *145*
    challenges of apartment living, 4, 16, 146, 148, 170
    elevators, 110, 144–48, 155, 184, 238, 244
    penthouses, 110–11, 144
    Roman *insulae*, 1, 106–13, *107*, 115, 117, 142
    tenements, 13, 111, 140–45, 147, 160, 180, 188
    walk-up apartments, 106, 144, 177
    Westhausen, Frankfurt, 158–61, *159*, 163
    See also Hong Kong; New York City
Appleyard, Donald, 218
aqueducts, 97, 101, 102, 113, 115, 116
Arabian Desert, 70
Aravena, Alejandro, 189, *190*, 192
archaeology, 1–18
    "agrarian urbanism," 116
    burial sites, 25, 47–48, 66, 93
    dwellings and permanence in, 19–51
    evidence of social stratification, 32, 64, 187
    on the fall of civilizations, 118
    home as workplace, 91
    lidar (light detection and ranging) surveys, 117, 214

archaeology (*continued*)
    problems of interpretation in, 9–10, 28
    on the rise of cities, 65–69
architectural design. *See* design
architecture
    during the Agricultural Revolution, 10–11, 41–42
    the architect's role, 3, 14, 18–19, 101, 215, 239
    architectural imperialism, 165–66
    evolving through artificial selection, 17
    "florescence of architecture," 54–55
    during the Industrial Revolution, 10, 13–15, 106, 121, 133, 136, 153, 161, 188, 194–95, 212, 235
    the Sustainability Transition, 10
    as technology for human survival, 1, 3, 5–6, 31, 33–34, 88, 134, 195, 200, 240–41, 244–45
    during the Urban Revolution, 10, 11–13, 73, 76–79
    See also design; dwellings; construction
Architecture of Country Houses (Downing), 150–51
Aristophanes, 91, 202
Aristotle, 87–88, 90–91, 93
Arlington, VA, 222–24
artificial intelligence (AI), 14, 15, 214, 215
"A-Sitting on a Tell" (Christie), 62
asphalt, 80, 176–77, 222, 253
Athens Charter of 1933, 198
Athens, 88, 96. *See also* Greece
Atlantic Monthly, 154
atrium house design, 11, 96–106, *98*, 111, 200, 246
Austin, TX, 208–10, 216
Australia, 6, 150, 240
avant-garde, 161, 207

Baby Boom, 168
Bachelard, Gaston, 5
backyards, 16, 219
Ballard, J. G., 178–79
balloon-frame construction, 153–55, 225
bamboo, 230–31
Ban, Shigeru, 237–38, *237*
Bangladesh, 244
Barbican Estate, London, 178
Barcelona, 16, 112, 221
barley, 30, 36, 37, 55, 70, 73, 116, 122
barriadas of Lima, 188

batteries, 202, 205–6, 208
Bauer, Catherine, 159
Bauhaus, 161, 164, 166
beaver dams, 6, 7
Becquerel, Edmond, 202
Bedouins, 42–43
"bedroom communities," 174
Beidha, Jordan, 36–39, 42–43
Belfer-Cohen, Anna, 49–50
Bell Labs, 202
Bell, Gertrude, 58
Bellerophon mosaic, Olynthus, 92
Benyus, Janine, 233
béton brut (raw concrete), 178
Betsky, Aaron, 236
bicycles, 222–23
bio-based materials, 14, 15, 225, 228, 231, 232
"bioclimatic architecture," 196–97
biodiversity, 34, 116, 250–51, 253–55
Biomason, 232
"biomimicry," 233
biophilic design principles, 210, 249–51
Birkenhead's Hamilton Square, 134
bitumen, 70, 79–80
Black families, 173
"blower door tests," 198
blueprints, 15, 191, 215
Boelen, Siti, 243
Böer, Karl Wolfgang, 202–3
Boeri, Stefano, 251, *252*
Bosco Verticale, Milan, 251, *252*
Boston, 152
bourgeoisie, 13, 124, 130
Bowling Alone (film), 219
Brasilia, 186–87
Braungart, Michael, 236
Brazil, 44–45, 130, 186–87
bricks, 55–57, 66–69, 75–79, 85
    brick forms, 82
    brick-laying ceremony, 75–76
    facades of, 111, 137–38
    limitations of, 80
    perforated for cross ventilation, 249
    production process, 82
    repurposed, 112
    yellow klinkers, 130
Brides (magazine), 171
Bristol, UK, 221
Britain
    building codes in, 251
    competition with the Dutch, 130

INDEX

the English garden tradition, 151
House of Commons, 5
Liverpool terrace houses, 10, 13, 131–38, *136*, 140
London, 133–34, 136, 178, 188, 202, 239
Broadacre City, 166–67, 176
Bronze Age, 50, 88
Brookline neighborhood of Boston, 152
Brooklyn's brownstones, 137, 140, 147, 241
Browning, Elizabeth Barrett, 136
Bruniquel Cave, France, 24
Brunswick Centre, London, 178
Brutalist architecture, 17, 166, 178
bucrania (bull horn decorations), 47
building codes, 15, 77, 109, 111, 129, 134, 189–90, 200
Building the Dream (G. Wright), 170
building-integrated photovoltaics (BIPV), 202–3
built environment, 7–8, 17–18, 21, 59, 85, 105–6, 189–90, 207, 243. *See also* architecture
Built Robotics, 214
burial sites, 25, 47–48, 66, 93
Busan, South Korea, 215
Butterlin, Pascal, 60–61

California, 137, 172, 222, 231, 239
Callendar, Guy, 194
Calvinist austerity, 128–29
Cambodia, 117–20, *117*
Canada, *28*, 197
canals, 70, 84, 118, 121–31, *126*, 140, 150, 242, 247
Caracas, Venezuela, 187
carbon pollution
    embodied carbon, 199, 208, 212, 227, 231–32, 239
    global carbon dioxide emissions, 7–8, 194, 212, 220, 230
    global warming, 194, 199–200, 246
    life-cycle thinking to combat, 18, 236, 239
    reducing, 199, 212, 229, 234, 243–44
CarbonCure Technologies, 232
cardboard tube construction, 237, *237*
Carlsberg brewery, Copenhagen, 233
Carrier, Willis, 164–65
cars, 4, 156–57, 173–77, 218–23, 227
    electric vehicles, 205–6
    garages, 171, 175, 216, 219, 240
    parking, 18, 174, 180, 217, 219, 224, 240, 255
    See also suburban living

Çatalhöyük, Turkey, 2, 3, 43–51, *44*, 72
Caterpillar, 214
cats, 97
Cave Canem ("Beware of the Dog"), 104
cave dwellings/rock shelters, 9, 17, 19, 22–26, *22*
cedar, 83
cellae (single-room units), 106
Celts, 97
cement, 212, 230, 232, 235–36
Central Park, New York, 153
Cervero, Robert, 184
Chicago, 13, 150, 153–55, 172
"Chicago Construction," 154
Child Welfare Manual, 170–71
Childe, Gordon, 41, 73
China, 9, 31, 73, 210
    city of Anyang, 94
    People's Republic of China, 179–80
    Shenzhen, China, 188, 190–91
    siheyuan (courtyard houses), 75, *95*, 95
Christie, Agatha, 62
Churchill, Winston, 5
Cicero, 103, 109, 113–14
Cincinnati, OH, 152
CIRCL Pavilion, Amsterdam, 238–39
cities, 52–86
    the cost of, 83–86
    dense vs. dispersed urban living, 113–20
    informal settlements, 15, 44–45, 64, 185–92, 205, 236–37
    preindustrial cities, 13–14, 118, 233, 235
    proto-cities, 8, 62–69
    in the sky, 177–85, *183*
    walkable neighborhoods, 15, 16–18, 155–58, 191, 218, 221–23
    See also urban living; urban planning; *major cities around the world*
città giardini of Italy, 150
Clark, Desmond, 22
Clark, Edward Cabot, 145
class, 94, 97
    middle-class homes, 7, 111, 127–28, 141–42, 170–72, 175–76
    working-class homes, 13, 131–32, 135, 163, 165
    See also cities; suburban living; urban living
Claudius, 112, 113
clay, 14, 29, 37, 46, 72–73, 213. *See also* bricks
cleanliness, 127, 146, 162
Climate adaptation, 14 , 116–119 , 241–247
climate change, 8, 14–15, 88, 118, 120, 131, 219, 242–44, 246

climate control. *See* indoor temperatures
Climatic design, 87–88 , 90 , 100–101 ,
    164–166 , 194–197 , 200
climatic eras, 35, 115, 116, 118, 243
Cloaca Maxima ("Greatest Sewer"), 102
Clouds (Aristophanes), 202
coal, 136, 143, 147, 150, 159, 176, 200, 201, 205
Code of Hammurabi, 77
Cold War politics, 171
Colosseum of Rome, 109
comfort, 7–8, 24, 127–28, 193–200, 218, 255
commuters, 152–53, 173, 222
composite materials, 56, 61, 231, 243
concrete, 11–12, 18
    alternatives to, 231–33
    béton brut (raw concrete), 178
    formwork, 210
    high rises and, 179–80, 184
    precast components, 160
    radiant heat, 169
    reinforced, 56, 111, 232, 236
    Roman, 11–12, 108–9, 111
    in 3D printing, 208, 210, 213
    as waste, 235–36
    wood vs., 226–27, 229–30
condensation. *See* moisture control
Condition of the Working Class in England (Engels), 132
Confessions of a Recovering Engineer (Marohn), 219
Congrès Internationaux d'Architecture Moderne (CIAM-2), 163
construction
    balloon-frame construction, 153–55, 225
    circular construction, 235–40
    from a craft into an industry, 154
    improvisational, 54–55, 236–37
    life-cycle thinking in, 18, 236, 239
    mixed-use development, 15, 112, 182, 221–23
    as place-making, 2, 20–23, 29–30, 219–20, 223, 236–37
    planned, 52–56
    resilient, 14, 243–47
    retrofitting, 222, 238
    salvage, 233–41, *234*, *237*
    skyscrapers, 6, 15, 144, 155, 164–65, 179, 181–82, 190–91, 199, 252
    on spec (without buyers), 134
    3D printing and automation in, 14, 17, 208–16, *211*

    waste from, 212, 227, 236–37, *237*, 240
    See also houses; infrastructure
consumerism, 7, 127–28, 160–62, 174
"Consumers' Republic," 171
"contour crafting," 210, 213
Copán, 116, 187
Copenhagen, 233, *234*
"core housing," 189
corridors, 17, 57, 127
Costa, Lúcio, 186
COVID-19 pandemic, 221
Crabgrass Frontier (K. T. Jackson), 176
Crane, Jacob, 188–89
Crassus, Marcus Licinius, 107
cross ventilation, 16, 197, 200, 249
cross-laminated timber (CLT), 15, 226, 227
Culdesac neighborhood of Tempe, AZ, 216–24, *217*
cuneiform, 72–73
curtain walls on corporate towers, 164
cycling, 222–23

Dafen village, south China, 191
Dakota, The, New York, *145*, 145–46
Darwinian evolution, 5, 17
Das Neue Frankfurt (magazine), 160, 162
Davis, Alexander Jackson, 152–53
De Architectura (Vitruvius), 100
de Architekten Cie, 238
de Blok, Marjan, 241–43, *242*
de Ruyter, Michiel, 128
"Debate Between Bird and Fish," 52
deforestation, 42, 48–49, 83, 90, 112, 114, 123, 154, 237
Delft, Netherlands, 16, 128
Delhi, 188, 190
demography
    constraints on growth, 13, 65–66, 118–19, 194
    death rates, 131, 140
    life expectancy, 4, 115, 133, 223
    longevity "blue zones," 223
    low birth rates, 115, 188
    mass die-offs, 181
    population displacement, 179, 244
Denmark, 233–36, *234*, 239–40
density, 113–20
    architectural forms and, 3, 39, 54–55, 177–85
    dangers and costs of, 3, 4, 42, 77, 84, 195–96

decentralized growth, 63
historical memory and, 48
innovation and, 73, 184
low-density communities, 116–20, 175
sprawl, 54, 63, 85, 112–13, 117–20, 156, 173–74, 184–85, 216–17
sustainability and nature despite, 247–52
deserts, 6, 29, 42–43, 73–74, 84, 113, 165, 189
design
aesthetics, 57, 103, 134, 137, 165–66, 170, 178, 203, 213, 239
avant-garde, 161, 207
Bauhaus, 161, 164, 166
design for deconstruction (DfD), 238–39
Georgian architecture, 134, 137
for longevity in the face of obsolescence, 165, 208, 241
Metabolist movement, 207
modern architecture, 164–66, 179, 236, 240
for modularity, 17, 94–95, 238
roundness vs. squareness in, 6–7, 31–32, 36–43, *38*, 82, 151–52, 210–11, 213
for structural soundness, 6, 32, 108, 208, 212–13, 227, 230–31, 236
symmetry in, 27, 32, 125
See also modernist architecture; *specific house systems*
diabetes, 4, 220
Dickens, Charles, 138
Digest of Roman Law, 110
Disch, Rolf, 203–4, *204*
dogs, 33, 91, 104
"doing the step" with a Donkey Stone, 137, 138
domestication. *See* farming
domus (Roman atrium house), 11, 96–106, *98*, 111, 200, 246
Don't Build, Rebuild (Betsky), 236
Donkey Stone, "doing the step" with a, 137, 138
doors, 57, 59, 71–72, 93, 127
Dosier, Ginger Krieg, 232
Downing, Andrew Jackson, 150–53
"drive-in civilization," 175
"dumbbell" floor plan, 141
Duncan, William Henry, 131–33
Dutch East India Company (VOC), 123
Dutch Navy, 130
Dutch Republic, 124. *See also* Amsterdam; Netherlands

dwellings, 1–5
cave dwellings/rock shelters, 9, 17, 19, 22–26, *22*
evolutionary imperative of, 5–8
four transformations in, 10–14
the household as economic unit, 7–8
from huts to high-rises, 8–15
as permanent places, 19–51
the rise of cities, 52–86
for tomorrow, 15–18
a universal logic of habitation, 61
See also houses

earthquakes, 109, 210, 237
East 17th Street development, Austin, TX, 209
École des Beaux Arts, Paris, 143
"economy," 7–8, 91
ecosystems, 7, 24, 34, 49, 236, 250, 253–54. *See also* environmental impacts
"edible" space, 251
Edison, Thomas, 146, 152–53, 201, 206
efficiency, 3–4, 6, 13–14
in construction, 133–35, 137–38, 144
from economies of scale, 12, 70–71, 90, 184, 185
in energy usage, 61, 218, 223, 229–30
in food production, 41
scientific management, 3–4, 161
of solar power, 201–3
standardization and, 160
symbiotic exchange and, 240
in urban planning, 89, 218
in use of space, 6, 32, 54–55, 57, 81
vertical living and shared infrastructure, 147–48
Eichler, Joseph, 172
Eindhoven, Netherlands, 210–11, *211*
El Kahun, Egypt, 93–94
Elamites, 84
electricity, 146–47, 162, 194, 201
batteries, 202, 205–6, 208
Edison's Pearl Street Station, 146, 201, 206
electric vehicles, 205–6
elevators, 146, 155
smart grids, 206
trains, 155
See also solar energy
electrochromic glass, 206
elevators, 110, 144–48, 155, 184, 238, 244
Elgsaas, Øystein, 228
"embarrassment of riches," 128

"emergence," 64–65
"energized crowding," 73
energy
    coal, 136, 143, 147, 150, 159, 176, 200, 201, 205
    energy crises, 159, 196, 199, 202–3
    energy-intensive designs, 165–66
    fossil fuels, 194–95, 205, 223
    oil and gas, 146, 196–97, 199, 200, 201, 202
    operational energy use, 184, 223, 229–30
enfilade design, 57, 59
Engels, Friedrich, 132
engineered wood, 14, 226–30
engineering, 6, 17, 19, 21, 26–27
Enkidu (mythical hero), 83
environmental impacts, 9, 219
    acid rain, 176
    deforestation, 42, 48–49, 83, 90, 112, 114, 123, 154, 237
    erosion, 42, 77, 83, 112, 114
    extinctions, 28, 34
    gigantism and ecological collapse, 119
    global carbon dioxide emissions, 7, 194, 212, 220, 230
    landfills, 61, 235–36
    salinization of the soil, 83–84
    See also waste
Epic of Gilgamesh, The, 80, 81–83, 201–2
Erie Canal, 140, 150
erosion, 42, 77, 83, 112, 114
estates in Hong Kong, 180–81
Etruscans, 97–98
Euphrates, 37, 52–53, 70, 78, 79, 84
Europe
    during the Ice Age, 25–27, 30, 35, 115, 118, 243
    the lawns of the aristocracy, 175–76
    medieval Europe, 116, 123–24, 129, 142
evaporative cooling, 246
Evelyn, John, 129
extinction, 28, 34
eye idols, 62, 67–69

famines, 23, 84, 140
farming
    domestication of animals, 10–12, 41–42, 47, 49, 54, 116, 254
    domestication of plants, 11, 116, 254
    irrigation, 11, 57, 61, 63, 70, 84, 113, 240
    plows, 70, 88

Farnsworth House, IL, 164, *165*
favelas of Rio de Janeiro, 44–45, 187
Federal-Aid Highway Act of 1956, 173
feed-in tariff for renewable energy, 204
Feist, Wolfgang, 193–94, 198, 200
feudalism, 123–24
Fez, Morocco, 75
"15-minute city," 16, 85, 221–22
fire, 21–24
    fire resistance/safety, 90, 108–9, 228–29, 246, 250
    hearths, 22–29, 32, 45, 46, 90
    wildfires, 14, 246
Flannery, Kent, 40, 54, 55
Fletcher, Roland, 118–19
floods, 39, 55, 70, 77–78, 83, 121–22, 187, 194, 242, 243–46, 249, 253
floor space demand, 7, 229
"florescence of architecture," 54–55
folkhemmet public housing, 163
formaldehyde, 229
Fort Steurgat, Netherlands, 240
fossil fuels, 194–95, 205, 223
foundations, 27, 32, 36, 37, 46, 56, 82, 89–90, 123–25, 130, 168, 231
France, 130, 134, 151
    prehistoric humans in, 9–10, 24–26, *24*, *25*
    sustainable building policies, 232, 239
Frankfurt, 158–64, *159*
Frankfurt Kitchen, 3–4, 161–64
Fraunhofer Institute for Solar Energy Systems (ISE), 203
freedom, 123, 167, 174–77, 189, 223
Freetown, Sierra Leone, 246–47
Freiburg, Germany, 203–4, *204*
French drains, 50, 79
"French flats," 142–44
frescoes, 99, 103, 104–5
fresh air, 71, 198. *See also* windows
Fritts, Charles, 201–2, 208
frontage, 125
Frontinus, Sextus Julius, 101
Fuller, Buckminster, 18
"functional diagrams," 161

Gans, Herbert, 174
garages, 171, 175, 216, 219, 240
garden suburbs, 149, 150, 152–55, 157, 167, 170
gardens, 97, 103, 105–6, 128, 151, 153, 240, 245, 250–51

INDEX

gas lights, 146
gated communities, 152
GDP, 12, 134, 222
gender, 4, 48, 91–93, 139
Genesis (bible), 78
Georgian architecture, 134, 137
Germany, 130, 134, 145, 150, 163, 193, 199–200
    energy policy in, 200, 203–5
    Frankfurt, 3–4, 158–64, *159*
GI Bill of 1944, 170
Gilgamesh (mythical hero), 80, 81–83, 201–2
Glasl, Sascha, 243
glass skyscrapers, 164–65, 252
Glendale, OH, 152
global carbon dioxide emissions, 7, 194, 212, 220, 230
Global South, 188, 236
glued laminated timber (glulam), 226–27
Goldberger, Paul, 169–70
"golden triangle" of the kitchen, 161–62
Goldfinger, Erno, 178
Goring-Morris, Nigel, 49–50
GPS, 214
granaries, 33–35, 59, 71
Grand Central Hotel, New York, 139
Grand Hotel, Paris, 138
gray water, 240, 251
"Great Arctic Office Conspiracy," 195
Great Depression, 168
Great Fire of Rome (64 AD), 109
"Great Flood," 77–78
Greece, 7–12, 88–96, *89*, 100–102, 114, 195, 217–18
green roofs, 198, 250, 253
green space, 156, 159, 177, 247–48
Green, Michael, 230–31
Gruen, Victor, 174
Gudea of Sumer, 75–76
gynaikonitis, 91, 92
gypsum, 46, 57, 77, 240

Haber-Bosch process, 160
Habuba Kabira, 71–74
Haeckel, Ernst, 8
Hafford, William, 81
"Half a House," 189, *190*, 192
Hall, Edward, 181, 184
Hamilton, J. R., 142–43
Hammink, Hans, 239
Hammurabi, 77

"handshake houses," 190–91
Hanoi, 249
Hardenbergh, Henry Janeway, 145, *145*
Harris, Jack, 22
Hassuna culture, 53–55, *54*
heart disease, 4
hearths, 22–29, 32, 45, 46, 90
heating, 61, 96, 102–3, 147, 246
    heat exchangers, 193
    heat pumps, 223
    heat-recovery ventilators, 198
    passive, 193–95
    radiant heat, 169
height caps, 109. *See also* vertical living
heliocamini (solar furnace rooms), 102–3, 202
Heliotrope, 203–4
hempcrete, 212, 231
Herodotus, 12
Hidalgo, Anne, 221
High Baroque architecture, 20
High-Rise (Ballard), 178–79
Hippodamus of Miletus, 94
"History Houses," 48
Ho Chi Minh City, 247–50, *248*
Hodder, Ian, 48
Hodgkinson, Patrick, 178
Holston, James, 186
Home Insurance Building, Chicago, 155
homelessness, 180, 209, 216. *See also* informal settlements
homeownership, 103, 140, 172–73, 188
homes, 1–5
    comfort, 7–8, 24, 127–28, 193–200, 218, 255
    home maintenance, 12, 46, 50–51, 61–62, 80, 203, 251
    the ideal home, 87
    modern concept of home, 124
    safety, 23, 108, 187
    See also households
Homo sapiens, 20–21, 24, 26
Hong Kong, 13, 15, 16, 179–85, *183*, 188, 195–96
"horse-cars," 155
horses, 70, 152
hospitals, 249–50
hotel flats, 138–42
House for Trees, Ho Chi Minh City, 248–49, *248*
House Form and Culture (Rapoport), 17
house mice, 33, 97, 109
House of the Tragic Poet, Pompeii, 104
House of the Vettii, Pompeii, 104–5

INDEX

households
- divine households in temples, 2, 8, 9, 12, 60, 62–63, 67–72, 75–77, 81, 90, 97, 100, 119
- division of labor in, 11, 42, 54, 65
- as economic unit, 7–8
- gender divisions in, 4, 48, 91–93, 139
- servants, 115, 124, 139, 142, 147, 162, 215

houses, 1–5
- of ancient Greece, 87–96, *89*
- for basic shelter, 19–30, *22, 25, 27–29*
- evolution from huts to high-rises, 8–15
- floor space demand, 7, 229
- house sizes, 32, 91–92
- indoor air quality, 4, 146, 176, 194, 228
- lot sizes, 153, 175
- as a machine for living in, 177
- as a machine for parking, 219
- next to other houses, 43–51, *44*
- open-plan layout, 157, 171
- pit houses, 11, 30–35, *31*
- as powerplant, 201–8, *204, 207*
- "primitive hut" theory of architecture, 9–10, 19–21
- as symbolic unit, 26, 60
- *See also* cities; design

housing shortages, 112–13, 140, 160, 168, 177, 216
Houston, TX, 175, 244
Hunt, Richard Morris, 143
hunter-gatherers, 2, 4, 24–41, 50, 119, 220, 250.
   See also Natufian people of the Levant
hurricanes, 244–46
huts, 1, 8–11, 17, 19–21, 25–28, *27*, 30–31, 57–59, *58*, 97, 108, 186
HVAC systems, 195, 200. *See also* indoor temperatures
hydrogen tanks, 203
hygiene, 45–46. *See also* cleanliness; health
hypocaust systems, 102

Ice Age Europe, 25–27, 30, 35, 30, 115, 118, 243
ICON (company), 208–11, 216
Illinois, 149–57, *156*, 164, *165*. *See also* Chicago
immigration, 140–41. *See also* migration
impluvium (sunken basin), 98, 102
indoor air quality, 4, 146, 176, 194, 228
indoor temperatures
- air conditioning, 16, 164–66, 174–77, 194–96, 198, 245, 249
- airtightness, 4, 193, 197–200
- cross ventilation, 16, 197, 200, 249
- evaporative cooling, 246
- extreme heat, 245–46
- insulation, 30, 37, 187, 193, 196–201, 203, 212, 231, 238, 239, 243
- passive solar design, 14, 87, 96, 193–201
- *See also* heating

"industrial ecology," 240
Industrial Revolution, 10, 13–15, 106, 121, 133, 136, 153, 161, 188, 194–95, 212, 235
informal settlements, 15, 44–45, 64, 185–92, 205, 236–37
infrastructure, 7, 13, 18, 70
- climate impacts on, 118–19
- cutting the cost of, 159–60
- efficiency of shared, 147–48
- leapfrogging the fossil fuel infrastructure, 205–6
- population decline and, 115, 119
- social infrastructure, 163, 181
- transportation, 171, 181–82, 184–85

Ingels, Bjarke, 216
Insula of Diana, Ostia, *107*, 111–12
insulae, 1, 106–13, *107*, 115, 117, 142
insulation, 30, 37, 187, 193, 196–201, 203, 212, 231, 238, 239, 243
insurance, 123, 244, 246
International Building Code, 232
International Energy Agency, 206–7
International Exhibition of Modern Decorative and Industrial Arts in Paris, 177
International Style, 165
"intimate distance," 184
Inuit igloo, 27, *28*
Iquique, Chile, 189, *190*
Iraq, 53, *53*, 55, 57–58, *57, 59*, 83, 113
Irish Potato Famine in 1845, 140
Iron Bamboo, 230
irrigation, 11, 57, 61, 63, 70, 84, 113, 240
ISE. *See* Fraunhofer Institute for Solar Energy Systems (ISE)
Israel, 11, 28–29, *29*, 30, *31*, 49, 52–53
Italy, 124, 134, 150, 246, 251, *252*. *See also* Rome

Jackson, Kenneth T., 176
Jacobs House (Solar Hemicycle), Madison, WI, 196, *197*
Jacobs, Jane, 241
Japan, 202, 209, 213, 225, 237
Jeffersonian ideal of independent homeownership, 140

INDEX

Jencks, Charles, 179
Jenney, William LeBaron, 155, *156*
Jericho, West Bank, 39
Jobs, Steve, 223
Johnson, Ryan, 217
Jones, David, 209
Justinian Code, 103, 202
Juvenal, 108, 110

Kahn, Louis, 196
Kalambo Falls, Zambia, 21
Kalundborg eco-industrial park, Denmark, 239–40
Kellett, Peter, 187
Kennedy, Brook, 213
Khirbat al-Fakhar (Hamoukar), Syria, 62–69
Khmer empire, 118
Khoshnevis, Behrokh, 209–10
Kin Ming Estate, *183*
Kindel, Peter, 218
kindergartens, 162, 178
King, Moses, 147
kitchens, 3–4, 16, 46, 99, 101, 128, 132, 143–44, 157, 161–64, 172
Kobe earthquake, Japan, 237
Kodama, Hideo, 209
Korea, Republic of, 215, 253
Kostof, Spiro, 12, 37, 73
Kuhn, Steven, 21, 23
Kulla (brick god), 76
!Kung people in the Kalahari Desert, 12, 29
Kunstler, James Howard, 153, 175
Kurokawa, Kisho, 207–8, *207*

La Folie camp, France, 25–26, *25*
labor
    commuting to work, 152–53, 173, 222
    maintenance and upkeep, 12, 46, 50, 61–62, 77, 80, 184, 251
    migrant labor, 64, 132–33, 140, 160, 186
    nonunion workers, 169
    slavery, 71, 95–96, 107, 123
    work from home, 221
Lagos, Nigeria, 187, 190
"Lament for Ur," 85–86
landfills, 61, 235–36
lapis specularis, 102–3, 202
lasers, 209–10, 216
Late Antique Little Ice Age, 115, 118, 243
lateral forces, 226
Laugier, Marc-Antoine, 9, 19–20

laundry, 110, 112
lawns, 4, 103, 106, 149, 151, 175–76
Lazaret Cave, France, 23
Le Corbusier, 177–79, 182, 186, 189–90, 198
Lebanese cedar, 83
Lendager, Anders, 233–35, *234*
Levitt, Alfred, 171, 172
Levitt, William "Bill," 167–68, 169, 170–72
Levittown(s), 167–74, *168*
Levittowners, The (Gans), 174
liberalism, 123
Licht, Luft und Sonnenschein (light, air, and sunshine), 158–59
lidar (light detection and ranging) surveys, 117, 214
Life (magazine), 169, 173
life expectancy, 4, 115, 133, 223
light. *See* electricity; natural light
Lima, Peru, 185–86, 188–89
lime, 46, 49, 108–9, 212, 231
Limits of Settlement Growth (Fletcher), 118–19
linseed/linoleum, 55, 231
Livable Streets (Appleyard), 218
Liverpool terraced houses, 10, 13, 131–38, *136*, 140
livestock, 65, 254
Livy, 106
liwan (Middle Eastern long room), 71
Llewellyn Park, NJ, 152–53, 157
London, 133–34, 136, 178, 188, 202, 239
Long Island, NY, 167
Loos, Adolf, 161
Los Angeles, CA, 236
lot sizes, 153, 175
"Lower Manhattan Expressway," 240–41
L-shaped house plans, 157, 172
Lucan, 114
lumber. *See* wood
Lysias, 92

malaria, 112, 114–15
Malé, Maldives, 244
Mallowan, Max, 62, 67
malls, 174–75, 191, 222
mammoth-bone huts, 1, 25–28, *27*, 30–31
"Man Who Loved Levittown, The" (Wetherell), 170
Manchester, UK, 132
Manhattan. *See* New York City
mansard roofs, 139, 143
manzanas of Barcelona, 221

marble, 96–97, 99–100, 104, 105, 235
Marina One, Singapore, 250–51
"Mark I" buildings, 180
Marohn, Charles, 219
Marrakech, Morocco, 75
Marseille, 177, 178
Marsh Arabs, 58
Martial (poet), 110
Maslow's hierarchy of human needs, 2
mass production, 71, 160, 162, 167, 172, 195, 209, 235
mass timber (engineered wood panels), 14, 228–32
Mass Transit Railway Corporation (MTRC) of Hong Kong, 182
mass transit. *See* public transit
material passports, 238–39
materials
  adhesives, 229, 238
  bio-based materials, 14, 15, 225, 228, 231, 232
  cardboard tubes, 237, *237*
  composites, 56, 61, 231, 243
  lapis specularis, 102–3, 202
  See also bricks; wood; *other common construction materials*
May, Ernst, 158–63, *159*, 166
Maya urban centers of the Central Lowlands, 94, 116–17, 119, 187
McCarthy, Joseph, 171
McDonough, William, 236
medieval Europe, 116, 123–24, 129, 142
Medieval Warm Period, 116
Mediterranean Sea, 30, 37, 42, 88, 96
megacities, 64, 188
megastructures, 178–79, 181
Melenbrink, Nathan, 214
Mellaart, James, 43
Mesopotamia, 52–86
  the Tigris and Euphrates, 37, 52–53, 55, 70, 79, 84
  Ubaid culture of, 57–62, 67, 71
  Ur, 3, 77, 78, 80, 82–86
  Uruk, 8, 69–75, 81, 82
  Zagros Mountains, 70, 84
Metabolist movement, 207
Metropolitan Museum of Art, 68
Mezhirich, Ukraine, 26–27, *27*
Miami, FL, 244
mice, 33, 97, 109, 181

micromorphology, 10
middle-class homes, 7, 111, 127–28, 141–42, 170–72, 175–76
Mies van der Rohe, Ludwig, 164, *165*
migrant labor, 64, 132–33, 140, 160, 186
Milan, 251, *252*
"missing middle housing" in North America, 15, 138
Mithen, Steven, 27, 47
mixed-use development, 15, 112, 182, 221–23
Mjøstårnet, Brumunddal, Norway, 226–29, *227*
modern architecture, 164–66, 179, 236, 240
Modern Housing (May), 159
modernist architecture, 3–4, 13–14, 161–66
  Brutalism, 17, 166, 178
  California modernism, 172
  Farnsworth House, IL, 164, *165*
  flaws in the modernist mindset, 187–92
  the Frankfurt Kitchen, 3–4, 161–64
  French modernism, 177–78
  mantra on form, 235
  Westhausen, Frankfurt, 158–61, *159*, 163
Mohenjo-Daro in the Indus Valley, 93–94
moisture control, 77–80, 89–90, 197–99, 208, 210
Monderman, Hans, 220
Montessori, Maria, 162
moon rocks, 216
Moreno, Carlos, 221
Morocco, 75
Morris & Essex railroad line, New Jersey, 152, 157
mortar, 37, 79–80, 82, 90, 91, 125, 216, 235
mortise-and-tenon joinery, 154
mosaics, 72, 91–92, 96, 100, 104, 111
Moses, Robert, 240
Mount Vesuvius, 105, 109
mudhif (long, arched guesthouse), 58, *58*
multistory construction. *See* vertical living
Mumbai, 188
Mumford, Lewis, 73
mycelium composite insulation, 231
Mykonos, Greece, 217–18

nails, 153, 154
Nakagin Capsule Tower, Tokyo, 207–8, *207*
Napier, Mark, 187
Napoleon III, 139
NASA, 216

INDEX

Native Americans of the Sonoran Desert, 31
Natufian people of the Levant, 11, 30–35, *31*, 36–39
natural light, 4–5, 89–90, 115, 147, 158–59, 182–83, 200, 240. *See* solar energy
nature
   in false dichotomy against civilization, 253–56
   harmonious proportions and natural shapes, 100, 210
   the myth of "pristine" nature, 34, 253
   "natural fallacies," 251–52
   our relationship with nature, 3, 35, 50, 121, 130
   See also environmental impacts
Nazi Party, 163
Neanderthals, 20, 24–26, *25*
Neo-Assyrians, 81
Neolithic period, 36–37, 39–41, 44, 49–50, 85
Nero, 109, 111
Netherlands, 18–19, 121–24
   Amsterdam's canal houses, 121–31, *126*, 133
   bourgeoisie of, 124
   building standards in, 200
   disaster year of 1672, 130
   Eindhoven's 3D printed houses, 210–11, *211*
   growing up Dutch, 18, 223–24, 247
   Oostvaardersplassen rewilding, 254
   polders, 18, 123
   repurposed buildings in, 240
   row houses, 13, 15–16
   traffic control in Oudehaske, 220
   Utrecht, 166, 251
   the *woonerfs* ("living streets") of, 220–21, 223–24
   See also Amsterdam
New Orleans, 245, 246
New Scientist (magazine), 209
New York City
   Brooklyn's brownstones, 137, 140, 147, 241
   Central Park, 153
   The Dakota, *145*, 145–46
   high-rise apartments of, 138–48, *145*
   housing crisis of the 1830s, 140
   "Lower Manhattan Expressway," 240–41
   Metropolitan Museum of Art, 68
   railroad flats of, 140
   SoHo neighborhood of, 241
   Stuyvesant Flats, 143–45, 148

Stuyvesant Town–Peter Cooper Village superblock, 179, 180
   tenements of, 13, 111, 140–45, 147, 160, 180, 188
New York State, 141, 161, 176
New York Times, 139, 140, 142, 169, 195, 202
New York Tribune, 138, 143
Newlands, James, 133
Nghia, Vo Trong, 247–50, *248*, 254
"niche construction," 5–6
niche-and-buttress facades, 60
Niemeyer, Oscar, 186
Nigeria, 187, 190
nitrogen dioxide, 221
Nixtun-Ch'ich' (city), 94
nomadism, 2, 12, 33, 35, 42–43, 50, 83–84
Norton, Peter, 219
Nothus, Ancarenus, 106
Núcleo Bandeirante neighborhood of Brasilia, 186
Nugent, Thomas, 127

oak, 30, 83, 128
"obese buildings," 200
obesity, 4, 220
obsidian, 44, 45, 64
Oeconomicus (Xenophon), 91
off-grid, 203, 246
office cubicles, 99
Ohalo II, Sea of Galilee, Israel, *29*
oikeiôsis ("belonging"), 95
"oikos units," 90–91
oil and gas, 146, 196–97, 199, 200, 201, 202
Ökologie (ecology), 8
Olduvai Gorge, Tanzania, 1, 20
Olgyay, Victor and Aladar, 196–97
Olmsted, Frederick Law, 149–50, 152–53, 157
Olthuis, Koen, 245
Olynthian House style, 88–96, *89*
On the Murder of Eratosthenes (Lysias), 92
Oostvaardersplassen, Netherlands, 254
open spaces, 62–63, 64, 172, 183, 217, 241
open-plan layout, 157, 171
Opticos Design, *217*
Orr, Harold, 197
Ostia, Italy, *107*, 111–14
Otis, Elisha, 144
Oudehaske, Netherlands, 220
Owens, Peter, 175
Owens, Richard, 134–36, *136*

Palestine, 11, 30, 49, 52–53
Palladio, Andrea, 134
Pantheon of Rome, 109
paper architecture, 237
Paris, 16, 112, 138–39, 142–43, 146, 177, 221–22, 251, 254
parking spaces, 18, 174, 180, 217, 219, 224, 240, 255
Parthenon of Athens, 88
Passive Houses, 193–201, *197*
passive solar design, 87, 96, 196, 198
passive survivability, 245–46
Passivhaus Institut, 198
pastas (roofed colonnade), 89, *89*
Pearl Street Station, NYC, 146, 201, 206
"pea-soupers," 136
Peking Man, 9
penthouses, 110–11, 144
People's Republic of China, 179–80
Perdiccas II of Macedonia, 88
peristyles (colonnaded courtyards), 98–99, 100, 103
Perlin, John, 96
Perovskite solar cells, 206
Perry, Clarence, 221
Persians, 194
pesticides, 4, 176, 250
Peter the Great of Russia, 129–30
Petra, Jordan, 36
Petronius, 110–11
Philip of Macedon, 96
The Phoenix affordable housing complex, Oakland, CA, 231
Phoenix, AZ, 176, 218
photopolymerization, 209
photovoltaics, 202–3, 205–7, 216
pit houses, 11, 30–35, *31*
place-making, 2, 20–23, 29–30, 219–20, 223, 236–37
Plague of Justinian, 115
"Plan Voisin" (Le Corbusier), 177–78
"planned picturesque," 151
plano-convex bricks, 82
plastic, 209, 235, 236
Plato, 187
Pliny the Elder, 114, 121
Pliny the Younger, 105
plumbing. *See* sanitation
Plutarch, 93, 107
polders, 18, 123

policy
    building codes, 15, 77, 109, 111, 129, 134, 189–90, 200
    housing shortages, 112–13, 140, 160, 168, 177, 216
    incremental housing solutions, 8, 191–92, 214
    taxes, 110, 125, 129, 170, 173, 223
    zoning, 15, 18, 174, 189–90, 205, 219
    See also water management
Pompeii, 28, 103–6
Pontine Marshes, 114
post-and-girder systems, 144
poverty, 237. *See also* informal settlements
prefabrication, 154, 160, 227
Pre-Pottery Neolithic people, 37, 39
"primitive hut" theory of architecture, 9–10, 19–21
Pritzker Prize, 189
Project Milestone, Eindhoven, Netherlands, 210–11, *211*
property values, 222
"proto-cities," 8, 62–69
"proxemics," 181
Pruitt-Igoe towers, St. Louis, MO, 179
public health. *See* sanitation; *specific diseases and ailments*
public transit, 16, 147–48, 156–57, 181–82, 184–85
Puente Hills landfill, near Los Angeles, 236
Putnam, Robert, 219
Putnam's Magazine, 141
Pytheas of Massalia, 121

race/racism, 172–73
radiant heat, 169
radiation, 216, 253
rail, 13, 132, 136, 155
    "rail-residential" urbanism, 182–84
    railroad flats of New York, 140
    railroad suburbs, 149–57, *156*
"rainproofing," 245
Rapoport, Amos, 17
"rat utopia" experiments, 181
recycling, 199, 232, 233, 237, 238, 240, 251
Red Building, Tell Brak, 66–67
redlining, 172
reed construction, 10, 32, 53, 57–58, *58*, 82
Reimchen bricks, 82
reinforced concrete, 56, 111, 232, 236

INDEX

renting, 106, 140, 170
Resource Rows, Copenhagen, 233–36, *234*
restrictive covenants, 172
retrofitting, 222, 238
rewilding, 254
riads of Fez, 75
Rietveld, Gerrit, 166
Rijnvliet neighborhood of Utrecht, 251
Rio de Janeiro, 44–45, 187
Ritchie, Hannah, 251
Riverside, IL, 149–57, *156*
roads and highways, 72, 93–96
   American highways, 171, 173–74
   asphalt roads, 176–77, 222, 253
   curved roads with no function, 149–50
   density and reducing the need for, 184
   environmental impacts, 219, 253
   leading to Rome, 113, 115
   woonerfs ("living streets") of the Dutch, 220–21, 223–24
Roaf, Michael, 71
Rome, 96–106
   apartment buildings (*insulae*), 1, 106–13, *107*, 115, 117, 142
   aqueducts of, 97, 101, 102, 113, 115, 116
   Great Fire of 64 AD, 109
   houses (*domus*), 96–106, 111, *98*
   Justinian Code, 103, 202
   limits of, 113–16
   patron-client system, 99
   Pompeii, 28, 103–6
   Via Teatro di Marcello, 235
Römerstadt, Germany, 162
Rosslyn-Ballston corridor, Arlington, VA, 222–23
row houses, 10, 11, 13, 15–16, 134, 136, 137, 143, 204, 233
Ruhr crisis of 1923, 159
Rural Settlement Authority, 161
Rwandan refugee camps, 237
Rybczynski, Witold, 124, 172
rye, 36, 122

safety, 23, 108, 187
salvage, 233–41, *234*, *237*
Samarra culture, 55–59, 82
San Francisco, CA, 137, 218
sanitation, 13, 84, 101–2, 109–10, 131, 160
   cleanliness, 127, 146, 162
   sewers, 50, 102, 110, 122, 132–33, 219

terra-cotta pipes, 72, 102
toilets, 72, 79, 84, 101–2, 110, 113, 135, 141, 145, 180, 244
U-shaped water traps, 102
Santana Row, San Jose, CA., 222
Santorini, Greece, 195
Saskatchewan Conservation House, 197
Satyricon (Petronius), 110–11
scarcity, 90, 241
Scarsdale, NY, 152
Schama, Simon, 128
Schermerhorn residence, Riverside, IL, *156*
Schoonschip, 241–43, *242*, 247
Schütte-Lihotzky, Margarete, 161–64, 166
scientific management, 3–4, 161
Sea of Galilee, 28–29, *29*
selenium solar cells, 201, 202
self-sufficiency, 156, 167, 246
Seneca, 96–97, 100, 109
Seoul, 253
servants, 115, 124, 139, 142, 147, 162, 215
settlement. *See* dwellings; houses
sewers, 50, 102, 110, 122, 132–33, 219
Sheetrock, 169
Sheffield's Park Hill Flats, 178
Shek Kip Mei squatter town, Hong Kong, 180
Shenzhen, China, 188, 190–91
Shibam, Yemen, 195
shipping containers, 191, 230, 234, 238
shophouses of Southeast Asia, 137, 248
shopping malls, 174–75, 191, 222
Shorto, Russell, 123
Sierra Leone, 246–47
siheyuan (courtyard houses), 75, *95*, 95
silicon, 202
Singapore, 13–14, 15, 137, 185, 250–51
single-family homes, 15, 123–24, 137, 149, 151, 155
   cultural inclination toward, 169–70
   L-shaped house plans, 157, 172
   within multiunit structures, 140–43
   3D printed, 211–12, 231
Sinhalese people of Sri Lanka, 119
skyscrapers, 6, 15, 144, 155, 164–65, 179, 181–82, 190–91, 199, 252
slate roofs, 136
slavery, 71, 95–96, 107, 123
smog, 136–38, 149, 150
smoking, 4, 174
Socrates, 87

sod-covered houses of rural Norway, 198
SoHo neighborhood of NYC, 241
solar energy, 201–8, *204, 207*
    passive solar design, 14, 87, 96, 193–201
    "right to the sun," 103, 202
    solar gain, 100, 196
    "sunflower architecture," 203
solar glass, 206
Solar Hemicycle (Jacobs House), Madison, WI, 196, *197*
Solar One, 202–3
Solar Settlement (Solarsiedlung), Freiburg, Germany, 203–4, *204*
soot, 137, 147, 150
soundproofing, 144, 145, 148, 213
South by Southwest festival, 208
South Korea, 215, 253
Southdale Center mall, MN, 174
Southworth, Michael, 175
Soviet Union, 163
Space&Matter, *242*
space
    creating a hierarchy of spaces, 32, 59–60, 72, 144
    green space, 156, 159, 177, 247–48
    "intimate distance," 184
    open spaces, 62–63, 64, 172, 183, 217, 241
    spatial thinking, 23–25, 127
    the use and experience of, 181
    when at a premium, 184
Spain, *22*, 100, 122–23
Spirn, Anne Whiston, 50
sprawl, 54, 63, 85, 112–13, 117–20, 156, 173–74, 184–85, 216–17
St. Petersburg, Russia, 129–30
Stalinism, 163
steam power, 13, 136, 152, 154–55, 157
steel, 1–3, 13, 109, 144, 155, 165–66, 178, 184, 228–30, 235–36, 238
Stiner, Mary, 21, 23
Stoics, 95
stoops, 126
"Stop de Kindermoord" (Stop the Child Murder) campaign, 220
straw, 37, 56, 76, 97, 122, 212, 231, 236
Stuyvesant Flats, New York, 143–45, 148
Stuyvesant Town–Peter Cooper Village superblock, 179, 180
Stuyvesant, Rutherford, 143
suburbs
    early railroad suburbs, 149–57, *156*
    lawns, 4, 103, 106, 149, 151, 175–76
    Levittown(s), 167–74, *168*
    purpose-built, car-free development in the, 216–24, *217*
    racialized, 172–73
    the rise of the, 166–77, *168*
    shopping malls, 174–75, 191, 222
    See also cars; single-family homes
Sugrue, Thomas, 173
sulfur dioxide, 147
Sumerians, 52, 67, 69–86
Sunbelt cities, 175
"sunflower architecture," 203
sunlight. *See* natural light; solar energy
"superblocks," 159–60, 179, 186, 190, 221
Superstorm Sandy, 244
Superuse (firm), 237
survival, 1–2, 23
Sustainability Transition, 10
sustainable living, 9, 10, 14, 15, 212, 218, 240–41
    forestry practices, 154, 227, 230
    hunter-gatherers, 2, 4, 24–41, 50, 119, 220, 119, 250
    in prehistory, 36, 50–51, 61, 116–17, 138
    urban, 138, 148, 184, 251–52
swarm intelligence, 8, 64–65, 88, 214, 245
Sweden, 163
Syria, 37, *38*, 60, 62

tabernae (store-fronts), 99
tablinum (study), 99, 111
taxes, 110, 125, 129, 170, 173, 223
Taylor, Frederick, 161
Tell Brak, Syria, 8, 62–69, 187
Tell es-Sawwan, 55, 57
Tell Gawra, 59
Tell Hamoukar, 62–69
Tell Hassuna, 53–55, *54*
Tell Madhur, Iraq, *59*
Tempe, AZ, 216, *217*
temperature control. *See* indoor temperatures
temple construction, 2, 8, 9, 12, 60, 62–63, 67–72, 75–77, 81, 90, 97, 100, 119
Temple, Sir William, 127, 128
"Tenant's Lament," 106
Tenement House Acts of New York State, 141
tenements, 13, 111, 140–45, 147, 160, 180, 188
tensile strength, 80, 227

INDEX

termites, 6, 8, 64–65
Terra Amata, Nice, France, 10
terraced houses of Liverpool, 10, 13, 131–38, *136*, 140
terra-cotta, 72, 90, 97, 102
thermopolia (food stalls), 112
3D printing, 14, 17, 208–13, *211*, 216
Thucydides, 88–89
Tigris River, 52–53, 55, 70, 79, 84
Tikal, 116, 119
timber. *See* wood
toilets, 72, 79, 84, 101–2, 110, 113, 135, 141, 145, 180, 244
Tokyo, 207–8, *207*
"tombstone urbanism," 163
Tonle Sap Lake, 118
Tower of Jericho, 39
"township" model, 181
transportation
    canals, 70, 84, 118, 121–31, *126*, 140, 150, 242, 247
    cycling, 222–23
    public transit, 16, 147–48, 156–57, 181–82, 184–85
    See also cars; rail
Trellick Tower, 178
triclinium ("three couches"), 100
tripartite house design, 59–62, 67, 71
Trypillia settlements (now Ukraine), 63
tuberculosis, 23, 131
"Tulip Mania," 129
Turkey, 53, 83, 129
Turner, John, 188
two-by-four studs, 153

Ubaid culture of Mesopotamia, 57–62, 67, 71
"ultrasocial engineers," 21
UNESCO World Heritage Sites, 50, 130
Union Square, Hong Kong, 182
Unité d'Habitation, Marseille, 177–78
United States
    Federal-Aid Highway Act of 1956, 173
    GI Bill of 1944, 170
    "missing middle housing" in the, 15, 138
    Sunbelt cities of the, 175
    See also cars; suburban living; *major American cities*
Ur, 3, 77, 78, 80, 82–86
Ur, Jason, 65, 67
urban living
    biophilic design for urban ecosystems, 249–53
    the future of, 7
    problems of, 50
    proximity to others, 12, 23, 73, 148, 149, 155–57
    the rise of, 63–69
    undeniable advantages of, 12
    vertical living, 11–14, 16, 81, 106–8, 144, 147, 155, 179–85, 190–91
    walkable neighborhoods, 15, 16–18, 155–58, 191, 218, 221–23
    See also apartment buildings; cities
"urban mining," 237
urban planning, 15, 129–30, 150
    in ancient Greece, 83–96
    "15-minute city," 16, 85, 221–22
    "superblocks," 159–60, 179, 186, 190, 221
    walkable neighborhoods, 15, 16–18, 155–58, 191, 218, 221–23
    See also roads and highways
Urban Revolution, 10, 11–13, 73, 76–79
urbanism. *See* cities; urban living
Ur-Nammu of Sumer, 78
Uruk, 8, 69–75, 81, 82
US Environmental Protection Agency (EPA), 211–12
US Housing and Home Finance Agency, 188
US Public Health Service, 147
U-shaped water traps, 102
Utrecht, Netherlands, 166, 251

Valla, François, 33
van Putten, Maartje, 220
Varro, 114–15
vaulting, 109
Vaux, Calvert, 139–40, 142, 149–50, 153
Vermeer, Johannes, 127–28
vernacular design, 58, 165, 248, 249
vertical living, 11–14, 16, 81, 106–8, 144, 147, 155, 179–85, 190–91. *See also* apartment buildings; skyscrapers
"vertical slum" of Caracas, 187
Vespasian, 110
Vienna's converted gasholders, 240
Vietnam, 247–50, *248*
Villa El Salvador, Lima, Peru, 189
Villa Welpeloo, Netherlands, 237–38
Ville Radieuse (Le Corbusier), 186
Vingboons, Philips, 125–26, *126*

Virgil, 113
Visigoths, 115
vitrification, 78
Vitruvius, 100–101, 107–8
volatile organic compounds, 4, 212
Voll Arkitekter, *226*, 228
von Siemens, Werner, 155
VTN Architects, 248, *248*

Wah Fu estate, Hong Kong, 180–81
walkable neighborhoods, 15, 16–18, 155–58, 191, 218, 221–23
walk-up apartments, 106, 144, 177
WASP (World's Advanced Saving Project), 212
waste
   construction, 212, 227, 236–37, *237*, 240
   human, 33–34, 45, 49, 102, 110, 141, 187
   waste heat, 240
   See also sanitation
water management
   aqueducts, 97, 101, 102, 113, 115, 116
   canals, 70, 84, 118, 121–31, *126*, 140, 150, 242, 247
   gray water recycling, 240, 251
   irrigation, 11, 57, 61, 63, 70, 84, 113, 240
   locks, 122, 124
   shared struggle against, 122–23
   water pollution, 34, 42, 49
   water pressure, 145–46
Waterstudio, 245
wattle and daub construction, 97, 108
Weimar Germany, 161
Welsh Streets neighborhood, Toxteth, Liverpool, 135, *136*
Westhausen, Frankfurt, 158–61, *159*, 163
Wetherell, W. D., 169, 170
wheat, 30, 36, 37, 55, 116
wheel, invention of, 4, 45, 70, 105
"white flight," 173
White Temple of Uruk, 72
Wikado playground, Netherlands, 237
Wilson, Alex, 246
Wilson, E. O., 250
Wilson, Peter, 41
wind, 32, 226
windbreaks, 25–26, *25*
windcatchers, 194

windows, 45, 71, 80, 93, 110, 127, 137–38
   electrochromic glass, 206
   with *lapis specularis*, 102–3, 202
   laws governing, 141
   triple-glazed windows, 166, 193, 197
   window-to-wall ratios, 199
   wraparound corner, 166
Winter, Kawika, 253
Wohnkultur ("dwelling culture"), 161
Wolf, Michael, 182
wood, 28, 118, 225–29, *226*
   bamboo, 230–31
   concrete vs., 226–27, 229–30
   foundations, 125
   lack of, 80–81
   mass timber (engineered wood panels), 14, 228–32
   Mjøstårnet, Brumunddal, Norway, 226–29, *227*
   natural workability of, 233
   new technologies in, 231–33
Woolley, Leonard, 57, 77, 79
woonerfs ("living streets") of, 220–21, 223–24
work from home, 221
working-class homes, 13, 131–32, 135, 163, 165
World Green Building Council, 229
World War I, 160
World War II, 168, 177, 179–80, 188
Wright, Frank Lloyd, 166–67, 172, 176, 196–97, *197*
Wright, Gwendolyn, 170
writing, invention of, 72–73

Xenophon, 87, 91

Yellen, John, 28
yellow klinkers, 130
Yellow River Valley of China, 31
Younger Dryas period, 35
Your Solar House (book), 196

Zagros Mountains, 70, 84
Zambia, 21
Zeilenbau (row-building), 158, 163
Zille, Heinrich, 160
zoning, 15, 18, 174, 189–90, 205, 219